W9-DDB-056

FIRE IN
THE HOLE!

FIRE IN THE HOLE!

THE UNTOLD STORY OF MY TRAUMATIC LIFE AND EXPLOSIVE SUCCESS

BY BOB PARSONS
WITH LAURA MORTON

Forefront
BOOKS

Published by Forefront Books, Nashville, Tennessee.
Distributed by Simon & Schuster.

Library of Congress Control Number: 2024901339

Print ISBN: 978-1-63763-298-7
E-book ISBN: 978-1-63763-299-4

Cover Design by G Sharp Desgin
Interior Design by PerfecType, Nashville, TN

Printed in the United States of America

DEDICATION

This book is dedicated to the American men and women who fought in the Vietnam War.

Welcome home, brothers and sisters. Welcome home!

CONTENTS

PREFACE

Fire in the hole!" is a phrase often used as a warning that an explosive detonation in a confined space is imminent. It's believed by some to have originated with miners, who used it as a way to alert workers that a charge had been set. Others think the saying was first used by soldiers before firing a cannon during battle. The types of cannons used during the Revolutionary War had a tiny hole where the cannoneer would pack a small amount of gunpowder, which would be lit. The gunpowder would then burn in the hole until it reached and ignited the main powder charge. Just before the explosion, soldiers would shout, "Fire in the hole!" as a way of letting their side know the cannon was about to blow. While writing this book, I toyed with many titles—and believe me, some would have really grabbed your attention—but ultimately none were as appropriate as *Fire in the Hole!*

I say this because I come from a long line of folks who were very familiar with coal miners. Generations of my dad's family lived in a northeast Pennsylvania mining town. While my father's grandfather Eugene and other relatives were definitely coal miners, exactly who else was a coal miner has been lost to history. Pop once told me that when the guys went to work in the mines, they would descend into the shafts in the morning and come back up after dark with every inch of their bodies covered in coal dust. Even their tongues and gums were jet black. When they finished work, instead of going home to their wives and families, many of them would hit the local bar and drink themselves silly. Then they'd get up the next morning and do it all again. In those days, miners usually died in one of two ways: either from an accident inside the mine or from black lung disease. Both are brutal ways to go, though Pop told me black lung is the absolute worst way to die. Compared to the miners who lost their lives to that horrific malady, some of those who perished in accidents inside the mines may have suffered a lot less.

Fire in the Hole! also seems like an appropriate title because, as a kid, I often found myself alone in my basement bedroom playing with my plastic toy soldiers. I'd set up battles and attacks, calling "*Boom!*" as if mock bombs were going off and "*Rat-a-tat-tat*" as if make-believe gunfire was taking out the enemy. I loved to play these battles out. I could be in my pretend world for hours. This may also have been the origin of my use of "ka-boom," which I've been known to say a lot over the years.

Moreover, "Fire in the hole!" took on an important meaning to me once I joined the United States Marine Corps and served as a combat rifleman during the Vietnam War. Whenever our rifle squad or platoon found an enemy tunnel, C-4 plastic explosives would be thrown into it. One or more of us would call out "Fire in the hole!" and then detonate the C-4, triggering a large explosion that would clear the tunnel of any booby traps, Vietcong, or North Vietnamese Army (NVA) soldiers that might be lying in wait for us.

Given the fact that today I'm a billionaire entrepreneur and philanthropist, I'm often asked if I've ever stopped to think about all that I've accomplished in my life. The answer is no. Don't get me wrong—I'm proud of my accomplishments, and even with all the success I've had, without a doubt, the thing I'm most proud of is being a United States Marine. But when answering this question, I don't think about the past. Instead, I think about everything I still want to do.

In the pages that follow, you're going to read about a different side of my life—one that may be unexpected and, for many of you, unfamiliar, especially when it comes to my time as a rifleman during the Vietnam War. Some of you will not understand, because unless you were there, you can't possibly comprehend what happened or why. You can't imagine the things I experienced and saw. There are days when I still have a hard time with all of that myself. But my involvement in the Vietnam War had the most profound impact on me as a man, a son, a husband, a father, a businessperson, and a patriot.

When I first began writing this book, I did so hoping it would potentially change people's lives—and *your* life too. This is because my path has taken me places I never imagined possible. I was always a big dreamer, even declaring in my high school yearbook that someday I would be a millionaire (an unimaginable amount of money for us back then). In so many ways, that declaration was laughable, if not absurd. The cards were heavily stacked against me. At the time, I was flunking almost every class. Also, I came from nothing—less than nothing, really. My story isn't at all like what you may have read about the Rockefellers or the du Ponts. I certainly wasn't born with a silver spoon in my mouth. My spoon was more like a dirty, broken plastic one. But that didn't stop me from carving a path to success in business and in life. Oh, baby, it's been a jagged, uphill climb, and I worked my tail off to get here, but I wouldn't change a thing. Not one thing. And nothing—I mean *nothing*—came easy. It's true what they say: if it were easy, everyone would be doing it. But let me tell you this: if I can do it, maybe you can too.

One thing you will quickly come to know about me is that no matter how hard or uncertain things get, I'm always good with the outcome. There's a question I heard as a young boy that has stayed with me: "Do we smile because we're happy, or are we happy because we smile?" In so many words, that question is meant to remind us that being happy is more or less a choice. I believe that we're happy because we choose to smile. Even in the face of adversity or challenging times, I'm generally a happy guy, and that's a good place to be. One of my earliest lessons in life was to never worry. As a kid, I went through a lot of tough times, but I learned at a very young age that worry is a beast, especially when you're in the middle of a crisis. Worry will never change the outcome of what you're stressing about. What it *will* do is make you miserable and hold you back. So I never worry. Ever. Because I know that what seems insurmountable here and now will often be a tiny blip on the radar tomorrow, a week from now, or a year down the road. It's been a blessing not having to wrestle with that beast. What I know for sure is that if you can't control it—whatever it is—put your focus and attention on something you can control, and you'll be better for it. I've lived that way my entire life.

To help you develop an understanding of how I became the calm, worry-free, determined individual I am today, you should know that I attended an inner-child workshop in 1997, and while I was there I wrote three documents. The lifetime of events that led to the creation of these documents, in many ways, forms the basis of this book.

At this workshop, I was tasked with (1) writing a letter to my younger self; (2) responding as the younger version of me to that letter; and (3) writing an essay on how I became me. At first, it wasn't as easy as it seemed. What did Big Bob want to tell Little Bob after so many years? And, realistically, how would Little Bob respond to such a letter? I had to dig deep. Way down. But then the words just flowed like a river.

While collecting my thoughts for this book, I came across all three of those documents, and it was amazing how closely the things I wrote in each one resemble the life I've ultimately lived.

I struggled with whether I wanted to share these letters with you, especially in the opening of my book.

I thought about it.

A lot.

And then I said, "What the hell. May as well step right out there and fire away on page one."

The three documents are as follows.

(1) Letter from Big Bob to Little Bob:

August 21, 1997
Little Bob Parsons
425 N. East Avenue
Baltimore, MD 21224

Dear Little Bob,
I am writing to you from 38 years into the future. I am the man you grew up to be, and I know more about you than anyone else in the world. Because of that, I love and admire you very much.

I know exactly what is happening to you now and how you feel about it. I also know everything that is going to happen to you.

I know you are scared most of the time and do not understand why your mother makes all her awful problems your problems and why your father isn't home. I know about all those other horrible things that are happening to you at school and at other places. Knowing how bad and guilty you feel about this breaks my heart. I want you to know that one day you will learn that none of it is your fault.

One day, you will rise above everything bad that happens to you. When you grow up you will realize how unfairly you have been treated and what an extraordinarily strong, courageous, and wonderful little boy you really are. You will know success at a level that is reserved for only a very few. And sweetest of all, you will achieve something that is rare indeed: you will know yourself.

So Little Bob, when bad things happen to you, trust yourself to do what seems right at the time. You know more about the right thing to do than you can possibly imagine. And most important, no matter what, keep dreaming about being in a better place and time, because more than anything else, that will be what saves you.

I love you very much.
Big Bob

(2) Return letter from Little Bob to Big Bob:

Dear Big Bob,
I cannot wait to be you. I do not like it here. Everything is sad. I hope you are happy. Thanks for writing to me. I love you too.

Love,
Little Bob

The third document I wrote during that weekend workshop is an essay on how I became me. Despite the fact that, after reading this, you might think that I was under the influence of some substance when I wrote it, I wasn't. One thing I know for sure is that I had to visit some painful memories to find these words. I had to travel way down to the dark places I'd spent most of my life avoiding (something I would ultimately pay a high emotional price for doing). If I wanted to finally be free of whatever was holding me back, there was only one way to do so—and that was to face my demons head-on. So I sat down, pen in hand, and wrote from the depths of my heart and my soul. I can't remember if I cried as I set down my thoughts. I probably did. I could feel my heart melt as I released my feelings onto the page. I hadn't expected it, but I found this exercise immensely healing.

(3) Essay on how I became me:

How I Became Me—An Unfinished Essay
I believe I was born a dreamer. As far back as I can remember I was always imagining doing fantastic things. As a small child, I used to lie in bed at night and dream of leading armies or sailing to foreign lands. In my dreams I saw myself slaying dragons, riding fast horses, or flying planes. With my imagination I could go anywhere, be anyone, or do anything.

My parents most certainly had a firm hand in creating the dark side of me that resides at my most basic level. To help protect me from the damage they and others did, the Dreamer somehow created several other parts. And it was those parts who were responsible for keeping the Dreamer alive. Ultimately this was my salvation.

The Dreamer somehow developed a Wise Old Man who shows me what to do when faced with a dilemma. And the two of them created the Tiger, who gives me the courage and the strength to do those difficult things we all sometimes must do.

Out of the Dreamer, the Wise Old Man, and the Tiger was born another important part, the Adventurer. The Adventurer loves new experiences and discoveries. The Adventurer is not often afraid of risk and creates new enterprises.

The Banker came about as the business part of me. This is the part that sizes up risks, makes deals, and ensures my investments are proper. The Banker is really a go-between. He operates between the Wise Old Man and the Adventurer.

Out of all these, the Survivor was born. It's with the wisdom of the Old Man, the imagination of the Dreamer, the courage of the Tiger, and the daring of the Adventurer that the Survivor seems to be able to overcome just about any threat or obstacle.

On the dark side of me is the Wounded Child. This part lives at my most basic level. The Wounded Child was created by my parents and others who neglected and abused me.

Above the Wounded Child lives the other dark part of me. That's the Vietnam Vet. This part was created when I carried a rifle with the United States Marine Corps during the Vietnam War, when I saw things no one should ever have to see and have memories no one should ever have to have. And after returning from that godforsaken war, I came back to a country that not only rejected me but also couldn't bring itself to simply say "Welcome home!"

The Wounded Child in hopes of a better life and the Dreamer somehow created the Romantic, which is the loving part of me. It is the Romantic who feels love and also understands the bittersweet pain of sadness. The Romantic was created with the hope that I will one day learn how to find the love I've been incapable of giving and receiving.

All of the dark parts of me, the Dreamer, and the Romantic also created the kind and gentle side of me. That's Mr. Softy. Because he idealizes a better way and knows firsthand how unkind life can be, he can feel the pain carried by others. He always wants to help and do the right thing and is usually willing to take the little extra time it sometimes takes to make others smile.

Finally, the last remaining part of me is the Writer. It's the Writer who communicates with all my other parts. He knows the pain, joy, suffering, confusion, and clarity experienced throughout me. And it is this part that communicates with the rest of the world.

A Witch, a Thief, a Miner, Then Me

We all have a family history that, for better or worse, helps us become who we are. Mine is interesting, to say the least.

One of my earliest traceable ancestors in the United States was Mary Parsons. She lived in Springfield, Massachusetts, in the 1600s. I know this because my younger sister, Beverly, is into genealogy. Several years ago, Beverly sent me a book she'd compiled about our lineage. I was intrigued, so I began to read. The first thing I came across was Mary's story. Believe it or not, she was tried for witchcraft . . . *twice*.

Her trials had something to do with people's cows dropping dead or her neighbor's son's new wife suddenly dying. Those neighbors, who weren't exactly friends with Mary, accused her of having something to do with those incidents. I suppose back then it was easy to accuse someone of being a practicing witch, especially if you were involved in some type of feud. Maybe things aren't so different today. In both of her trials, Mary was found not guilty, although the second time she was locked in a tower for about a year while awaiting her hearing—all for no justifiable reason.

Fast-forward to sometime in the 1930s, when my uncle Eddie was arrested for robbing the Glyndon Bank in Glyndon, Maryland. "Uncle Eddie" wasn't my actual blood relative. Edwin Monroe was married to my mother's oldest sister, Evelyn. Edwin and Evelyn lived with my grandmother. My aunt Agnes (another one of my mother's six sisters), was probably in the first grade when Eddie robbed the bank of $9,000. To hide the money, they sewed it into the lining of Agnes's coat. She went back and forth to school every day with all that money on her. Although Eddie was arrested and the cops searched my grandmother's house repeatedly, often showing up in the middle of the night, they never found the loot.

Now, I was born on November 27, 1950, to Elsie (née Buck) and Ralph Shaver Parsons. Right after the bombing of Pearl Harbor in 1941, my dad joined the Navy. He was sent to Baltimore for boot camp, and that's where he met my mother. Thankfully, Pop never worked in the mines like his grandfather, and so, by default, neither did I. During the war Pop served as a Seabee and helped build and repair runways for our fighter planes and bombers. While on Guadalcanal, he took a photo from the beach of his ship, located not too far offshore, as the vessel exploded and disappeared into the Pacific. Pop said a Japanese suicide submarine, loaded with explosives, attached itself to his ship by drilling into its side, then detonated itself.

My mother's mother, Mary (née Gorecki) Buck, was a first-generation immigrant from Poland. She grew up with six siblings and became a homemaker. Her husband, Frank Buck, was a cooper, which for him meant he built and repaired whiskey barrels. It's mostly a lost profession today. I never met my grandfather, but Dad described him as the meanest man he'd ever met in his life. Frank was a big drinker. He would often come home late at night, drunk as could be, and pull my mother out of bed or wherever she was in the house to beat the living daylights out of her. He did this again and again. I'm not sure why he focused his anger on my mother and never laid a hand on her twin, Bertha (whom everyone called Bert), or her other siblings. For whatever reason, he took all his rage out on Mom. Apparently, his grandmother and others abused him terribly when he was a little boy, so the cruelty was surely generational and a product of his upbringing. Even so, it was a terrible way for my mom to grow up. Frank developed severe, debilitating stomach problems from drinking whiskey mixed with charcoal. Back then, charcoal was placed in the bottom of whiskey barrels to absorb the impurities, and there was always some whiskey thick with this stuff in the barrels he was given to repair. My dad told me that Frank would scoop the whiskey from the bottom of the barrel with a tin cup and gulp it right down. I find it hard to imagine my grandfather actually drinking that shit, but he did, and the physical damage to him was awful.

Frank was a brutal man in every sense of the word. When he was no longer able to work, he committed suicide. Even the way he killed himself was harsh: he died from asphyxiation by crawling inside an oven after turning the gas on high.

> "You can raise a puppy to be a warm, lovable, fun pet, or you can treat it mean and abuse it and it will grow up to be a vicious dog. That's the way it is with most people."

I remember talking to my friend, the world-renowned singer Andrea Bocelli, about what made certain people violent. He said, "You can raise a puppy to be a warm, lovable, happy pet, or you can treat it mean and abuse it and it will grow up to be a vicious dog. That's the way it is with most people." And he was right. If your parents were kind and loving to you when you were growing up, you hit the lottery. And if they weren't, well, there was a steep price to pay. My mom surely paid, and eventually I did too.

With me, it wasn't so simple. The abuse I suffered was more emotional than it was physical, and much of it stemmed from neglect. And that made it confusing to me, and nearly impossible for anyone else to see. Even so, it stung just as badly.

My mother was never intentionally cruel, but I can't remember her ever giving me a hug or telling me she loved me. Mom was a stunningly beautiful woman who had all the love beaten out of her as a child. As a result, she didn't know how to give love—at least, not in the way I saw other moms expressing affection to their kids.

It was heartbreaking.

I have a hard time looking back on my youth and remembering any loving moments with my parents, but especially with Mom. It wasn't my parents' fault, and I don't blame them. I can't hold them responsible for things they didn't know or weren't in control of.

My parents lived in East Baltimore, a blue-collar neighborhood on the edge of Highlandtown. The community was made up mostly of folks with Polish, German, and Czech ancestry. Our neighborhood was a collection of small row houses. We didn't live in the nicest house in the area, but it also wasn't the worst.

I'm the oldest of three kids. My little brother, Allan, and I shared a makeshift bedroom my dad created for us in the basement, while my baby sister, Beverly, and my parents lived on the second floor. Pop fixed up our bedroom as best he could. The walls were made of painted cinder blocks, and the floor was covered in twelve-inch-square linoleum tiles. Of course, the paint Pop used on our bedroom walls was full of lead and asbestos, so who knows what damage we received from breathing in that poison night after night for so many years.

My dad owned a little variety store in our neighborhood on the corner of McElderry Street and North East Avenue. It was called Ralph's Variety, and it was like a 7-Eleven without the gas pumps. He sold ice cream, cigarettes, over-the-counter medicines, and other basics there. It was nothing fancy. Just convenient.

Pop loved a good deal, but most of his "good deals" turned out to be disasters. He would repeatedly fall prey to some huckster pawning off inferior products for a ridiculously low price, making it too good for Pop to pass up. Somehow, he always ended up paying heavily for his frugal decisions in business. Here's what I mean: Every once in a while, a supplier would offer Dad a special deal on, say, hot fudge. The problem was, once he heated up the fudge and put it on ice cream, it would turn hard as a rock. You couldn't break off a piece with a hammer and chisel, much less your teeth. Another time, he got an incredible deal on Christmas trees. Within days, all the needles fell off. Everyone who bought one of those trees wanted their money back. Even my friends at school harassed me about their trees after that debacle.

"What do you want me to do? I feel worse about it than you do. I didn't sell you the tree!" I'd say with my palms turned up. I'm lucky I didn't get my ass kicked.

Ralph's Variety made us appear well-to-do in a neighborhood of mostly poor folks. It wasn't that we had money—we didn't. It was no secret that my dad wasn't much of a businessman. He was more of a gambler, and not a good one. He was also a womanizer. His gambling addiction and his love of the ladies were a deadly combination when it came to running a business.

To be certain, he always left whatever money he had at the track. I can't think of a time when Pop hit it big. And if he did, it didn't last long. He'd gamble it all away in a matter of hours. Seldom did things go his way. I remember once he got a tip about a horse that was going to be doped at the racetrack at Timonium Fairgrounds, now known as the Maryland State Fairgrounds. It was supposed to be a sure thing, and best of all, the horse was a big long shot. That meant for every dollar Pop bet on it, he'd receive twenty or thirty times the amount when he won—*if* he won. So Pop put every nickel he could scrape together on the nose of that horse. He bet it all to win. Was that horse doped? You can be sure it was. When the bell rang to launch the horses out of the starting gate, Pop's horse came out like a rocket. At the first turn, it was ahead by three or four lengths; at the second turn, it was leading by six lengths. It seemed to be running faster and faster. At the far turn, it was leading by twelve lengths. *My God! Pop was finally going to be a big winner. It was going to be fat city.* Then Pop's horse blazed into the turn at the home stretch, and instead of continuing to run along the inside rail, it swung out wide—really wide. The horse was so doped and running so fast that it couldn't make that final turn. Instead, it bulleted right into the fence that lined the outside of the track, instantly killing itself and damn near killing the jockey. Pop went from the pinnacle of betting glory to being just another knucklehead who'd wagered on a loser.

The reality is, we were always flat-ass broke and in perpetual debt. We seldom went hungry, but quite often the meals we had weren't the best. Mom was a reasonable cook, and there were certain dishes she liked to make, such as meatloaf, sour beef and dumplings, and manicotti. Occasionally, she'd serve a tuna sandwich with beef gravy—what my mom called surf and turf. I'll tell you something: when you're hungry, most everything tastes good. Every now and then she would make me a white bread sandwich with mayonnaise slathered on it. *Mmm-mmm.* To this day, I love the taste of that.

My mother was just like my old man in that she also loved to gamble—and she was almost as bad at it as Pop was. If there were ever two people who were exactly right for each other, it was Mom and Dad. Boy, did she love going to bingo with her sister, Aunt Bert, while Dad spent most of his free time either at the track or playing golf.

While their gambling habits sure made for some thin financial times growing up, there were a few upsides. When I was a little boy, maybe six or seven years old, Mom taught me how to read the racing form. Some of the races covered distances of seven-eighths of a mile or maybe one and one-sixteenth miles. I remember when Mom explained how one-eighth is a larger number than one-sixteenth like it was yesterday. I was a terrible student throughout elementary, middle, and high school, but thanks to Mom, I nailed fractions.

Although my mom was a striking woman, she never had the confidence to feel good about herself. She didn't have faith in her ability to do much of anything. She also never learned how to drive. As a stay-at-home mom with three children, she didn't think she could get or keep a job, so she often felt stuck, like a prisoner. She was able to leave the house on occasion, usually to go to the bingo hall. Somehow, she always had money for that, but she had to rely on other people to drive her there. The same was true if she needed to go shopping or anywhere else.

Despite her insecurities, Mom was one of the smartest women I've ever known. All the smarts I have most certainly came from her. She was so sharp. Mom could just look at a garment and then crochet it perfectly. Her memory was extraordinary. Whenever she played bingo and one of her numbers was called, she never marked her cards. She could just recall what she had and what had been played. Her memory also made it impossible for me, Allan, and Beverly to put one over on her, so we rarely tried. And she was always brutally direct. She spoke her mind, whether you wanted to hear it or not. (I inherited that from her too.) Even so, none of that translated into her having many friends or living a better life. If I had to pick a word to describe her back then, it would likely be *miserable*.

We were just getting by when Pop's business failed. At one time, Ralph's Variety was a viable entity, but my dad had racked up so much debt from gambling and credit cards that everything came tumbling down. In the end, he practically gave the business away. And when he did, we went from not having much to having nothing. I mean absolutely *nothing*. Everything my father ever bought was on credit, and the debt was compounded by high interest rates. There was no bouncing back from that. Humiliated by his loss, he wasn't around much after that—not that he ever was before.

Right around this time, my dad started having an affair with a woman who lived around the corner from us—or at least that's what my mom thought. The woman's name was Mrs. Beverly. She had dark hair and was a real looker. I thought she was gorgeous. Whenever Mom suspected that Mrs. Beverly was home and that Dad was with her, she would put my baby sister in the stroller and walk by Mrs. Beverly's house, looking to catch them together. To the best of my knowledge, she never did. I knew my mother was upset by Pop's behavior, so anytime we were home watching television, if there was a woman on TV with black hair who even slightly resembled Mrs. Beverly, I'd try to change the channel. I thought it would help prevent Mom from feeling hurt or jealous. It didn't, of course, but I tried anyway.

No matter where he was, Dad would eventually come home at night pretty tanked from drinking whiskey and beer. A lot of times, especially after Pop lost the store, Mom would be waiting for him. She'd hide behind the door with a metal pot or a broomstick in her hand. When he walked in, she'd clock him. She knocked him into next week many times. One thing I will say for the old man is that he never hit her back. I never saw him raise a hand to her. And even though he surely knew he'd get clobbered again, he always came home. Although he wasn't home much, he never deserted us. I respected him for that.

I guess you could say Mom had a bit of a temper. Sometimes when I misbehaved, she would whack me across the back of my legs with a leather strap she had doubled up. Oh, man—that got my attention. It didn't happen often, but I've never forgotten the sting.

Pop did his best to support the family in those months that followed the collapse of his business, but ours wasn't a happy household at that time—not that it ever was. I was out late with him one evening when I was nineteen years old and had just come home from the Vietnam War. He turned to me that night and said, "You know, Robert, when you're married and you come home late, you'll get to the point where you're only going to catch so much hell. And when you hit that point, you might as well stay out all night." That was the kind of advice I'd get from my dad growing up. (He was pretty right on about that one.)

Things started to get really bad for the family when I was around eight years old. We were constantly being harassed by bill collectors, and Mom was emotionally falling apart. Allan was five and Beverly was just an infant when my mom had what I believe was her first nervous breakdown. She was always so sad, and that broke my heart, but even then she was hard to live with. Every once in a while, she would repeatedly call out my name in the middle of the night: "Robert! Robert! Come upstairs." When I did, I just stood there in front of her, skinny as could be in my Jockey briefs while she faced me while sitting on the edge of our La-Z-Boy chair.

"Where's your father?" she'd ask, quietly at first.

"I don't know, Mom," I'd respond.

She'd raise her voice and say it again, much louder this time. "Where's your father?"

"Mom, I don't know."

Then she would start screaming as loud as she could, *"WHERE IS YOUR FATHER?!"*

Her screams were so loud, so filled with desperation and agony, they seemed to pierce my soul.

And I would shout back, "I don't know!" I didn't know what else to say.

Things often escalated to the point where Mom would start pulling her hair out of her head in clumps while repeatedly banging her head against the wall. She'd make these awful noises that sounded like a trapped, wounded animal.

Whenever Mom went nuts, it was such a hard thing for me to watch. All I knew to do was to call her twin sister, Aunt Bert, who lived nearby. Sometimes she would come over and try to calm Mom down, and other times she wouldn't. I suppose when she didn't come, it was because she couldn't bring herself to witness her sister once again possessed by the devil, in the throes of insanity. Other than calling Aunt Bert, I never really knew what to do, so I'd take slow steps backward until I could escape, unnoticed, back down to the isolation of my basement bedroom.

I'd put my head on the pillow and wonder why Mom was like this. I wasn't scared so much as ashamed. I'd think about my friends, who all appeared to be so happy with their nice, normal parents. I wanted to understand why my mom was the way she was, but at the time I couldn't really comprehend it. It seemed so wrong; that much I knew. I understood that she was somehow broken, but I couldn't grasp the depth of her pain. Not then, anyway.

Sometimes she even threatened to kill herself. I'd beg her not to. "Please, Mom, don't do that," I pleaded with her.

I didn't want my mom to die. The threats alone made me feel terrible. She'd describe in the most graphic detail how she would do it by putting a plastic bag over her head. She never talked about shooting herself. And she never talked about slitting her wrists or anything like that. It was always pills or a plastic bag.

Looking back, I can see that she manipulated me in the worst ways. As brutal as it was to see her in this state, I would usually just go numb. I wouldn't allow myself to react emotionally. At that young age, I quickly figured out that I couldn't do much to help her and that her extreme misery was making me miserable too. And so I learned to remove myself from her craziness by retreating into the basement, where I could be in my own little world. It was the only place I truly felt safe.

I'd stay in the basement and play with my toy soldiers. I had all different types, and together they were more like a ragtag gang than a true battalion. I combined my cowboys and Indians, Vikings, medieval knights, and Civil War soldiers with my little green plastic army men. I'd set both sides up, and I never played any favorites. I just let them battle. When I was done, there would be pieces scattered all over the basement. It was more than a distraction from the sadness upstairs. It was a source of happiness.

I also turned to reading comic books as often as I could. I really polished my reading skills by doing that. I never liked the stories about villains as much as I liked the ones about heroes such as Superman, Spider-Man, Batman, and the Incredible Hulk. I also loved Casper, Hot Stuff, Wile E. Coyote, and the Road Runner. There was nothing better than drifting off into another world where superheroes conquered villains and Archie, Veronica, and the Gang lived their best life. There I'd dream of the kind of life I wanted to live someday.

As with most things growing up, I had to teach myself how to tie my shoes. Mom was in no condition to show me, and Pop was seldom home, so I had to figure it out by myself. I started by tying small knots. That kept my shoes on, but those little knots were buggers to untie, and I was left with long laces hanging off the sides that I then had to tuck into my shoes so I wouldn't trip on them.

Later, I noticed that the bows other kids tied had two loops. Whenever I was alone—and I was *usually* alone—I played around with tying my shoes until I got the hang of my own two-loop method. My approach was unconventional, to say the least, but it did the trick. Figuring out how to do it took quite a while, but the result was still a knot with two large loops. My bow did for me what every other kid's did: it looked good, was easy to untie (I just had to pull one of the shoestrings and it came completely undone), and because my bow used up a lot more string than the little knots I used to tie, I no longer had to tuck my laces into the sides of my shoes. It was efficient. Plus, my way was fast. I still tie my shoes the exact same way I taught myself, alone in my basement bedroom, all those years ago.

Once in a while, if I had the money, I'd buy a roll of wild cherry Life Savers. Boy, oh boy, I loved them. I'd sit back in bed, pop one in my mouth, and savor the delicious candy. I would challenge myself to make each Life Saver last. I'd stretch it out as long as I could, slowly letting it melt down to a sliver. I would never eat more than one each night. A roll of wild cherry Life Savers and a good comic book (especially a brand-new one I hadn't yet read)—man, that was the perfect night. To this day, whenever I enjoy a wild cherry Life Saver, I get the feeling that everything is okay. It's a strange comfort, and one of the few good memories I have of growing up. Every now and then, someone will give me a gift of butterscotch Life Savers; butterscotch is good, but wild cherry, well . . . for me, they are like striking the perfect golf shot. You immediately know when it's right.

Despite the chaos and drama around me, there were times when I would lie there and think, *I'm so lucky*. And I really did feel that way. I also believed that someday, life could and would get better.

I must have been nine years old when Mom went berserk one night and I retreated to my basement bedroom, where I dropped to my knees and prayed to God. I was as serious as I ever was. I didn't ask for a way out of my situation. Instead I said, *Dear God, when I*

grow up, if I have a family, I promise you they will always have what-
ever they need. I never broke that promise.

Our family never talked about Mom's illness, and I never
shared what was happening at home with anyone. They already
knew my mom had problems. If
any of us kids were outside playing with our friends, Mom would
find some reason to start screaming at them, calling them terrible
names like "shit heels." The kids
would go home and tell their par-

Dear God, when I grow up, if I have a family, I promise you they will always have whatever they need.

ents about it, and then suddenly they were no longer allowed to
play with us. At the time, I resented her terribly for treating our
friends that way. I don't anymore, but I sure had a difficult time
with her erratic and unpredictable behavior back then.

I remember some of the kids had swimming pools in their
backyards. They were round, aboveground pools made with cor-
rugated metal and plastic lining. They weren't big, so people could
fill their pools with garden hoses. A boy named Harrison lived up
the street from us, on our side of the alley. When his family got a
new pool, his mother held a big party and invited a lot of the kids
from the neighborhood. Of course, Allan and I weren't included.
I remember walking up the alley that day and coming upon their
house. I saw Allan standing by the fence outside Harrison's yard,
holding on to it as he peered inside.

"Brother, what are you doing?" I asked.

He said, "I'm watching everyone play in the swimming pool."
This just broke my heart. Then Allan turned to me and said, "I
asked Harrison's mother if I could watch, and she said I could."

I took a deep breath and said, "Brother, you don't want to be
doing this. Let's go do something ourselves and have some fun."
And on we went.

To be fair, while I didn't have the closest relationship with my parents, I loved them both. If I had been given the option to trade them for someone else's parents, I wouldn't have done it. They both had their faults, but given the circumstances, I think they did the best they knew how to do. And there were times when my dad tried to step up. He would occasionally take Allan and me to hit baseballs and play catch. I loved that time together. Sometimes one or two of my uncles, Dad's brothers, would come over and we'd throw a football around with them too. Just us guys. It was so much fun—and so important as well. It felt good to have that small amount of male influence.

After he started working as a furniture salesman at Montgomery Ward, Dad would occasionally come home with some cheap steaks for Mom to broil. He'd cut the gristle off his steak and let me eat it. Man, it tasted so good. I loved it. After dinner, he'd watch his favorite show, *The Untouchables*, starring Robert Stack. Once in a blue moon, he'd let me watch it with him too.

The happiest times in our home were the simple times—a nice tree at Christmas, my brother and me getting to sleep on the floor in my parents' bedroom next to the air conditioner on a hot summer night, or a game of catch with the old man. But the best day of the year in our house by far was Christmas morning. I mean, what kid doesn't love Christmas morning? One year, my brother and I were up at the crack of dawn. It may even have been before dawn. We quietly crept up the stairs to the tree and started opening gifts before anyone else was awake. Another year, my father made the mistake of getting my brother and me pellet guns. We loaded them up, and after holding them for a bit in awe, we agreed to each shoot just one of the antique bulbs off our Christmas tree. I shot first, and then Allan went. *POP! POP!* Then we decided to each shoot one more, but Allan just kept going, so I joined him. In no time we shot all the bulbs off the tree. Pop sure was pissed about that—almost as pissed as he was when we crashed his new Lionel trains into each other on the railroad track he'd laid around the tree. *BAM!* He read us the riot act both times but never punished us. Allan and I loved him for that.

There was one Christmas, though, that I'll never forget. I must've been around eleven or twelve years old and was still playing with my plastic soldiers, always acting out some type of battle scene. Stanley's grocery store was up the street from our house, and right around Thanksgiving, they'd showcase maybe a dozen larger-size toys they were selling for Christmas. The toys, which were shrink-wrapped in see-through plastic, sat in colorful cardboard displays. To keep kids' hands off the various toys, they were placed on the store's top shelves. None of us could reach them, but we could still see everything about them. Most of the kids in the neighborhood would go inside and daydream about what they wanted. There were dolls and kitchenettes for the girls and toy guns and footballs for the boys. This particular year, there was a toy destroyer called *The Fighting Lady*. It had guns that shot darts and hidden wheels so it could "sail" around on the floor and still look as if it were in the ocean. This thing was the ultimate, most epic gift a kid could possibly get—at least to me. I went down to that store most days to look at the fighting ship.

I finally told my parents about it. The destroyer was the one thing I really was hoping for that year.

"Well, you never know what Santa is going to do," Mom said. After Mom told me that, I told Mr. Stanley or his wife, Mrs. Molly, when I was at the grocery store, "My mom and dad are going to get this for me for Christmas, so make sure you don't sell it." They would always reply, "We hear you."

Both Mom and Dad kept saying things for weeks that led me to believe I was going to find that ship under our tree on Christmas day. But that never happened.

When Christmas rolled around, I went up the basement steps early that morning, wide-eyed and happily looking forward to putting *The Fighting Lady* into action. I looked all around our Christmas tree, but I couldn't find it. I didn't want to believe it wasn't there. Instead, I got a new pair of pants. I was devastated. It was embarrassing, but even more so crushing. I had been so looking forward to that thing, and everyone knew it. Mom and Dad's excuse was that they didn't have the money to buy gifts that year, but I knew where the money had gone. I remember thinking that the horses they bet on meant more to them than I did. I'm fairly certain I didn't cry, but I know I wanted to. I sat there that morning with a giant hole in my heart. I wasn't angry so much as deeply disappointed. Even writing about it today, I'm surprised that it still hurts so much. I could have one hundred *Fighting Lady*s today if I wanted them, but that's not the point. My parents knew how much that plastic ship would have meant to me, and they sure had no problem with letting me down.

Believe it or not, there's always a silver lining when life doesn't go the way we plan or want it to. For me, from that day on, I learned not to look forward to anything too much. *The Fighting Lady* taught me that. Nothing is a sure thing in life until it's a done deal. Period.

In the end, my parents were married for over fifty years. That's not to say they had a perfect marriage. Who does? But as their son, I certainly would have protected both of them from being hurt at any time, in any way I could.

For all his flaws, Pop could be quite levelheaded. He did his best to impart his thoughts and beliefs to us, and often he had really memorable advice. Sometimes it was clouded by alcohol, but the words stuck with me. He told me that we're all in this thing called life together. At some point, you're going to need other people, and they will need you. He believed that deep down, almost everybody was a good person, and that we were all equal, regardless of our religion or the color of our skin. He also told me to treat people the way I wanted to be treated. And he once told me that life was short, so I might as well live where the weather was good. It was simple advice, but it made a wonderful difference in my life. I owe that to my dad.

It wasn't until I started writing this book that I realized I loved my father and my mother as much as I did. Sometimes we have to look back on life and

> **Sometimes we have to look back on life and search for its meaning and purpose.**

search for its meaning and purpose. I'm so grateful for both of my parents. I wouldn't have become who I am today without them.

"Fair" Is What You Pay
When You Get on a Bus

I spent my early years attending Public School 83. I loved it. It was a place where I remember always feeling happy. When I was there, everything was positive. It was the opposite of being at home.

I basically stayed in our basement until junior high school, with no real friends to speak of. I played Little League for a brief time. I was never a great athlete, because I didn't play enough to be any good. The only time I ever got on base was because I was hit by a pitch. I was so excited. Full of confidence, I took a big lead. Then I took a bigger lead. And *bam!*—just like that, the pitcher turned and threw the ball to the first baseman. I was picked off! I remember telling my father about it, and him saying, "Son, the world needs spectators too."

A parent knows when their kid has it and when they don't. And I didn't. Pop laughed about it. He never made me feel bad about my inability to thrive as an athlete. It wasn't an expectation, and so there wasn't any pressure around sports.

As I got older, I came out of the house more and more and developed some really good friends. I'm not sure why, but all my closest friends were the best friends anybody could ask for. They were intelligent, principled kids who had a positive influence on me. There was Paul Kolb, who liked to read a lot, like me. He got me into playing roller hockey on metal roller skates. If you've never played, it's a tough sport. The surface you play on is hard, usually concrete. When you fall or get knocked down, man, it hurts. Quite often I'd come home from a game pretty bruised up. Mom would notice and say, "What the hell happened to you?" I'd tell her, "Mom, I was playing roller hockey and got a little beat up." She'd say, "If you want to get beat up, just tell me and I'll beat the shit out of you." Rather than trying to tell her how much fun playing hockey was, I'd just walk away.

As often as we could, Paul and I would take a city bus downtown to watch professional ice hockey and basketball games. After the games ended, usually around nine or ten o'clock at night, we'd walk about ten city blocks to a section of town called the Block, where all the strip joints were located. There was a pizza place there that made the best pies. We'd each buy a slice and walk back and forth past the strip clubs as we ate. Their front doors were usually open, so we'd try to get a peek at one of the strippers in action. We never really did. The doormen who worked at those joints made sure of that. But once in a blue moon we'd catch a quick glimpse of a star-covered breast and that put us over the moon. We'd talk about it all week. Once, a few of us were wondering why it was always a star. Our friend Edgar chimed in and asked, "Maybe it's a celebration of America?" Paul and I just laughed. It wasn't until much later we learned those patriotic stars were required by law.

Ron Perone was a good guy too. One thing I liked about him was that he always had interesting plans for his future. I remember him talking about working for Merrill Lynch in the financial and investment industry someday.

And then there was James Tankersley, who was four or five years older than me. He was a gentle, kind dude. We met when I was around twelve years old and James was sixteen. He was living with his mom and grandmother. I think his dad had passed away a few years earlier. I went to James's house a lot. I liked the way I felt when I was there. I'd knock on the door, wait for his mom or grandmother to answer, and ask if James was there. They always made me feel welcome. Sometimes his mom would bring me a freshly baked cookie and a tall, cold glass of milk. They were a very sweet family.

There was a chess set in James's living room that caught my eye every time I stopped by. Intrigued, I asked James if he would teach me to play, and he did. After I learned how each piece moved and how to capture opposing pieces, we played quite a few times over the months that followed, so I got a general idea of how the game flowed. Then he began teaching me a few strategies. I'll never forget his kindness or the gift he gave me by introducing me to chess.

James had a conviction about him that was admirable. Even at a young age, I understood that he was a guy with a lot of integrity. Years later, James became a fireman. While out fighting a fire one day, he ran into a burning house to rescue some children. He found one and came out, then went back into the burning building a second time, found another kid, and made his way out again. Finally, he ran in a third time, but he never came out. I still tear up when I think about that. It was a hard way to lose a friend. To this day, every time I play chess I think of James.

After my dad's business failed, for one reason or another, he decided to become Catholic. Up until this point, I had been raised with no religion. We never went to church. However, because of Pop's new faith, he pulled my brother and me out of PS 83 and enrolled us in a Catholic elementary school called Saint Elizabeth of Hungary. The teachers were all Franciscan nuns, which meant that they wore big penguin-like outfits. You could only see their faces, most of which looked old and mean to me.

I was in the third grade and didn't really understand why I had to change schools. My grades took a dive; from that day on, I just wasn't a good student. I never did any homework. I didn't participate in anything unless I had to. And I was very upset by our situation at home. I was terribly confused and distraught. I just wanted to be happy, but after leaving PS 83, that was never the case. And if there were moments of happiness at Saint Elizabeth, they didn't last long. Everything at home seemed to be melting down. The place was drenched with screaming and turmoil.

The first day I walked into Saint Elizabeth, I saw a large crucifix with an effigy of Jesus hanging on it. In my mind, it looked like a guy nailed to a plus sign. *These people are* really *serious about math!* I thought to myself.

We had to go to school early and sit through mass first thing in the morning. Back then, the entire service was conducted in Latin, and I squirmed through the whole thing. When I look back, I realize I probably had undiagnosed ADD, but in those days, there was no name for my restlessness. These days I would have been pumped full of Ritalin, but at that time, it was just seen as a behavioral issue that made me more of a pain in the nuns' asses than anything else.

It wasn't unusual to find me chewing on the yellow number 2 pencils we had to use in class. I could turn a pencil into a toothpick in one day. I'd gnaw on those pencils until there were little yellow paint chips stuck between my teeth and all over my lips. I must have looked like a little rabid beast. I had a lot of nervous energy that was hard to control. My classmates and I would sit in

> I quickly earned a reputation for misbehaving, which meant I was usually on the wrong side of the nuns.

the pews on those mornings we were in church and play with our coats and hats, just fiddling with anything to pass the time. There were little clips on the benches in front of us where we could hang our hats. I'd play with one, occasionally pushing it back and then letting it go so it would snap. And when it did, it made a loud-enough noise that the nuns were immediately on me. I quickly earned a reputation for misbehaving, which meant I was usually on the wrong side of the nuns.

It didn't take long before a few of my classmates and I started skipping mass. When the nuns realized some of us weren't there, they would search for us and chase us through the alley behind the school. We thought it was funny, and as fast as they could run in those habits, they never did catch us.

My third-grade teacher was a nun named Sister Louis Gonzaga. Every now and then she would tell us that the world was going to end in 1960 and our parents were going to hell, and more than likely so were we. She was what I'd call a real Debbie Downer. Once she asked a boy in class what he wanted to be when he grew up.

"A lawyer," he proudly said.

"That's a shame, because the world is going to end in 1960 and you and your parents will probably fry in hell."

No doubt about it: she was nuts.

From the day I started at Saint Elizabeth, it had been burned into my head by Sister Gonzaga that the world was going to end in 1960, so when my parents had a New Year's Eve party on December 31,1959, and they and their friends counted down and celebrated as midnight approached, I sat in my dad's La-Z-Boy anticipating doomsday. I was waiting for it all to end, expecting an avenging angel to come down and take us all out. But then nothing happened. Nothing. It was all bullshit. Everything Sister Gonzaga told us in third grade—that the Blessed Mother had appeared to her and told her the end of the world was coming—all of it was false. After that, I had even more trouble buying into religion.

I suppose the nuns weren't all mean, but most of the ones I came across during those early school years were pretty awful. When my aunt found out we were changing schools, she warned me that when I got to Saint Elizabeth, the nuns would beat the shit out of me if I didn't behave. Forewarned, but hardly forearmed. I got whacked across the palms of my hands with the back of a big wooden-handled brush or smacked across the knuckles with a yardstick more than a few times. They would hit you hard enough for you to feel it and not want it to happen again, but never hard enough to really hurt you. If I went home and said anything about this to my parents, I would get it again. For the most part, they figured I must have done something worthy of that type of punishment. In their eyes, the nuns could do no wrong. In my eyes, they could do no right.

I was never fully beaten by the nuns. But shaken down? Now, that's a different story. When the nuns would collect money for the archbishop's relief fund, they took it very seriously. They would have a contest to see which row of kids in each classroom could give the most. There were times when my brother saw a nun turn one of the guys in his class upside down and shake him for the loose change in his pockets. I wasn't the biggest kid, but I wasn't the smallest either, so thankfully I escaped that treatment.

My brother and I never really took to our Catholic school experience. I can't even say we took to becoming devout Catholics either. It just wasn't for us.

On Sundays my mother would give each of us a quarter for the collection box and then send us to church. We actually went a few times, but when the weather got nice, we'd head across the street to Patterson Park instead. We'd play for a while and then walk over to the local pharmacy, which was open on Sundays, to buy ice cream with our quarters. We'd get our cones, head to a hill by the local soccer fields, and watch whatever game was being played.

"Doesn't it seem more like *this* is what God wants us to do?" I'd ask Allan.

Being with my brother, whom I absolutely loved and adored, meant more to me than being in church, that's for sure. It was almost worth the price of going to hell for it.

> Being with my brother, whom I absolutely loved and adored, meant more to me than being in church, that's for sure. It was almost worth the price of going to hell for it.

We never told our parents about our special Sundays. If we had, we would have gotten clobbered. Instead, we kept it between us brothers. And I loved every minute of it.

When I was in the fifth grade, Allan was in the second grade. He was the cutest kid, with white-blond hair and crystal-blue eyes. Allan never met a stranger; he could talk to anybody. He wasn't an introvert like me. He was polite, polished, and charming and could have sold you the Brooklyn Bridge if he wanted to. And people loved him for that.

Sister Trina was a nun at Saint Elizabeth who had an Avon business on the side. She saw something special in Allan—so special, in fact, that she used his sweet innocence and charm to sell her Avon products door to door. The women loved it, and therefore Allan sold a ton of cosmetics, closing sale after sale for Sister Trina. In return, she'd give him time off from school. When he reached the third grade, there was a lot he didn't know that he would have known if he hadn't missed all that class time selling beauty products or playing on the swings at Ellwood Park. He struggled for a while but eventually caught up.

By the time I'd gotten to fifth grade, I had all but given up on my education. I'd barely passed third grade. In fourth grade, I had a lay teacher named Miss Vicky Kenny. She didn't like me one bit. If I asked to go to the restroom, she'd say no. If I asked again, she'd still say no. One time I raised my hand a third time and said, "I really need to go to the restroom."

"I told you no," she said again.

Sure enough, I pissed all over myself. I was horrified. All my classmates saw it happen too.

"What is wrong with you?" Miss Kenny asked, as if I hadn't already explained that I *really* needed to go.

I was so embarrassed, I started to cry. And when I did, Miss Kenny started calling me a big baby, which made me feel even worse. It surely wasn't my fault. When you've got to go, you've got to go, right? I got gibed about it a little bit, but much to my surprise, the other kids also didn't like what happened. After all, it could have happened to any one of them too. I was always grateful for that.

The worst thing Miss Kenny ever did, though, happened during one of her class spelling bees. Since I had spent so much time reading comic books, I was a reasonably good speller. I never studied the vocabulary words; I just had a knack for knowing them. The prize for the winner of this particular spelling bee was a special mass card with an image of Jesus on it for protection. You were supposed to keep it in your pocket or wallet and always carry it with you. I really wanted that card. And I wanted to win the spelling bee, especially against Tyrone Smith. Tyrone was a good kid who was always nice to everybody, but he was also Miss Kenny's pet student—by far her favorite. As best I could tell, other than being a good student, Tyrone hadn't done anything to become Miss Kenny's pet. For whatever reason, she just really liked him.

The final round came down to one word between Tyrone and me: *astonishment*.

Tyrone stumbled on it.

Then it was my turn, and I was feeling really confident because one of the comic books I read as often as I could get my hands on it was called *Tales to Astonish*.

I knew that word left, right, and center.

I nailed it and won.

Tyrone sat down as I relished my victory.

That is, until Miss Kenny walked over and handed Tyrone the mass card instead of me.

"You should have won," she said as she gave Tyrone the coveted card.

What?

I didn't understand what had just happened.

And then it dawned on me. She favored him and despised me and had decided Tyrone deserved to be the winner even though he'd lost.

It wasn't fair, and I'm not going to say it didn't hurt me, because it did. A lot.

Tyrone felt bad, and being the good guy he always was, he came over and said, "You can have the mass card. You deserve it."

"Tyrone, she gave it to you. Just keep it." I knew I'd won. So did Tyrone. The other kids knew it too.

This was the moment when I realized that *life is not fair*. As a matter of fact, since then I've always said, "You'd do well if the only meaning *fair* has to you is what you pay when you get on a bus." (Of course, as a crackerjack speller I know that the word for a bus payment is actually spelled f-a-r-e.) From that day on, I never had any expectations that life would be f-a-i-r.

While I did move on to fifth grade, I was barely making it through school. I hated it and was giving up any hope that things would ever get better. My fifth-grade teacher was Sister Brenda, who was kind of laid-back compared to the other nuns I'd encountered at Saint Elizabeth. But at the same time, she was also quite mean, and for whatever reason, she also didn't like me at all. I suppose that by this time I'd solidified my reputation for being a troublemaker, and I was certainly someone who didn't like complying with the rules. As a result, throughout most of the school year I was kept late after school for detention. It was never anything bad—mostly talking in class when I shouldn't have been or goofing off.

There could be ten kids talking and Sister Brenda would always single me out and say, "Robert Parsons, you're staying after school." And she'd do it often.

I'd drop my head and say, "Yes, Sister."

I walked Allan to and from school, so when I was in detention, he'd have to stay after school with me. Every now and then, Sister Brenda took pity on Allan for having to wait and let me go early.

On the last day of school that year, I was filled with excitement for a nun-free summer. I couldn't wait to get out of there and away from Sister Brenda. I remember it being an especially hot and humid early summer day. Sister Brenda started handing out report cards to her students like they were Academy Awards. "Nice job, Debbie"; "Excellent work, Steve"; "Well done, Carl"; and so on.

Once you received your report card, you were supposed to stand up and get into line, and then she would walk all of us around the entire complex to meet our parents, who were waiting for us on the corner across the street. The campus was fairly sizable, so it was a decent march. The church, school, and convent were on one side of the street, lined up one after the other in that order. The rectory was on the other side of the street, directly across from the church, with residential housing completing the rest of that side. The front of the convent faced the houses adjacent to the rectory. The corner where our parents waited for us was across the street from the back of the convent.

Sister Brenda came to the end of her stack of report cards. Everyone had received one except Anthony, Frankie, and me. Three losers. Our classmates made a point of not looking at us as they stood in line.

"You three stay here until I get back," she said sternly.

She left the classroom with the line of kids following happily behind her.

Holy shit. The three of us are going to fail, I thought as I sat there in the sweltering heat.

At first, I was numb. I stared at the door for maybe another minute before deciding right then and there that when Sister Brenda returned, she wasn't going to find me in her classroom.

I got up from my desk and, without saying a word to Anthony and Frankie, walked out of the classroom, ran through the halls and down a flight of stairs, then escaped out the back exit. From there, I hightailed it down the street behind the convent and up along the fence that surrounded it. When I reached the far corner, I looked around and saw my class and Sister Brenda walking toward me. Most nuns on the last day of school would walk with their class all the way to the street, then cross so everyone could join their waiting parents. If Sister Brenda did that, my goose was cooked. But there was one thing I knew for sure would save me: Sister Brenda was one lazy nun. She never did anything she didn't have to. During the dozen or so times when she *didn't* keep me after school, she always broke off from our group early and headed right into the front entrance of the convent, letting us kids go on by ourselves. As I peeked around the convent fence, I saw, to my relief, that Sister Brenda wasn't going to let me down. She left my classmates, turned around, and started heading back to the classroom to crucify the unholy threesome. I waited by the fence for my class to walk by and was amazed that they were all so preoccupied with school being over for the summer that none of them paid any attention to me as I stood there. *Whew!* I fell in at the back of the line and walked across the street, joining my brother and father, who were waiting for me. My father always made it a point to pick Allan and me up from school on our last day.

"Where's your report card?" Dad asked.

"Sister didn't give me one," I responded, which was true— she hadn't.

"How come?"

That's when I told him a fib. I said, "Dad, this year, if you passed, you didn't get a report card."

I was stone-faced.

"So, let me get this straight: if you passed, you don't get a report card?"

"No, Dad. I didn't." Again, I stood by my story as if it were the gospel.

Now, my brother had already given Pop his report card, so I'm sure he thought something was fishy. He stood quietly for a moment, with a racing form under his arm and a Tareyton cigarette in his mouth. He took one last drag from his cigarette, looked at me, flicked the butt into the street, blew the smoke out of his mouth, and said, "Whatever. Get in the car."

All I could do was breathe a sigh of relief and hope he didn't discover the truth.

Dad drove Allan and me to Louis J. Smith's sporting goods store. As a reward for graduating, he allowed us to pick one thing. "Go ahead and get yourselves something," Pop said.

My brother loaded himself up with stuff only to have Dad tell him to put most of it back. I didn't pick anything. I couldn't help feeling guilty, knowing I was on death row and I would be executed the moment he found out I'd failed and lied to him about it.

"Robert, what's the matter? Don't you want anything?" Dad asked.

"Dad, I've got plenty. I don't need anything," I said, knowing we literally had nothing. I wasn't sure where he was getting the money to pay for our things that day.

"Go ahead and pick something out, son," he said.

Reluctantly, I chose a first baseman's mitt. I felt the way folks must feel when they know they're writing a bad check.

When we got home, Allan bolted into the house to show my mother his report card like he was in a relay race. I moseyed in slowly.

"Where's your report card, Robert?" Mom asked.

"Sister didn't give me one," I said.

"Why not?"

I had to keep the same story I gave to Pop, so I told her, "If you passed, you didn't get a report card." I paused for a moment before blurting out, "Call Sister Brenda. She'll tell you."

"You know what? I think I will call her," Mom responded.

"If it makes you feel better, Mom," I said, "you should call her."

But she never did.

And though I waited for days and weeks for the other shoe to drop, the school never called my parents either. I thought about what I might say when Sister Brenda made that call, how I would explain it to my mom and dad. Every time the phone rang, I would practically jump out of my skin. But it was never her.

Thus began the longest summer of my life.

It took me a couple of weeks to realize they weren't going to call. I'd wake up in the morning so happy it was summer, until it would slowly begin to sink in that I was a dead man walking—a prisoner waiting to be shot by a firing squad once my parents discovered the truth. The thought never left my mind. If I was playing ball with some of the guys, I'd be thinking about it. I would get so deep in thought that the guys would constantly ask me what was wrong. I knew that if I told anybody it would quickly spread, so I never said anything to anyone.

I even tried to tell my dad the truth one day near the end of summer. Baltimore was a hot place in August. Our house was small, and the heat would get trapped in our tiny living room. Pop was sitting in his drawers and a white T-shirt reading the newspaper. He held it up with both hands, covering his face.

I mustered up enough courage that day to say, "Dad."

Nothing.

"Dad," I repeated.

Still no response.

Finally, after I called his name a few more times, he slowly lowered the paper. Sweat was running down his face. He looked at me, a man in misery, and, with his eyes bugged out, said, "What?"

I paused.

"Nothing," I said.

The newspaper went slowly back up, and I never did confess. When the end of summer neared and it was time to buy my school supplies for the next year, I acted as if I would be starting sixth grade with the rest of my friends.

On the first day back, somehow Allan and I got a ride to school with Mrs. Molly, Stanley the grocer's wife. Mrs. Molly picked us up in a little red Volkswagen Beetle. To say there were a lot of kids in her car that morning would be an understatement. We all jammed ourselves in there. I remember my hands were by my waist, holding my small knapsack, and we were so pressed up against one another that I couldn't raise my arm. When Mrs. Molly pulled up in front of the school to drop us off, it must have looked like kids would never stop coming out of that little Beetle.

After we got to school, I stepped into line with the other sixth graders. I looked over at Sister Brenda's fifth-grade line, and sure enough, Frankie and Anthony were standing there. Both of them must have been looking for me, because they saw me instantly and waved for me to come over and join them. I remember thinking, *Lord, have mercy.* I waved back at them while I shook my head no, then turned away.

When the bell rang, the kindergartners went in first, then the first grade, then second, third, and so on until it was our turn. As I walked through the doors, I saw the sixth-grade teacher, Sister Saint Thomas, there in the hallway waiting for me. She pulled me out of line and backed me up against the wall. She bent down, put her face in mine until our noses were about an inch from each other, and, somewhere between a whisper and her normal voice, said sternly, "Sister Brenda told me what you did, that you failed her class and didn't wait for her to come back like she told you to. She didn't know what to do, so she passed you."

So
She
Passed
You.

The four most beautiful words anyone had ever uttered to me.

"You give me any grief and you're going right back to fifth grade," Sister Saint Thomas said. And I could tell she meant it.

"I won't, Sister. I promise," I responded. And you'd better believe I was being sincere in that moment.

I had already given myself up for dead. I'd punished myself all summer long worrying about the truth coming out. However, I learned two very important lessons from this experience. First, I learned how important it is to keep your own counsel. If I had told anybody, I would have been in hot water. What I'd done would have been out there, and then there wouldn't have been anything I could do to prevent the inevitable.

The second thing I learned was that most of the time, if you just hang in there, things work out. I applied that knowledge throughout my life after that, and it has never failed me. I relied on it during the Vietnam War, when building my various businesses, and even to this very day.

I wish I could tell you I was better with Sister Saint Thomas in sixth grade than I had been before that, but if I was, it wasn't by much. The only difference was that Sister Saint Thomas didn't have it in for me. She actually treated me nicer than the nuns before her had. I still ate my pencils and was a rabid little beast. I barely passed her class, but it was still a pass. When I showed my mom my report card that year, she looked at my grades and said, "Well. This is nothing to be proud of, but you did pass." After a few moments she said, "I like it a lot better when you get a report card." I certainly understood what she was saying.

All I could say was, "So do I, Mom. So do I."

Learning How to Turn a Buck

I've always been a pretty optimistic guy. By no means am I a blind optimist, though. I somehow inherently understood that, even as a kid. You might say I've always had the entrepreneurial spirit. Now, to be clear, that doesn't mean that every business I've ever started was a success. My early years as an aspiring entrepreneur were, well, full of mistakes that I had to learn from.

When I was ten years old, I decided to set up a lemonade stand. I had never made, let alone tasted, lemonade before, but I thought, *How hard can it be?* Lemons, sugar, water. Easy enough. My mother kept fresh lemon juice in a bottle marked "Lemon." I grabbed that bottle, poured its contents into a large pitcher full of water, and added sugar. I tasted it. It was awful. But then I thought, *Maybe that's the way it's supposed to be.* Even so, I added more sugar and tried it again, but it still tasted weird to me. I kept adding sugar to get it right.

I set my stand up at the edge of our front porch steps, put up a handmade sign that read "Fresh Lemonade—5 cents," and then waited for people to come by. It was a hot day in the middle of summer—so hot, in fact, that you could see shimmers of heat rising from the asphalt in the street.

Back then, especially in East Baltimore, life insurance men would walk what was called a debit route. They'd come to collect insurance premiums every week. One of those men was Mr. Hill. He made his way toward my lemonade stand with his sport coat flipped over one shoulder and his porkpie hat atop his head. He had loosened his tie and unbuttoned the top button on his collared shirt. He looked hot, tired, and thirsty. *Bingo.* He was my first customer.

"Man, do I need one of those," he said as he pointed toward a fresh cup of my soon-to-be famous homemade lemonade. He flipped me a dime he'd fished out of his pants pocket and said, "Keep the change." I couldn't believe my luck. I handed Mr. Hill a lemonade and watched him take a giant swig.

Mr. Hill's eyes grew wide and bulged before he spit that big gulp of lemonade into the street.

"Jesus Christ, kid. That's the worst lemonade I've ever tasted!" He threw his cup down and walked away mumbling something I couldn't quite make out.

I was surprised by his reaction, but not deterred. Soon thereafter, Suzanne Hamel, a girl who lived across the street, stopped by to see me. I sold her a cup of lemonade, but I could tell she didn't like it either. A few minutes later, Suzanne came back and told me her mother said I needed to give her back her nickel—which I did. This happened a few more times, until word had spread to stay away from my lemonade. After that, I shut the stand down.

My attempt at launching my first business was a total bust. I couldn't figure out what I'd done wrong. When my mom came home from whatever she was doing that day, I told her I was selling lemonade but no one seemed to like it. She asked how I made it— what did I use? I told her lemon juice, water, and sugar.

"Where did you get the lemon?" she asked.

I told her from the bottle in the refrigerator that said "Lemon" on it.

"Robert! I keep vinegar in that bottle, not lemon juice!" my mom said.

Well, how was I supposed to know that?

Now it all made sense.

I hadn't made lemonade. I'd made *vinegarade*.

My mom helped me make a new batch, only this time with all the right ingredients. But it was too late: everyone in the neighborhood knew about my horrible lemonade. I never sold another cup. But I did learn an early lesson that the quality of your product is very important. This also taught me that if your only goal is to make money, chances are you won't—or at least not in the long run. I know that last part goes against everything most people think they know about turning a buck, but believe me, it's how I built all my businesses and made them successful. To make real money, you have to create enthusiasm around your product, and you have to serve your customers'

To make real money, you have to create enthusiasm around your product, and you have to serve your customers' needs.

needs. Finally, you must get their attention up front. No doubt I got their attention that day, but for all the wrong reasons.

I was naturally creative with my business ideas. Again, not all of them were great businesses, but they were resourceful. I once bought some tropical fish I thought I could mate and then sell. They were Siamese fighting fish (bettas). You can tell which fighting fish are male by their beautiful fins, especially when they're ready to breed. You have to put glass inside the aquarium to keep the male and female fish apart until the time is right. When the male is in full bloom, he's ready to go. My male fighting fish was building the most incredible bubble nest. I watched as it got bigger and bigger. When it got huge, though, I still didn't put the two fish together. The male finally gave up, shriveled, and died. I suppose you could say I learned a valuable lesson there as well. Maybe two. First, you can wait too long for something. And second, you need to strike when the iron is hot—or when the fish is ready.

One of my favorite jobs was the paper route I had as a young man. A few of my buddies would come by my house to wake me up around three o'clock every Sunday morning. They'd come to the window over the basement and whisper, "Robert." As soon as I heard that, I'd shoot straight up like I'd seen a ghost.

"What?" I would whisper back.

The guys and I would roar with laughter.

I worried that my parents would kill me if they were awakened at that hour, but they never did. I'd quietly go out the back door and meet my friends in the alley behind our house. We'd each pick up our stacks of papers that had been dropped on the street corner and deliver them to everyone in our neighborhood. I had a big strap for carrying the papers in. I shoved as many papers in there as I could carry and then slung it over my back. When it was full, it was so heavy that I thought it would break my back. I tossed those papers out as fast as I could, lightening my load along the way.

The newspaper charged me for every paper, and it was my job to deliver papers and collect the money to pay for them. After I'd paid for the product, the profit was mine to keep. I occasionally had a hard time collecting, but I never put pressure on anyone. My customers were all usually very nice. If for some reason they couldn't pay, they always promised to make good the following week. And for the most part, they did. As for the few customers who didn't pay? Well, I'd knock on their doors in hopes that they'd come up with the money, but I never really expected them to. I chalked that up to the cost of doing business. I didn't really mind, because I liked socializing with my buddies who were busy doing the same thing I was.

Sometimes after I'd finished delivering the papers along my route, usually at around five in the morning, I'd go down to the White Coffee Pot diner. Outside the diner there were two newspaper dispensers, one for *The Baltimore Sun* and the other for *The News American*. I'd put a quarter into each and take out all the papers, then set them in front of me on the sidewalk next to the diner as if I were in charge of selling them to the customers. There weren't a lot of places to buy the paper early on a Sunday morning, so I created a way.

> Whenever someone asked, "What if it doesn't work?" I'd always say, "But what if it does?" I've followed that philosophy for most of my life, and it has always served me well.

The diner was an ideal location because there was the Monumental Bus Tour terminal next door. The buses from Philadelphia or New York would stop at the terminal to gas up, and the passengers would get out to stretch their legs and grab a cup of coffee and a newspaper. I sold each paper for fifty cents, or a dollar if I was feeling bold. I usually sold out the stack. But if I didn't, I'd put the remaining papers back in their respective boxes and insert a quarter for every paper I sold. In other words, I paid for the papers I sold *after* the sale. I usually made a profit of five or six dollars, which was pretty good scratch for a young kid. I never told anyone what I was doing. I knew that if I told my buddies, they'd come down and screw it up for me.

I could always find ways to make money, and I mostly did it doing things I enjoyed. That kept it fun, interesting, and profitable. I never worried about whether something would work. If I didn't know how to do something at first, I'd just figure it out. Whenever someone asked, "What if it doesn't work?" I'd always say, "But what if it does?" I've followed that philosophy for most of my life, and it has always served me well.

Where the Rubber Meets the Road

I'm glad to report that my time at Saint Elizabeth ended almost as abruptly as it started, midway through the seventh grade.

My seventh-grade teacher, Sister Vincentia, brought classroom punishment to a new level. She was very old, she never smiled, and she was in a league all her own. I know this won't come as a surprise, but I was her whipping boy. It was the same routine: everyone was talking, but I got nailed. I glanced out the window—busted.

She enjoyed whacking me with a yardstick as much as any of the nuns, but her favorite form of torture was to drag me up to the front of the classroom and shove me under her desk. The space beneath that big desk was made for a pair of nun's legs, not a pair of nun's legs plus little Robert. I'd squeeze in there, Houdini-like, and all I could see was dusty wood, that Sister's nun suit, and her clunky black shoes. I breathed in so much dust down there that I felt damn near asthmatic.

As tough as I had it, it was worse for my classmate Sandra. That little girl just couldn't sit still. So Sister Vincentia came up with a plan: she took a piece of rope and tied Sandra's hands behind her back. To ensure she didn't move, Sister Vincentia pushed pins through the rope with the points aimed at Sandra's back. If Sandra leaned back, even slightly, those pins would stick her. As I think back, though, what's amazing is that Sister Vincentia's pin punishment wasn't that shocking to the rest of the class. Only, say, a beheading would have shocked us. Maybe.

It was plenty shocking to my mom and dad, however. When I told them what happened to Sandra and explained how I spent as much time under Sister Vincentia's desk as I did sitting at my own, it began to occur to them that maybe Catholic school wasn't such a great idea after all. That's when Dad pulled Allan and me out of Saint Elizabeth and enrolled me in Hampstead Hill Junior High, a local public school, while Allan was back at PS 83. That was one happy day for us.

But God apparently wanted to make sure that I understood just how unfair life could be. The day after I transferred out of Saint Elizabeth—just *one* damn day—Sister Vincentia somehow managed to tumble down a flight of steps, and *bam!* . . . she was dead. Sister Vincentia's tumble into the next life wasn't what bothered me. The real crusher was that the entire school—yup, every student at Saint Elizabeth of Hungary—got the week off. I know it sounds heartless, but I felt cheated. I didn't get any time off, and I spent more time in Sister Vincentia's gulag than any of them.

Son of a bitch, I remember saying to myself before it occurred to me that—horror of horrors—I would see Sister Vincentia again. I knew I'd probably meet up with her in hell someday. After all, that's where she always told me I would end up, and I could think of no reason why she wouldn't be there too.

Boo!

She'd get the last laugh.

As grim as Saint Elizabeth was, Hampstead Hill was the complete opposite. The atmosphere was relaxed and fun, and it was a place where we laughed *with* our teachers, not *at* them. This was also the place where I started to make new friends, including my buddy Paul Kolb.

My homeroom teacher was Mrs. Caldwell. I sure liked her. Up until then, I had never met a teacher I really liked, but she was a pretty cool lady and taught me that not all teachers were out to get me like those nuns were.

For lack of a better place, I used to keep a little white mouse in my shirt pocket. I was a sucker for animals like that. I remember that, back in the fifth grade, a few of us kids would go over to the local graveyard and push the small tombstones over. Sometimes, little garter snakes would be underneath. One of the guys sold me a snake, and I carried that thing around everywhere. There was a kid in my class who was kind of a bully who wanted my snake. He was mean, and much bigger than me. I think he was older than me too, but he'd failed a few grades some years before. Anyway, he was huge. I remember him walking out of school and kicking me in the back of my ankles to try to take my snake. I never gave it up, though. I was tough when I needed to be, but I was never a bully like that guy. By now, you know I was always doing stupid stuff I shouldn't have done, but nothing so horrible. Mrs. Caldwell never seemed to have a problem with my pet mouse. Then, one day, she turned to me and said, "Robert Parsons, let me ask you a personal question about that little white mouse. When you keep it in your pocket all day, where does it go to the bathroom?"

"I guess in my pocket," I said.

I hadn't really thought about it until she asked me the question. I didn't carry the mouse around after that. It seemed kind of gross.

Now, I could tell you that once I got to Hampstead Hill, I suddenly became a better student—that I somehow saw the virtue of working hard and getting good grades. But I didn't. The truth was that I chugged along through school doing what I always did: very little, at least when it came to schoolwork. When I finished Hampstead Hill, there were a number of high schools I could have attended, and I chose an engineering high school called Baltimore Polytechnic Institute. It sounds fancier than it was. I had to take a bus to get there, as it was downtown. It was safe, as long as I didn't stay past dark. If I ever found myself at the bus stop after dark, I would get shaken down for any loose change I might have in my pockets. It was not a good place to be.

Polytechnic was an all-boys school. It was pretty hard academically, and I disliked it—especially the all-boys part. I focused on what I needed to and was excellent in certain subjects, such as geometry. But other than that, I started failing most of my classes. I just quit paying attention to my studies. Pop could see I was on a clear path to failure, so he yanked me out of there after the tenth grade and put me into Patterson High School, a big school about a mile from our house where most of the neighborhood kids went. If Patterson is known for anything, it's that it was the setting for the play and movie *Hairspray*, which takes place in Baltimore in 1962, a few years before I attended the school.

My Patterson experience wasn't exactly *Hairspray*, but there were a lot of similarities I appreciated—a lot. Especially my discovery of girls, alcohol, rock music, and Motown. Girls at Patterson wore skirts that fell below their knees and had their hair pulled straight back or done up in a beehive. All the guys tried to look tough, with James Dean–style ducktails or long hair and bell-bottom jeans. This was the 1960s in America. The British Invasion was underway, America's involvement in Vietnam was escalating, and change was in the air.

Patterson could be a rough place, especially for a new student coming in. On one of my first days there, in fact, I was in printshop class, and this kid named Lou took my pen. Lou was a big dude, born a year earlier than me. For whatever reason, he wouldn't give me back my pen.

"Lou," I said, just as it was time to leave class, "can I have my pen back?"

"No," he said, acting like a dog protecting his bone.

"But I need my pen."

"It's my pen now. Besides, what are you going to do about it?" he asked.

Lou was taller and heavier than me, but I knew that if I let him keep my pen, I'd be seen as a pushover. As we stood in line waiting for the bell, with Lou standing behind me, I tried once more.

"Hey, Lou, I want my pen back."

"No," he replied. I faced forward again, waited a couple of beats, and then, without hesitation, I swung around and punched big Lou in the face as hard as I could. *Smack!* Right in the chops. I mean *BOOM!* I clocked this guy.

He just stood there snarling at me. "I'm going to kill you!"

"Oh shit," I said.

Lou rushed at me and I went at him, down between his legs. I came out behind him—the size difference was that great—and when he reached through his legs to grab me, I got hold of both his arms and hung on for dear life until the shop teacher pulled us apart and escorted us to the principal's office.

The funny thing was, as we were waiting to see the principal, our tempers cooled, and Lou smiled at me as he handed back my pen. "You know what?" he said. "You're crazy. We should be friends." I smiled to myself, thinking that sometimes it's good to establish yourself as a little crazy from the get-go.

Lou was my buddy from then on. He even started looking after me. But the relationship was born of fire. Now, I'm not advocating fighting. I didn't really like to get into those scuffles. In some ways,

I think it was generational—perhaps a high school coming-of-age, *Summer of '42* type of thing. Maybe that doesn't go on as much today, but I'm sure it does to some degree. At the time, I couldn't just let someone push me around. In the split second before I hit Lou, I accepted that he was going to beat the shit out of me, and that was okay. The way I saw it, it was better than a life of torment, which is what I'd envisioned had I let him keep my pen.

So that was Patterson High. I actually liked the place. Looking back, I think moving over to Patterson is what saved me. I climbed out of my shell, although after years of being in the basement, I had the social skills of a gnat.

I had started smoking around the age of fourteen. My mother used to light me up a cigarette and send me off to school. As a result, I smoked all the time. Back then, you could smoke on the school campus. Everyone did it.

On weekends, Allan and I used to sneak out through the basement trapdoor to go get smashed with our buddies, drinking Colt 45 malt liquor. In the winter, some of our neighbors would store their beer outside on their porches to keep it cold. In a neighborhood full of teenage boys, that was a dumb idea. I spent my junior and senior years doing typical teenage stuff: I discovered pot, I played street hockey, and I read, generally about war: Julius Caesar's *The Conquest of Gaul* and memoirs by Ulysses S. Grant and William Tecumseh Sherman. I tried playing the drums; I was awful, and never got any better. I had a couple of jobs—pumping gas at a nearby Sinclair station and working construction on the weekends.

> Eventually, when I was a senior, the greatest opportunity in a teenage boy's life came my way: I had the chance to get laid.

Eventually, when I was a senior, the greatest opportunity in a teenage boy's life came my way: I had the chance to get laid. I had a buddy in high school named Danny Thorne; he was older than me and was the guy who knew everything I didn't. It was Danny who explained the birds and the bees to me, which I appreciated. That was a conversation I never had with my dad, that's for sure.

Danny was in a relationship with a pretty girl named Toni. Toni lived at home with her mom, who was going out of town for the weekend. Danny invited me over to hook up with Pauline, one of Toni's friends. She and I knew each other, and from what I was told, she was all in. So was I. Pauline was absolutely stunning. She had luscious black hair, even darker eyes, and the smoothest skin imaginable. Most of what I knew about sex—or thought I knew—I'd heard from Danny or gleaned from reading *Playboy*.

"Come over on Friday night. Toni and I will be upstairs. You and Pauline can have the basement rec room," Danny said with a wink and a smile.

I had never gotten close to anything like this. I was beyond excited. After school on Monday I went to the pharmacy and bought a condom. I had only enough money to buy one. After school on Tuesday, I took the packaged condom out and set it down on my dresser. I looked at it. And it looked at me. In my head, I was having a conversation with it.

You know, this will be my first time, I said.

Mine too, the condom responded.

Friday couldn't arrive fast enough. I had the same conversation with the condom every day for the rest of the week.

Finally, it was Friday.

Man, was I excited.

I came home from school, scrubbed down, put on my best clothes—which weren't great, but they were the best I had—and put my condom in my pocket. I was raring to go. And then I noticed it was just three o'clock. I still had three hours before I could head over to Toni's house. I took the condom out, just like I'd done all week. I sat there and looked at it.

Well, three more hours, I said.

I can't wait, said the condom.

Neither can I!

For whatever reason, I opened the condom and I put it on.

Are you sure you want to do this? the condom asked.

I wanted to see what it would feel like. It felt great.

Sitting there in my bedroom with the door locked, I decided I would leave it on so that when it was time, I would be ready.

This would prove to be a *very* bad decision.

Inevitably, between that time and meeting up with Pauline, I went soft. And when I did, unbeknownst to me, the condom rolled up into my pubic hair. Even so, I never took it off.

When I got to Toni's house, Pauline and I went down to the rec room and started making out on the couch. A switchblade couldn't have popped up faster than I did. When I sprang to life again, the condom didn't unroll, and it was now yanking on my pubic hair. It felt as if my crotch was tied to the bumper of a Chevy and the driver had just floored the accelerator.

Man, did that hurt.

At first I thought I could tough it out, but there was no way that was going to happen. A seasoned spy would have talked from the pain. Suddenly, I hit the floor. I crawled into the tiny makeshift bathroom they had down there.

No matter what I did, I couldn't get the condom off. I was in there saying Hail Marys and thinking about ugly nuns.

"Are you okay?" Pauline asked as she knocked on the door.

"Yeah, I'll be right out," I squeaked while trying everything I could think of to get back to normal. Nothing seemed to work. I don't know how much time passed before I was finally able to take the condom off. When I did, there was hair everywhere. Then I put it back on. *Ahh!* I finally felt some relief. I was ready to do this. I opened the bathroom door like some superhero ready to save the damsel in distress—but there was one problem: Pauline was long gone. And that was that. Understandably, she wasn't very happy. Pauline told her girlfriends she had been in Toni's basement with me and kissed me a few times, but when it came time to get busy, I'd run and locked myself in the bathroom!

Needless to say, that knocked me out for some time, and any hopes I had of having sex were dashed for quite a while.

"How did you fuck that up, Parsons?" Danny asked. "That was a sure thing!"

I never told him or anyone else what happened until I wrote this book. I have no secrets from you, dear reader.

And Danny was right. It was and should have been a sure thing. Looking back, though, I think it was one of the luckiest things that ever happened to me. I had only one condom, and a pre-worn one at that. If we'd had sex, we probably would have done it more than once, and I surely would have gotten her pregnant. Because I was a knucklehead, I got lucky—but not in the way I'd hoped. Even so, I did learn a very valuable lesson: sometimes you can be *too* prepared.

Sometimes you can be *too* prepared.

This Is a Stickup

As I mentioned, when I was sixteen, I took a summer job working at the Sinclair station on the corner of Highland Avenue and Fayette. My job was to pump gas, check oil, put air in tires, wash windshields—basically whatever needed to be done to make the customer happy. Sometimes I'd work during the day, but more often than not I worked the graveyard shift. There wasn't usually a lot of action during those hours, which I liked. It gave me time to do other things.

On July 4, 1967, I was working with another guy, John Tumenelo. John was in his mid-thirties but looked like he was in his fifties. He stood around five foot four and was a stocky dude with thick Coke-bottle glasses. He was missing most of his teeth too. I always thought he looked like a turtle.

I had gotten my hands on some bottle rockets and was shooting them off over the houses that were across the street. I had the station's garage door raised just enough to get a jack handle underneath it. I aimed the jack handle just over the houses, placed the bottle rockets in the end of it, and lit them with a cigarette. They'd shoot up into the sky and go *BOOM! BOOM!* I'd quickly put the garage door down when the homeowners came outside looking all over to see where the bangs were coming from. I'd just laugh as they scratched their heads, trying to figure it out. They'd go back inside their homes, and then after five or ten minutes had passed, I'd do it again.

Around one in the morning, I heard John call me to the front office. I thought I was in trouble for sure. I grudgingly rolled my jack back, closed the garage doors, and walked to the office. When I got there, I noticed a guy with a handgun pointed at John. *Whoa.* I hadn't expected that.

I could see John struggling to get his gold wedding band off his fat finger, but it wouldn't budge. I looked to my right and noticed another guy standing there too.

"Give me all your money," one of them demanded.

I had seven bucks in my pocket, so I reached into my jeans and handed it over. I also had a loose pack of Marlboros, which they took.

John was shaking with fear, but I wasn't. For whatever reason, I was cool as a cucumber. I had never seen anything like this before in my life, and I just felt numb.

The two thugs pushed John and me into the back of the service station, where there were three lifts. Toward the end of the wall that divided the office from the garage there was a sectioned-off tool room. That room had cinder block walls and a pocket door, which we usually kept closed. One of the guys opened the door and shoved John and me inside.

"Don't shoot us," John begged as he started to cry.

"Shut the fuck up," the guy said before hitting John across the face with the side of his revolver. When he did that, the gun accidentally fired, sending a single bullet ricocheting all over the place. Somehow, none of us were hit.

At this point, John was lying on the ground, whimpering. As for me? Well, I still wasn't scared. Not one bit. When someone is pointing a gun at you, your mind just goes blank. You can't really think of anything else—at least, not in that moment.

I was still standing there when I realized the guy was now pointing his gun at me. For whatever reason, he didn't shoot. Instead, the two thugs slid the door closed and latched it from the outside. They jammed a screwdriver over the latch so we couldn't get out.

> "Don't shoot us," John begged as he started to cry. "Shut the fuck up," the guy said before hitting John across the face with the side of his revolver.

I waited a few minutes and then tried to open the door. When I did, the two guys came back. I heard them remove the screwdriver before they abruptly slid the door open. When they came in, the same guy pointed his gun at me. I was sure he was going to shoot me, but he couldn't do it. Eventually, they shut the door and left, the same as before. A few minutes later, they came back one last time. I kept expecting to get shot, but the guy never pulled the trigger. After they'd shut us in again, a little time passed, and I realized they were finally gone. To be absolutely sure, I waited about ten minutes. When I knew they'd really left, I grabbed a pipe wrench and beat the vent out of the door. I crawled through to the other side and unlocked it to let John out.

I needed to call the police to let them know what had happened. There were only pay phones in the gas stations back then, and there was no such thing as an emergency call. You either had the money or you couldn't make the call. Since the two guys had robbed me, I didn't have any money; they'd taken all our change, everything they could scrounge up.

I walked out onto Fayette Street and tried waving down a police car, but none of them stopped. Normally, they'd be chasing me all over the place, but on that night, they weren't interested in the likes of me. I shook my head in total disbelief before walking back to the station.

There was a man who used to sleep in the nasty dumpster next to the service station. His name was Jimbo. He was the epitome of a hobo. I don't think he ever bathed, and he always slept with six or more stray dogs. Jimbo didn't bother anyone, as long as no one bothered him. I knew him well enough to wake him, get him out of the dumpster, and tell him we'd been robbed. I explained that I needed to call the police but didn't have any money. Jimbo reached into his pocket and handed me enough change to make the call. As soon as I did, cops were everywhere.

The owner of the station was Mr. Ziglar. Somehow he got wind of the robbery and came down to the station late that night. When he arrived, he asked John and me how much money the thieves took from each of us.

"Seven dollars," I said.

"Three hundred," John chimed in.

I don't think John had ever seen three hundred dollars, let alone had it, and Mr. Ziglar didn't seem to buy his story either. Still, he asked, "Where did you get three hundred dollars from, John?"

"It's what I had on me," he said.

Yeah, right.

Much to my surprise, Mr. Ziglar gave us our money back. I was absolutely stunned. And for a moment I thought, *Why didn't I say three hundred dollars too?* Except for one thing: it wouldn't have been true. I've always been honest when it comes to money and business. I never wanted to take advantage of anyone, certainly not someone I worked for. It didn't feel right. John may have gotten away with his ruse, but it kind of pissed me off that he did it.

Later that night, as I was lying in bed, I thought about what had happened. It was only then, in the quiet of my bedroom, that

I realized I'd gotten lucky. Very lucky. I was beside myself when I had that epiphany. Someone must have been looking out for me from above; of this I was certain.

A few days later, the two guys who robbed us were arrested. They'd been getting hopped up on something and doing the same thing at other stations all over town. Crime wasn't uncommon where I lived. It was kind of a crazy, rough neighborhood. I'd hear horrific stories about guys getting whacked, beaten so badly that their teeth were knocked out, or stabbed with pool cues. I never liked that those things happened. It was terrible and I was sad about it for sure, but it was the way things went down in East Baltimore. And for better or worse, I learned to see the world through that lens, so I never gave it much thought. It was all I knew.

> I've always been honest when it comes to money and business. I never wanted to take advantage of anyone, certainly not someone I worked for. It didn't feel right.

Some guys' dads taught them how to fight and defend themselves. My pop wasn't that kind of father. I had to teach myself. And it wasn't really in my nature to be aggressive unless I was pushed into a corner. I certainly didn't look for trouble that way. Occasionally, there would be a couple of knuckleheads doing stupid shit, and I'd get caught in the crossfire. I remember planning to go to a Catholic Youth Organization dance at Saint Elizabeth. It would have been the first school dance I ever went to. I wanted to look nice, so my mother bought me a brand-new short-sleeved shirt. It was warm enough to wear the shirt without any type of jacket. On my way to the dance, I cut through the small playground at Ellwood Park. It was pretty dark out, but going this way would get me to the dance quicker. Halfway across the park, I felt a terrible sting in my back, just above my right kidney. Two guys who were hiding there had shot me with a pellet gun. You better believe it hurt. I confronted them. I didn't know them, and they didn't know me. They were older; I knew that from their size. Before I could tell what was happening, they beat the shit out of me. They were jackasses for shooting strangers in the park, and bullies for beating me up when I stood up to them. They ripped my new shirt right off my back. When they were through, I went home, made my way straight to the bathroom, turned on the water, and filled the tub. I just sat there and soaked. I threw the shirt away and never told my mother what had happened. I was too ashamed and embarrassed.

When the assailants who robbed John and me were arrested, the cops asked us to go to the police station to see them in a lineup and confirm that they were the same guys who'd robbed us. I took one look at the lineup and saw them there. I identified them both right away, as did several other victims. But there was one possible victim of theirs who couldn't be there—my friend Charlie Brown. He worked at the Hess gas station around the corner from the Sinclair station where I worked. He was shot in the head and killed while working the night shift. I don't know if it was the same guys who robbed us or not, but what I did know for sure was that it didn't seem right for him to take a bullet in the head. He was a kid my age. Although we didn't speak often, I knew him well enough to know he left behind a family who loved him. Their pain would be eternal with this loss. After that shooting and our robbery, the local service stations started closing at 9:00 p.m. for safety.

The two thieves were booked for armed robbery. A few months later, they stood trial. The police wanted the witnesses, including John and me, to testify against them. By this time, school was back in session and I had started my senior year. When it was time to go to court, the police came to get me at my home. I can't remember if I rode in a squad car or a detective's car. As it turned out, I was the only witness who showed up. No one else wanted to get involved. Even my parents didn't go that day. I don't know if these thugs had friends who got to the others and perhaps scared them away from testifying. All I know is that I felt it was my responsibility. These were not good guys— certainly not the kind you'd want your sister to bring home. I wasn't scared to do it; I just felt like it was something I had to do. They needed to be put away.

After I told my story of what happened, the judge turned to me and said, "Master Parsons, I want to congratulate you on what you just did. It took a lot of courage." I loved that he called me Master Parsons. It made me feel good, whole, important. But I was even more appreciative that he'd complimented me on my behavior.

> I loved that he called me Master Parsons. It made me feel good, whole, important.

For most of my life, people had usually complained about it, so this was a nice change.

I'm not certain what happened to those guys. I'm pretty sure they were found guilty, but I never saw or heard of either of them again.

I often tell people that any event can change the trajectory of their lives. It's like playing pinball and hitting the bumpers at random as the ball bounces here and there. Every once in a while it will hit one of the flippers. That can change everything. The robbery had that effect on me.

In a weird way, the robbery was good training for what was to come. I realize now that this experience taught me how to step out of any situation at hand—to get outside of myself, in a sense—and deal with what I had to deal with. You can't assess anything correctly if your knees are shaking, and it's hard to make good decisions when you panic.

I've learned that's true in all aspects of life, but in business, it's absolutely critical. The definition of courage is being afraid of something and doing it anyway. You have to be able to stow your fear, maneuver around it quickly, and make yourself into a dispassionate, rational observer of any dicey situation you face, instead

> The definition of courage is being afraid of something and doing it anyway.

of participating in it. You've got to learn to stand your ground.

Now, if that ground is the stinking, soul-sucking rice paddy mud of, say, Vietnam in 1969, that's a little easier said than done.

Security Is for Cadavers

Most people spend a lifetime chained to the familiar. They get locked into a way of thinking that makes it impossible to move beyond that mindset. I've spent most of my life learning and accepting that nothing of any significance happens when we're in our comfort zones. As I like to say, security is for cadavers.

At Patterson High, I had a buddy named Aggie Sirokis. His mother owned a local bar. After Aggie's dad died, she kept the business running to provide for her family.

One afternoon, I was standing at my gym locker changing clothes after class when Aggie and another classmate, Charlie Mason, asked about my plans after graduation. I hadn't given it a lot of thought. I just laughed and said, "Well, I think I'll still be in high school." It was the last semester of my senior year, and the writing was on the wall. I honestly didn't think I would graduate. You see, my grades weren't looking good,

> Most people spend a lifetime chained to the familiar. They get locked into a way of thinking that makes it impossible to move beyond that mindset.

which meant my prospects for getting my diploma with my class-mates were bleak. I suppose I owed that outcome to spending most of my high school years drinking and occasionally doing drugs. Nothing outrageous—mostly pot and pills I bought at school from Dave the Dude. Uppers and downers. When you took one of each, we called it a set. Hey, it was the sixties; no excuses, just the facts.

I was aware that Aggie had joined the Marines. I had a lot of respect for that decision. As we spoke that day, Aggie asked Charlie and me if we wanted to go see his Marine Corps recruiter on Conkling Street.

"Sure, why not?" I said.

We walked into the Marine Corps office and met the recruiter, who was tall and wiry. He was in tip-top shape. I also noticed that his clothes were crisp and pressed, with perfect creases. I loved it.

"How are you men doing?" he asked as we walked through the door.

I'll admit that I liked hearing that. No one had called me a man before that day. In the eyes of everyone else, I was a knuckle-head kid.

We started talking, shooting the breeze. I noticed him fumbling around, rummaging through his cupboard like he was looking for something. Then he turned toward us and said, "I owe you an apology. I wanted to pour you men a drink, but I'm all out."

We would have loved it, of course. Then one of us said, "Not a problem."

The recruiter spent an hour or two talking about the history of the United States Marine Corps and the things that Marines see and experience. He also talked about what it takes to make it. Not long after that, the recruiter leaned across his desk and said, "You

> No one had called me a man before that day. In the eyes of everyone else, I was a knucklehead kid.

know, I like you two men. If you're interested, I'll see if I can get you fellas into the Corps."

"Oh, could you do that for us?" We were like moths to a flame, and he knew it.

Charlie was eighteen, so he didn't have to get his parents' permission to join up, but I was only seventeen. I wouldn't turn eighteen until the following November, so I would have to get my mother to sign the papers allowing me to enlist.

When we left the office, I went straight home. I couldn't wait to tell Mom about my plan. When I explained it to her, she wasn't nearly as excited as I was.

"Why would you want to join the Marine Corps?" she asked.

This was April of 1968, and the Vietnam War was raging.

"Mom, I want the adventure. I want to get over there and defend our country." I continued with my plea, thinking I would surely convince her this was the right thing to do.

"You really want to do this?" she asked.

"I do," I said. And I meant it. I was and still am a patriot. I love my country. And sure, I craved adventure, but I also needed a change of scenery. I wanted to feel like I belonged somewhere. Up until now, I'd been floating through life, trying to avoid conflict at home and goofing off at school. I inherently understood that the change would do me good, even if I couldn't articulate it at the time. All I really knew was that this was important for all sorts of reasons.

> I was and still am a patriot. I love my country.

Much to my surprise, Mom said yes and agreed to sign the paperwork.

I was so excited I could hardly contain myself. We went to see a neighbor who was a notary public so Mom's signature could be witnessed and certified.

Before signing, Mom hesitated. She held the pen to the paper but didn't write her name yet. Then she looked up at me and solemnly said, "I feel like I'm signing your life away."

"Mom, I know what I'm doing. Don't worry." I did my best to reassure her that everything would be all right, but she knew better than that. I was being naïve, but I really believed what I was saying. I was ready, willing, and more than able to go into battle. And proud to do it.

Since Charlie and I joined up together, we were on what the Marines refer to as "the buddy plan." We would go through basic training together, which included boot camp and infantry training. After that, we would most likely be split up and sent to different combat units in Vietnam. And, as a bonus, since we joined together, we didn't have to report for duty until August, when we were expected at Parris Island, South Carolina.

When I got my orders, I showed my teachers that I'd enlisted. Once they saw my papers, they passed me, and I graduated high school in 1968, at the height of the Vietnam War. After I'd shared my enlistment, one of my teachers, Mrs. Zvonar, pulled me aside and asked, "Do you know what you're doing?"

"Sure I do," I said. I wasn't on the dean's list, that's for damn sure. Had I not joined, I don't believe there was a shot in hell I would've gotten my diploma. But I would graduate, and that was all that mattered to me.

She started crying. I didn't understand why then, but she surely knew what was ahead of me and the danger I would be facing.

Before I left for Parris Island, my father took me down to Fort Holabird, an Armed Forces examining and entrance station located in the southeast corner of Baltimore that was at one time home to the US Army Intelligence School and the Counterintelligence Records Facility. This was where they processed incoming troops for their physicals and took care of some other clerical matters.

While I was being examined, I was placed in a soundproof room to test my hearing. I sat there facing the wall, wearing a headset. The examiner told me to push a button every time I heard a beep in either ear. I sat there for what felt like an eternity and never heard a damn beep. *Uh-oh.* I thought maybe my hearing was shot and I wouldn't be able to go to Vietnam.

Well, what happened was the soldiers doing the processing set me up in that room and then went to lunch. They never conducted the exam. Believe it or not, they forgot about me.

When they returned from lunch, one of the guys opened the door and said, "Holy Christ! You're still here?"

I just laughed, more out of relief than anything else. I got up and walked out of the room. They passed me anyway.

Once I was processed into the system, I was eligible for induction into the United States Marine Corps. Shortly thereafter, I took a bus to the train station, along with a bunch of other newly minted recruits. We boarded a train that would take us to South Carolina.

The day my father took me to Fort Holabird, he had tears streaming down his face. I'll never forget it. He said, "I would give anything if I could go in your place."

"I know, Dad."

Tell Your Mama to Sell the Toilet, 'Cause Your Ass Is Ours!

On the train to South Carolina, one of the guys had brought a couple of cases of Colt 45. They were the big ones too. We drank them until they got warm. That got us tuned up. After they were too warm to drink, we started throwing them off the train. They'd explode before they hit the ground. It must have been from the heat, the air, and the speed. We probably should have been calling out, "Fire in the hole!" We were definitely acting like new Marines. It was fun. Until it wasn't.

Once we got to South Carolina, we boarded a bus that took us to the Marine Corps Recruit Depot at Parris Island. When we pulled up, a Marine boarded the bus and bellowed, "What the fuck are you doing sitting around? Get the fuck up! Get off the bus. Get the fuck off the bus, *NOW!*" It was one expletive after another, and it made for a rather memorable welcome.

The next thing I heard was, "Tell your mama to sell the toilet, 'cause your ass is ours!" I remember thinking, *Oh, shit.*

It was hot as hell outside. We were told to stand on the yellow footprints that were painted on the ground and ordered not to move. We did as we were told. One guy passed out. When they were giving him smelling salts to bring him back, another guy started laughing.

"Oh, you think this is funny, huh?" the Marine screamed at the giggling knucklehead before grabbing him by his shirtfront and shoving smelling salts up his nose. He was kicking and putting up one heck of a fight. He didn't win.

When we were released from our spots, the first place we were sent was to get a haircut. While I didn't have long hair like a lot of the other guys, I still had a pretty good head of hair that I liked. Sure enough, they sheared it all off. I insist I wasn't crying, but I couldn't keep tears from running out of my eyes. I kept saying, "There's something in my eye." The only silver lining was that when we were done, none of us had any hair atop our heads. It certainly leveled the playing field.

For the first three days, we were holed up in staging barracks. I don't really recall those few days as being hard, but I do remember feeling a little homesick. One thing was for sure: nobody was calling us men or offering us a drink here.

We slept in narrow bunk beds, lined up in the barracks. It didn't bother me. It was an upgrade from the basement room I'd grown up in. Before dawn, drill instructors would get us up by raising living hell. They would run down the aisle throwing trash cans and blowing ear-piercing whistles. We ran drills until after dark—marching, doing calisthenics. We were smacked around a lot. But hey, this was boot camp: they strip you of everything—your personality, your self-esteem, your individuality—so they can build you back up as a Marine.

Some couldn't take it and disappeared, never to be heard from again. After a couple of guys tried to kill themselves with razors, our platoon sergeant gathered all the recruits for a lesson on how to properly commit suicide: slit your wrists lengthwise, not across, and have the fuckin' decency to do it in the goddamn shower so some other private doesn't have to clean up your lame-ass bloody mess. It made *Full Metal Jacket* seem like boarding school.

Once we were staged, we were known as platoon number 1010 Parris Island. Every recruit was given a number; mine was 61. When the drill sergeant told us to count off, we'd count our numbers in order, starting with one. If someone didn't call out their number, they'd likely taken off in the middle of the night. Three guys from our platoon just vanished. It's not like you could just quit the Marines, especially during the Vietnam War. They were absent without leave, or AWOL. If they were caught—and they usually were—the Marines weren't particularly cordial, and they certainly didn't send them home. It was either back to training or to the brig for their dumb asses. Once you signed up, you were in, baby. You became a Marine for life.

On my first morning there, as I counted off in my skivvies, Gunny Oliver, our drill instructor, or DI, asked me about my funny tan lines. Before joining the Marines, I'd worked for my uncle's construction company. I always wore half T-shirts. They weren't wifebeaters, just undershirts made with straps because they were cooler. As a result, I had a strap tan.

"Sir! Construction work wearing a strap T-shirt. It's from the sun," I said with conviction.

"Bullshit. I bet you were a queer, running around with a bra," he shot back.

"No, sir!"

"C'mon. You were a queer, running around with a bra, weren't you?"

"No, sir!"

"I'll tell you what: if I catch you looking at one of the other privates funny, your ass has had it. And don't you look at me, you little queer fucker!" And then he walked out.

He knew what he was saying was bull. He was doing his best to get my goat. And, I suppose, to toughen me up.

I'd love to tell you that this drill instructor was the worst of them during boot camp, but he wasn't. The job of the DIs wasn't to be your friend; it was to prepare you for the rigorous environment in Vietnam. There was one drill instructor I recall who was especially intimating. Staff Sergeant Knight had the biggest hands of any man I'd ever known. He was huge in every way. He would put his hand on my forehead and his fingers would reach the back of my shaved head. He was not a guy you wanted to mess with. For the most part, he was usually pretty decent, but every now and then he'd come after us in one way or another. It didn't take long to figure out that that was just what they did. It wasn't personal. Not usually.

One morning, I woke up early and got fully dressed in my fatigues and boots. When the drill sergeant came into our barracks, the rest of the guys were still in their skivvies, as they were supposed to be.

"Who the fuck told you to get dressed?" Staff Sergeant Knight yelled at me as loud as he could, his nose half an inch away from mine. He was so close that I could feel little droplets of his spit hitting my eyeballs and skin.

"Nobody, sir!" I answered.

"Private, you don't do anything unless you're told to do it! Stand in the middle of the room over here. Everybody, push your racks together!" He then punished the whole group for my mistake.

At first, I didn't catch on to why he did that. No matter what happens in Marine Corps boot camp, when somebody screws up, everybody pays. Quite often they'd punish everyone *except* the one who made the mistake. The lesson they were trying to teach was that we had to depend on one another. In a combat situation, everybody must do their part and pull their own weight. If they don't, the entire squad suffers. I would eventually come to understand that this was one of the reasons the Marine Corps was such an

> In a combat situation, everybody must do their part and pull their own weight.

excellent fighting force. They drilled that *all for one and one for all* philosophy into my head from day one.

After being at boot camp for a few days, I didn't necessarily feel duped by the recruiter. I knew what I'd signed up for. But even so, it was very different from what I'd expected.

Much to my surprise, the food was better than anticipated. Maybe it was because we'd worked up such a ferocious appetite by the time we were allowed to eat, but compared to the food I was used to eating before I joined the Marine Corps, it was uptown. We'd get to the chow hall and there would usually be a DI jumping up and down on a table and shouting, "Eat! Eat! Eat!" No one had to ask me twice. I was always hungry. The milk, especially the chocolate milk, was icy cold, just the way I liked it. Man, it tasted great, especially in the deep Carolina heat. Even so, one of the first lessons I learned was not to eat too much or too fast. If you did, you'd end up puking when you had to run after the meal.

We never knew exactly when it would happen, but there was often a five-mile run after chow. We weren't running in brand-new sneakers either. No, we ran in our combat boots, which meant a good number of us got shin splints, blisters, and twisted ankles. This prepared us for being in combat, where we could expect at least that level of pain and discomfort. If you needed to be treated from some injury, you had to go to sick bay, but then you'd have to start boot camp all over again if you missed training with your

platoon for more than a few days. *No thank you.* I was determined
to tough it out. I just put my mind to getting through each run and
working past any pain.

We were supposed to clap and sing during our runs. The songs
weren't very politically correct, and some were downright haunting:

> *If I should die in a combat zone, box*
> *me up and send me home.*
> *Place my arms across my chest and*
> *tell my girl I did my best.*

One time the drill instructor caught me not singing. The next
day, I was sent to motivation platoon. It's not what you're thinking.
Motivation platoon is a glimpse into total hell. I had to wear my
helmet and full fatigues, all buttoned up, and carry my rifle and
a full pack. We started marching in deep sand before sun up and
ended after dark the next day. It was brutal.

I remember when one of the guys in our group fell. I had been
thinking about dropping out myself, but thankfully I stayed with
it. The drill instructor shouted at him to get up, but the poor guy
couldn't stand. He tried but fell back to the ground.

"Get the fuck up!" the drill instructor screamed, standing over
the guy's limp body before pouring water on his face and kicking
sand at him. Just when we thought it couldn't get worse, the DI
called out, "Somebody get the ice wagon!"

The ice wagon was a pickup truck with a large ice chest in the
back. When the truck pulled up, the drill instructor opened this
guy's shirt and began stuffing it with ice. He called for another DI
to grab his feet while the first drill instructor grabbed his arms, and
they flung him up and into the back of the truck. Ice came flying
everywhere out of his shirt.

A few days later, someone told me another guy actually died
by drowning in his own puke. I was pretty sure that wasn't true,

but even so, I didn't want to be that guy. So I doubled down and made it a point to get even more serious about why I was there. Still, when I look back, I think the darkest moment of boot camp was motivation platoon. Keep in mind that this was August in Parris Island. The heat and humidity were suffocating. It was most definitely a glimpse into hell and made our normal training seem not so bad. One thing for sure, I never wanted to be sent back to Motivation Platoon again.

After that, you'd think I would have learned to straighten up and fly right. Still, there were things I did that unintentionally provoked my drill sergeants.

When I worked at the filling station in high school, I had a habit of keeping a yellow pencil tucked behind my right ear, just like the ones I used to chew on in grade school. If I needed to write something, it was the handiest thing. I could pump gas and then fill out credit card slips without going back into the station. One day during boot camp, I was headed from one class to another when Sergeant Little, a drill instructor, came flying at me and asked, "What have you got stuck behind your ear?"

"Pencil, sir."

"What the hell are you doing with a pencil there?"

"I used to work in a filling station, sir. I guess I do it automatically." It was the only response I could come up with.

"I'm going to give you the break of your life, maggot. I don't ever want to see that pencil there again. If I do, I'm going to jam it right up your ass! Am I clear?"

"Sir, yes, sir!"

The next day, I was marching with my platoon from one class to another when Sergeant Little came at me again. Sure enough, I had that damn pencil behind my ear. I didn't mean to; it was just an old habit. He pushed me over and over again until my back was up against the column of a building. He took that pencil and stabbed me at the bottom of my throat until I was sure he was about to give me a tracheotomy. "Next time, I'm going to kill you with it, asshole."

"Yes, sir!"

I'm not going to tell you I wasn't scared, because I was. I was pretty sure he meant it. However, the next day, I was leaving class when I saw Sergeant Little moving toward me. I reached up and realized I had that damn pencil behind my ear again. Lucky for me, I was able to grab it before he saw. After that close call, you'd better believe I never kept a pencil up there again. They say old habits die hard, but training as a Marine will make them die fast.

There were a lot of experiences I had during that first phase of training at Parris Island that were hard to understand at first, but everything the DIs did had meaning and purpose. Everything. Like when they taught us the naked stranglehold, a move in which you come up behind somebody, put your knee in the back of their knee, and put them in a chokehold from behind at the same time. When you do that, they lose their ability to breathe; and while they're gasping for air, you take your KA-BAR knife and stab them in the kidney. If you don't have a knife, you clasp your hand with your other hand and tighten your hold. Of course, during training we weren't actually stabbing one another because we didn't have knives, but we did learn this combat move, and then drilled it over and over until it became second nature.

> The Marine Corps taught me many things, but it especially taught me about strength and perseverance.

The instructors would get everyone set up and then pair us off so one guy would take the shot and the other would give it to him. At first we were led to believe that everyone would go one time. We all ended up doing it three times. By the end of this, none of us could talk. The first time it was my turn, I was the guy giving the shot. I came up to my partner from behind and took it easy on him. We switched, and the second time my partner gave me the shot, he didn't take it easy on me. Each time we hit the other guy's throat with the bone of our wrist, it got rougher and harder. When we finished, the drill instructor said, "Now, listen up, you idiots. If you haven't figured it out yet, you need to be nice to the guy you're doing this to—but only now. If you're ever in battle, you must go hard, or you will die." That's the Marine Corps.

The Marine Corps taught me many things, but it especially taught me about strength and perseverance. It taught me that you never know how strong you are until being strong is your only choice. It taught me that crawling is acceptable. Falling is acceptable. Puking is acceptable. Bleeding is acceptable. And pain is acceptable. But quitting is not. Failure is never an option.

Strength doesn't come from what you can already do. It stems from overcoming the things you once thought you couldn't do. When you've been trained as a United States Marine, obstacles won't stop you. Problems won't stop you. People won't stop you. Only *you* will stop you. By the time I left boot camp, I had come to better understand my role and purpose.

Infantry Training Was a Gas

Graduation from Marine Corps boot camp is like any other graduation day. It's a huge relief. We made it through the first phase of training, and for a moment, they cut us a little slack. Early on our graduation day, before we changed into our dress uniforms, I had to run back to the barracks for something and came across a big dude from Louisiana who had bullied me and many others the entire time we were there. I wasn't the biggest guy in camp, but I had developed a fiery temper and could certainly hold my own. When I got back to the barracks, this guy started picking on me like he always did. I snapped. I jumped on his back and hit him in the head as hard as I could. He went down like a brick, with me still hanging on to him. The other guys eventually broke it up. Thank God those guys were there, or one of us would have been dead. Probably me. The big guy got up, stood toe to toe with me, and threatened to kill me. I didn't waver. I just stared that bastard down. After that, he left me alone. Something happened at boot camp that I hadn't expected. I discovered I had a fire in my belly and a short fuse. Mentally, I was ready to get on with things without some jerk making it harder than it needed to be. It felt good to stand up to him. I wanted him—and all the others—to know that I was no pushover. Technically, this was my first battle as a Marine. I can't say I won, but I certainly didn't lose.

My parents and sister came down from Baltimore for graduation. Pop was really proud of me—perhaps the proudest he ever was. Mom couldn't stop crying. I overheard her say to Dad, "He's not like he used to be." And she was right. I had changed. I'd become cold and even more detached than I was before I went in. I knew I would continue to change with every passing day, but I had no idea how profoundly.

My family and I had only a couple of hours to spend together, so we went to IHOP and had pancakes. I loved it. Before I knew it, our time was up, and I had to report back to boot camp. We reluctantly said our goodbyes.

> I knew I would continue to change with every passing day, but I had no idea how profoundly.

Shortly thereafter, the other recruits and I boarded a bus and headed to Camp Lejeune for infantry training. I remember that the air was hot and thick with the type of humidity you get only in the South.

We were all fired up and so happy on that bus ride, belting out "The Marines' Hymn" as loud and proud as we could.

From the Halls of Montezuma
To the shores of Tripoli;
We fight our country's battles
In the air, on land, and sea.

All these years later, I haven't forgotten the words to that song. It chokes me up to sing it sometimes, although I often do so with great pride.

When we got to Camp Lejeune, I was assigned to Kilo Company. No sooner had we arrived than we were ordered on our first night forced march, something we would do almost every night. Afterward, we'd get the worst charley horses, usually sometime in the middle of the night. They were so bad that they would wake you from a dead sleep. You'd fly out of the barracks in terrible pain, grabbing your leg and jumping around until the cramp passed. I quickly learned to drink a lot of water so that it wouldn't happen to me—or at least not as often.

Just before one of those night marches, a gunnery sergeant said something I've never forgotten. He was a short fellow with a big presence. He said, "All of you privates are going to Vietnam, and many of you are going to come home with medals—metal arms and metal legs. And some of you are so fucked up, you'd be doing Uncle Sam a favor not to send your dumb ass there just to get killed. You won't waste the government's money." I hadn't really thought about getting wounded, but the sergeants would say stuff like this all the time. It got to the point where we learned to just tune them out. I didn't want to let them get into my head and make those thoughts my thoughts. No way, no how. The dialogue was pretty dark at times. If the instructors were trying to weed out the weak, I wasn't aware of it. All I could do was look for ways to keep moving forward and surviving while developing skills I knew would serve me well in Vietnam.

> I had to keep a strong mind and constitution so I wouldn't get killed.

The best thing that happened to me early in my training was being issued pants with buttons and not a zipper. Man, did I get lucky. Want to know why? While you were on those forced marches, whenever you had to take a leak, you didn't want to stop. If you did, you'd fall behind and then have to run to catch up with the rest of the group. While most of us were quick about it, ten times a night I'd watch certain guys fall to the ground. Why? They took their zipper down to pee and then they'd get their junk stuck in there when they tried to zip up. All I could think was, *You can't do that with buttons, baby!* I did, however, somehow rip those original fatigues and was eventually reissued a pair of pants with a zipper. Yup, you guessed it: it got me. It was excruciating. Like the words to "The Marines' Hymn," I never forgot that either!

My time at Camp Lejeune was all about getting better—getting optimal instruction on weapons, getting into peak shape, and getting in sync with my unit. One of the exercises we did at Lejeune to build togetherness involved spending time in a structure known as the gas house. We entered the gas house with our gas masks on, and each of us placed a hand on the shoulder of the man in front of us. The second we walked in, they detonated a CS gas canister. CS is the main ingredient in tear gas; exposure to it causes a burning sensation and tearing of the eyes, making it difficult to keep your eyes open. It also causes a burning irritation of the mucous membranes of the nose, mouth, and throat, resulting in coughing, profuse nasal discharge, disorientation, and difficulty breathing, all of which partially incapacitate you. Once the gas house was filled with thick CS tear gas, the drill instructor commanded us to start running in a circle as one unit. Then the instructor ordered us to remove our masks and sing "The Marines' Hymn." That got us breathing and forced the gas into our lungs, noses, eyes, mouths— everywhere. This was not fun in any sense of the word.

On command, we pulled our masks off and felt the most unbelievably painful sensation all over our bodies. Do you know what CS gas does to your skin? It isn't pretty or comfortable, that's for sure. Eventually, the instructor opened the door and we stumbled coughing and choking outside. It felt good to finally catch our breath as we waited for the pain to go away. After I did this exercise, I had to take a leak. I didn't think about possibly getting CS gas on my junk, but I should have, because it was all over my hands and it burned like hell.

Later that night, we got our first breather from training. We were allowed to go to the base exchange. In the Marine Corps, you never let anyone break through your formation. That night, I came out of the barracks and began running in between another group's formation. I didn't even think about it. One of the Marines who was standing in that formation took his M16 and hit me right in the face with the butt. My teeth are *still* rattling from that. I suspect I would have killed him if someone hadn't pulled me off him. When I think about that today, I'm still pissed about it, because he didn't need to do that. As Marines, we were all tough, hardened, and serious about why we were there—to serve our country and hopefully not get killed. And certainly not accidentally, by one of our own.

> I wanted to be the best version of myself that I could possibly become. The Marines gave me that passion, drive, and discipline.

With every passing day, I was getting clearer on what I wanted to do and who I wanted to become. There was a moment sometime during training at Camp Lejeune when I decided I would always try to do my job as best I could, just like I did in boot camp. I wanted to be the best version of myself that I could possibly become. The Marines gave me that passion, drive, and discipline.

From that day forward, I began cleaning my rifle every day. I was very proud of that, and I kept cleaning it regardless of whether anyone noticed or not. I kept my rifle clean because that was my job.

During a big inspection, eighty of us fell out to have our rifles examined by a number of troop handlers. Their job was to inspect everyone's rifle until they found something wrong. Whenever they did, they would throw the rifle in the dirt. If they didn't find anything, they moved on to the next Marine. Eventually, only two of us were left standing there—me and another Marine—and the handlers couldn't find anything wrong with our rifles. Sergeant Ryder came over to where I was standing at attention, looked at me, and asked, "You see the lint on the back of that trigger?"

"No, sir!" I said angrily. There was no lint on the back of the trigger. That thing was immaculate.

Sergeant Ryder took my rifle and threw it in the dirt. When I picked it up, it was filthy. Now I was pissed. But then I thought, *Screw this.* I had been putting all my attention on keeping my rifle clean, when they were teaching us how not to die. Did I go back and clean it? Well, I got all the big pieces of dirt off and cleaned my rifle, but not obsessively like I had been doing. I realized that the effort I'd put into making my rifle insanely clean wasn't necessary. And that was the message. I still cleaned my rifle after that, but I learned never to let it get to the point of obsession again; the juice wasn't worth the squeeze. Instead, I decided to let loose a little. I spent time with the rest of the guys goofing around, and I realized I could never win an inspection. It was no different from the spelling bee in grade school that taught me "fair" (fare) is what you pay when you got on a bus.

Shipping Out

While I had certainly endured my fair share of fistfights growing up, it was only during infantry training that I learned a few things about boxing. The fights and scuffles I'd been in during grade school were a far cry from taking on an opponent in the ring.

Back when I was at Hampstead Hill, I got into a fistfight with a guy named Tony Pelekakis. He and I clashed over something stupid—just guys being guys. However, everyone knew we were going to fight after school. It was like two Roman gladiators meeting in the Colosseum. Tony and I sparred as the crowd around us grew. No one even tried to break up the fight. They were cheering for either Tony or me. I noticed that when he made a certain move, he'd come in with his face, so I set him up to do that, and *BOOM*—I clocked him.

"You motherfucker!" he yelled, and then he took a big swing at me. But I ducked, and instead of hitting my face, his fist smashed into a Formstone wall. His knuckles looked like they had exploded. He went straight down to the ground.

One of the guys who was watching put his arm around me and said, "Looks like you won." So I left. I didn't feel like a winner; not at all.

The next day, I got called into the principal's office. Tony was sitting there next to his dad, with his hand all bandaged up. That's when I got suspended. Why? Because Tony was bandaged up and I wasn't. I didn't start the fight, but I had to defend myself or he would have crushed me. Tony was trying to hit me in the head when he missed and hit the wall instead. It was really that cut-and-dried. Yet another reminder that fare is what you pay when you get on a bus. Thank you, Tony!

In the Marines, I was boxing as a lightweight, weighing in at somewhere around 140 pounds back then. Kilo Company set up a boxing ring, and I decided to try it. I can't really recall why, but I wanted to do it. I fought only a couple of guys in my weight class and beat them both. After those victories, I should have been done for the day, but then a heavyweight stepped into the ring. The troop handler asked if anyone wanted to box him, and I volunteered. This was a very bad decision. A real idiot move on my part. After I got into the ring, he threw the first punch and hit me really hard. I felt like I had been hit by a car. I went down hard. Stupidly, I got back up, and the next thing I remember is being outside the ring. One of my shoes was missing, and they were giving me smelling salts to bring me around.

> It was then and there I discovered I'm a lover, not a fighter.

I had a headache for three days after that match. Back then, nobody talked about concussions, but I'm pretty sure I had one. It was then and there I discovered I'm a lover, not a fighter.

In between Camp Lejeune and advanced infantry training at Camp Pendleton, I was allowed to go on leave. I headed back to

Baltimore to spend thirty days with my family. Aggie, who had already been through boot camp, came back to Baltimore on leave too. Some random guy was giving his mother a lot of grief over something at the bar. Aggie got in the middle of their argument, and the guy plunged a knife into Aggie's heart, killing him. He never made it to Vietnam, and I lost my good friend, which broke my heart.

The night before I left for Camp Pendleton, I went out and whooped it up something good. At a sub shop I ran into a buddy of mine who was with a beautiful woman he was dating named Martha. The moment I saw her, I was smitten. But she was dating my friend, and I was leaving for Vietnam.

The morning of my departure to Camp Pendleton, my mother came into my bedroom around nine or ten and woke me. She said, "Morning, Robert."

Still groggy from sleep, I mumbled, "Hi, Mom."

"I'm going to the racetrack with Aunt Bert. Don't get yourself killed," she said.

"I won't, Mom, I promise."

She might have given me a little peck on the cheek that day, but maybe not. I want to believe she did, but I honestly can't remember. It wouldn't have been like her to do that.

I rolled over and went back to sleep for another hour before getting up to call my cousin, who gave me a ride to the airport.

Pop left the house that morning without saying a word. I had to be at the airport around two o'clock that afternoon, and I'd hoped he might come back to say goodbye or drive me to the airport, but he didn't. All the other guys' parents were there to see them off, to wave goodbye and hug them,

> As it turned out, my mother had raised the perfect Marine without realizing it. And maybe that's the most loving thing she ever did for me.

many for the last time. Some were holding homemade cardboard signs wishing us Godspeed and good luck. And then there was me, by myself. I remember looking around before boarding the flight and thinking, *It's nice to have all these people here.* Even if they weren't *my* people.

I was used to being alone for most of my life, so I didn't really dwell on it. In many ways, I didn't need anybody—or at least up until that moment. As it turned out, my mother had raised the perfect Marine without realizing it. And maybe that's the most loving thing she ever did for me. Years later, I asked her why she chose to go to the racetrack that day. I wanted to know why she didn't at least wait until after I'd left. "I couldn't bear to see you leave," she said.

And I believe that to be true. A mother never wants to see her child go off to war, but especially to Vietnam at a time when there were a hundred bodies being shipped home in wooden boxes every week. I didn't get that at the time, but she did. And while I couldn't possibly understand my parents' decisions that day, it made total sense to me when we finally talked about it.

After leave, everyone came back to Camp Pendleton a little soft, at least according to the military. So, they had us running up and down mountains for a month or two to get back in shape while we awaited our orders to go to Vietnam.

Roughly two weeks into advanced infantry training, I got involved in a card game. Card games often sprang up in the afternoons right after we all got paid, which was usually every couple of weeks. We had a three-day weekend ahead of us, so six guys and I gathered to play some high-stakes poker—or at least it was high stakes for us. Over the nine hours we played, I won some and lost some. I was about to throw in my cards because I was pretty much out of money—that is, until I drew a really good hand. A full house of aces over kings. The others were betting big, and I bet right along with them—except I had no money.

"Parsons, where's your money?" one of the guys asked.

"Don't you worry. I've got it. If you win, I'll give it to you, so don't worry about it." I was being a little smug for someone who was bluffing about having the money.

"You better have it," one of the guys murmured.

Well, as it turned out, my luck changed with that hand, and I won the pot. I stayed in the game until two o'clock in the afternoon the following day and left with $3,000. That was a lot of money to me—perhaps the most I'd ever won in those days. After I gathered up all my winnings, I knew what would happen if I didn't act fast. I went over to the post office, bought a money order, and sent most of the money home to my family. I asked them to keep it safe so I'd have a nest egg when I got back. Of course, deep down, I figured that money was headed right to the track. I kept about twenty-five dollars on me so I'd have some cash in my pocket when I got to Okinawa.

Except for the guys in the game that day, no one knew exactly how much money I'd won. However, the word was out that I'd won big. That night after I fell asleep, I was woken up by three or four different groups of guys asking me for money. I showed them the receipt for the money order and explained that I'd sent it home. I had expected they would all come by one by one to try to shake me down, and they did. One guy asked me for twenty dollars, while others were looking for a big payday. Each time someone asked, I repeated, "I sent it all home."

Other than that poker game, my time at Camp Pendleton wasn't especially memorable. It was just another Marine Corps base with a nice view of the mountains and the ocean. I didn't go off base a lot because I didn't really care for being away from famil-iar surroundings and people. I didn't mind spending time alone, reading on my bed, lying in the grass, or taking a nap whenever I could sneak one in. I enjoyed that a hell of a lot more than chasing girls in Oceanside, California, with ten thousand other Marines.

When my orders to leave for Vietnam finally came, I was more than excited to get there. I wasn't really sure what to expect, but I was ready to go. The night before we shipped out to Okinawa, I started feeling sick. Not nervous, but more like a bug or the flu. The next morning, I had a wickedly uncontrollable gastrointestinal issue happening. It didn't matter; they put me on a plane at the Marine Corps air base in El Toro anyhow. It turned out that several other guys and I had contracted what was called the Hong Kong flu. It took an act of courage to go into the toilet on our plane because it was so nasty from everyone who was sick.

By the time we landed, I was exhausted, dehydrated, and ready for a comfortable bed. Yeah, that would have been nice. Instead, they took us to a local Marine Corps base where it was hot and very muggy. There was a troop handler waiting for us there.

"We're going to have a little three-mile run—or maybe five. Welcome to Okinawa, fellas. Fall in!"

The run lasted for what felt like an eternity. When I finally went to our barracks, I remember taking a shower, but man, oh man, I was still sick. I crashed in my bunk and didn't wake up until the next morning. Thankfully, the flu passed, and I was good to go. To this day I believe that run healed me, as only the Marines Corps knows how to do.

In Okinawa, my particular unit was part of the 9th Marine Amphibious Brigade. We were diverted to Kadena Air Base for riot control. They were expecting huge protests over the B-52 bombers that operated from there. While at Kadena, we learned all about riot control. We were taught how to make noises with our feet and how to bang on our shields like the ancient Romans did. They understood that to defeat your enemy, you must first defeat

> To defeat your enemy, you must first defeat their eyes. Make them afraid.

their eyes. Make them afraid. We never really had to do riot control at Kadena, but we learned the skills anyway. I'm not really sure how long I was in Okinawa—maybe a couple of weeks or so—but from there I went to Vietnam, baby. Vietnam.

The Marine Corps does this hurry-up-and-wait drill every time you're deployed. They get everybody ready, wherever it is they're going, even if they're not leaving for six hours, and then everyone just waits. They do it so that when it comes time to leave, they aren't scrambling and waiting for guys to show up. Some guys kept asking, "When are we leaving?" But no one ever really gave us an answer.

We were positioned in a long hallway at the Kadena Air Base, waiting to catch our flight. We waited, and waited, and waited, and still there was no word on when we were supposed to leave. So, William Parker Jr., a Marine I met from North Carolina, and I got the idea to go into an empty hallway just a few feet away and catch some shut-eye. We sat down, and before we knew it, we were fast asleep. When I woke up, everyone was gone. I shook Parker to wake him and we took off down the hallway, asking the first person we saw in uniform, "Where did everybody go?"

"They were looking for you guys everywhere. Your plane is going down the runway now. You're under arrest for being AWOL."

Yup—they took us to a holding barracks and locked us up. It was like the brig but without bars. The worst thoughts were racing through my brain. What had we done? Were they going to shoot us? Hang us? We'd fallen asleep. We didn't flee. The more I thought about it, the more I realized that they couldn't have looked too hard for us, if they looked at all. A few days later, a guy came by and said, "If you each give me fifty dollars, I can get you on the next flight to Vietnam." Right before we were supposed to ship out, we'd been given an advance on our pay, so we gave him the money. He looked at us and said, "It's your lucky day, fellas. You're going to Vietnam."

10

The Land of the Blue Dragon

I can't say what made me fall in love with Vietnam—
that a woman's voice can drug you; that everything is
so intense. The colors, the taste, even the rain.
—Graham Greene

The story of my time in Vietnam is one of hundreds of thousands. There's no doubt that plenty of guys saw far more than I did and had it much worse. More than 58,000 American troops came home in body bags; approximately 154,452 came back wounded, many in dreadful shape. But one thing we all share is that we were forever changed by the experience.

I think it's important to put the Vietnam War in perspective—especially for those of you who are too young to remember or who were just unaware of the casualties. The Vietnam War was much larger in scope than you might guess. It was enormous. The longest war our country has been in was the War in Afghanistan. Again, while the numbers can vary, the average number of killed and wounded on both sides totaled somewhere around 150 per week.

During the Vietnam War in 1969, the year I went over to fight, that number was around 32,700 a week.

There are many who served far longer than I did. All of us went through varying degrees of bloodcurdling combat, some on multiple tours, and many paid an unthinkable price for doing what they believed was their patriotic duty. My pal Charlie, who I enlisted with and who was by my side through boot camp, was wounded so badly that he lost both of his legs and one of his arms.

> I'm certain that had I not gone through Vietnam I wouldn't have accomplished all that I have over the years.

Despite and because of the gruesome things I saw, Vietnam shaped me in so many ways, and it changed me to the core. What I witnessed, what I went through, and how I survived is a big part of who I am today. My life was on a different path before I left Baltimore. I'm certain that had I not gone through Vietnam I wouldn't have accomplished all that I have over the years. From that perspective, I'm so very grateful. Every experience in life can be a gift. You may not understand the reason behind the pain and struggle in the moment, but there's always something to be learned from those experiences. It can take years of reflection to achieve that epiphany, but it's there.

These days, I don't know anyone who enjoys life as much as I do. Seriously. By now, you already know that wasn't always the case, especially in my youth, but today, a bad day is a rare day. And when something challenging comes along, I don't dwell on it; I know tomorrow will be a better day, and I just go with it. You see,

> These days, I don't know anyone who enjoys life as much as I do.

I'm a guy who loves to take action. I only want to move forward and rarely look in the rearview mirror. I'm willing to take (calculated) risks along the way and am always ready, willing, and excited to face new challenges. These traits are the results of what I went through in Vietnam—and I wouldn't change a thing about what got me here.

I'm proud that I served my country, and I would do it again.

It sure wasn't pleasant, though. Not for any of us.

I served in the Vietnam War as an 0311 Rifleman. I was stationed with Delta Company of the 1st Battalion, 26th Marines. We operated off Hill 190 in Quảng Nam province, Vietnam. My first vivid memory of the place was the endless rice paddies as far as you could see. I had been told that Vietnam would change me, that whatever was absent from my life I would find there. It didn't take long for me to understand that once you arrived in this beautiful country, you quickly understood a lot. But there were many things I would learn in Vietnam that would have to be experienced firsthand to fully comprehend. The heat, the smells—both overwhelm you on contact. I have never known anything like it before or since.

> I'm proud that I served my country, and I would do it again.

Our job was to operate on squad-level ambushes every night—well, almost every night. On many days, we had to help Explosive Ordnance Disposal (EOD) find dud bombs and blow them up, which meant there was not much sleep during the day or most nights.

Our primary responsibility was to keep the North Vietnamese Army from getting into the various small villages surrounding Hill 190 where they could confiscate rice, terrorize the villagers, and then feed their troops. For the most part, we did a pretty good job preventing that.

When I got to my squad on the first day, I wasn't all that surprised to learn that two other Marines and I were replacement troops, because our squad had been ambushed three days before and suffered five casualties, four of which were fatal. And to make things worse, they were the senior men, meaning they were the Marines who had been there the longest. Our new squad leader was a Marine by the name of Barry George. Barry was nineteen years old and had been in country for only six weeks, but he was now calling the shots. Even though it didn't seem like it at the time, our squad was in good hands with Barry. He turned out to be one of the finest Marines and best leaders of men I've ever met. He remains a great friend to this day.

After meeting with the squad, I had a little downtime, so I walked over and sat on one of the walls at the top of Hill 190, near our tent. I looked down at the vast valley below me. The colors were intense and beautiful. I don't think I'd ever seen anything as green—certainly not in Baltimore. As striking as those colors were, I wasn't paying much attention, because my mind was completely focused on one thing: *How was I going to stay alive?* I kept asking myself how would I ever make it through this. Clearly, nobody in my squad had been there for very long, and to top it all off, a Marine Corps tour is thirteen months, not twelve like those of the Army, Navy, and Air Force.

> Remember what they say: be careful what you wish for, because you might just get it.

Sitting there on that wall, I tried to picture how I could still be alive in thirteen months. I kept thinking that the senior man in my squad had been there for just six weeks. My prospects were grim. I had no idea what I was up against and no clear picture of what I had actually gotten myself into. Remember what they say: be careful what you wish for, because you might just get it. I found the situation impossibly dark and seemingly insurmountable. From where I was sitting, I was screwed with a capital S.

I started to notice that my heart was racing and I was finding it difficult to breathe. The air was thick and the temperature unbearably hot. My skin was clammy. I felt sick. Even though it was bright and sunny, all I could see was darkness. I think this was as close as I've ever gotten to an anxiety attack. Then something extraordinary happened. It hit me like a lightning bolt: I realized that, more than likely, I wouldn't survive this. This was where I was going to die. I was sure of it. I let out a big sigh and just dangled my legs over the wall.

That seminal moment changed everything. I sat there stunned for about five minutes after this revelation. And then, miraculously, I accepted that certain death was now my fate. With this understanding, I suddenly relaxed. I felt at peace, and the weight of the world was lifted from my shoulders. The darkness instantly let go of me, and I was able to see the light. What had seemed impossible moments earlier now seemed, well, manageable. As I stared out into the vastness in front of me, I could finally appreciate the incredible colors of the valley surrounding Hill 190. It was beautiful, in so many ways.

And I was surprisingly okay.

That's when I made myself two promises. The first was that I would do everything I could to perform my job well as a US combat Marine for my brothers in my squad and to make my friends and family proud. The second was to somehow, some way stay alive for mail call every morning. More than anything, it was that second promise to never look any further into the future than the next morning's mail call that got me through the short time I spent fighting in the Vietnam War. Do you know how to eat an elephant? You do it one bite at a time. What initially seemed like an overwhelming situation became something

I could deal with, as long as I did it day by day. And from that moment on, I was fine.

After coming to that realization and making those two promises, I took a deep breath, stretched out my arms as if to say *I've got this*, and then joined my squad on my very first ambush.

The action began soon after we left Hill 190 to set up the ambush. It was exhilarating and terrifying all at once. I had just turned eighteen in November and was in amazing shape, perhaps the best I've ever been. Even so, the rice paddies and mud were so thick that I didn't know how the hell I was going to take another step. It was the heaviest mud you can imagine. The water might have been only a foot and half deep, but the mud was also a foot and a half deep. Every step felt like I was trudging through shit and vermin. Sometimes the leeches were horrible too. I occasionally found them around my feet and ankles. I quickly learned to shake them out of my boots and to use a lit cigarette to make them back their heads out of my skin. To make matters worse, the boots the Marine Corps had issued me were two sizes too big, which made each step even harder.

It was dark—like, you-can't-even-see-your-hand dark. The only light we saw that night came in bursts from explosions and gunfire. My pack, my weapon, all the equipment I was carrying on my back were heavy, like the air, which was sweltering even at night. With every breath, it felt like I was inhaling hot muck into my lungs. As miserable as that was, the cherry on top of this shit sundae was the rancid stench all around me. I imagined that this was what death and doom—or perhaps hell—must smell like. It was unlike anything I'd ever experienced. I've never forgotten that smell. There were bloodsucking mosquitoes everywhere, especially all over me. They were drawn to my wet fatigues that were soaked from my sweat and the thick water splashing me with every step. I was usually covered in mosquito bites. One night, I had so many on my wrists that I couldn't tell where my wrist ended and my hand started.

About half an hour after our squad set up in the initial ambush site just outside a village, we received a radio call that a Marine was seriously wounded. His squad was lying in wait in another pagoda, about a thousand meters across the rice paddy from where we were positioned. I was staked out with a few other Marines facing away from the village, all of us as still as could be and poised to pounce, when the Marines facing the village saw enemy soldiers moving about in the distance—NVA or Vietcong, who knew?

After a short wait, the explosions began. They came fast, and they were bone-rattlingly loud. A call for help came across our radio, and we were ordered to move. We had a corpsman with our squad, and they didn't. A corpsman is an enlisted medical specialist in the United States Navy, who may also serve as a Marine. They are the first responders for injured Marines, especially in active combat zones. Marines consider them to be one of the most vital and effective members of their unit.

Hunt, a skinny six-foot-tall kid who, like the rest of us, was not yet twenty, had just fired a LAW—a light anti-armor weapon that was sort of like a bazooka. It was really powerful, made to take on tanks. You fire it once and then toss it away. I later learned that just after Hunt shot that thing, an enemy soldier popped out of a spider hole and threw a Chicom (our name for Chinese communist hand grenades) at him. Hunt was down on his right knee when the grenade landed between his legs. It didn't go off, though, so Hunt grabbed it, and as he was throwing it back—*BLAM!*

It exploded just as he let go, ripping off part of his arm and a chunk of his face and tearing small holes in him from top to bottom. Miraculously, it didn't kill him. When we got there, Hunt was actually trying to get himself together. He was in shock. A couple of guys were holding him back as he tried to use his right arm to reach up and feel his wounded eye. There was nothing to feel, and nothing to feel it with. The eye was gone, as was his right hand and most of his right forearm. Not that Hunt knew any of that. He moved around like a zombie—a limbless, mangled zombie. As all this went down, the Marines in Hunt's squad were firing like mad, so we figured a bunch of dead NVA would be lying in the muck.

I was in a rice paddy not far from that squad's sergeant, a Marine named Larry Blackwell. The medevac helicopter was coming in, bringing wind, noise, and total chaos. That chopper—a big Huey with propellers on the front and the back—was getting ready to land, and holy shit, it was going to land on Sergeant Blackwell. But Blackwell didn't notice. He was busy vomiting from the sight of Hunt. Without thinking, I dashed over, lunged at him, and pushed him hard until we both tripped over a dike in the rice paddy and went tumbling into the murky water. The chopper just missed us. But hey—we were alive. There's no doubt about it: I saved Blackwell's ass.

So, on my first ambush, I saved another Marine's life, and I also fired my rifle for the first time . . . at a snake. Allow me to explain: after the chopper took Hunt away, it was time to establish the body count. Confirmed body count was everything in the Vietnam War. All of us—Marines from both squads, many still weak from puking—were ordered into a long formation. Flares launched by artillery hung from mini parachutes, lighting the place up like Yankee Stadium. We plodded in a line through the rice paddies, tired to the bone, swatting mosquitoes in vain, and trolling for NVA corpses so we could take their rifles, cut off their clothes, and turn it all in to rack up points for the good guys. That night, though, we found none. Zero. It was as if we'd been fighting ghosts.

As I stood three feet deep in the paddies, I looked in front of me and saw a big red snake about fifteen or twenty feet away. This thing was huge. It was traversing the water, swimming toward me. I kept thinking, *Surely it's going to go left or right.*

Well, it didn't.

It got within about four or five feet of me, and with a burst from my rifle, I sent it to snake heaven. When I did, the bullets from my rifle hit that nasty, nasty water and splashed it up into my eyes. It took me a while to get it out. When I could see, I looked around, and everybody was gone. *What the hell?*

They were all in the water.

All my brothers went down when the gunfire started, which I

> "Next time, don't shoot the snake."

understand. They didn't know it wasn't enemy fire. I was so embarrassed. Later that night, I had a counseling session with my squad leader, and Barry advised me, "Next time, don't shoot the snake."

Afterward, I was beat. Physically and emotionally. I had never—and I mean *never*—done anything so grueling.

I had been with Delta Company for eight, maybe nine hours.

The next day, back on Hill 190, some guy offered me a pair of boots—size 10, my size. I tried them on, and they were a perfect fit. I asked him where they were from, and he told me they were Hunt's.

"Are you shitting me?" I asked.

I was wary of taking boots from a Marine we all figured was dead by now. I looked at them for a moment. Then I slipped those well-worn boots onto my aching feet, and man, they felt good.

Remarkably, I found out later that Hunt had made it. He ended up settling in western New Jersey, running a few antique stores and having a houseful of kids. When I reached out to him many years after the war, I told him about the boots. And when I did, he said he was glad that they fit me. But then he said he wanted them back.

War Is So Brutal

On my second night in the bush, we pulled ourselves together from what had happened the first night and set off to mount another ambush. A Marine Corps ambush is usually done in three phases: First you go out at dusk, you keep moving until after it gets dark, and then you settle in. You wait about an hour to an hour and a half, depending on your squad leader's call, and then you move again—*very* quietly, using a compass to guide you toward the second point. A while later, you move once again to your third and final spot. You do this so the enemy has less chance of knowing your location, which increases your chances of retaining the element of surprise. And in war, having surprise on your side is everything.

It was important that you also be at the right spot. If you called in artillery or mortars, your calls would be to predetermined firing coordinates around you. You always wanted to be in the middle of those coordinates. If, God forbid, you were in the wrong location, the mortar, artillery, or aerial bombardment might land right on top of you. In those days, there were no GPS or position beacons like there are today. We had only compasses to navigate with.

We were trudging through a rice paddy with a Marine by the name of Ray Livesey leading as the point man. Ray was tall and teasingly referred to himself as Sergeant Rock, the old comic book figure who was always fighting against World War II–era enemies. At that time, at least for us, the point man made the decision to walk on the dikes or not. Walking on a rice paddy dike is much easier and more comfortable than walking though the shit of the rice paddy, but the NVA and Vietcong knew that too—so that's where they put their booby traps. Ray got up on the rice paddy dike that night. He hadn't been walking for five minutes before an explosion mangled his legs. Ray was the only one who was hurt in that explosion. We made a stretcher out of the ponchos we had and started carrying him back. He was in a lot of pain. We were the better part of a mile away from where we needed to take him, just outside the perimeter of Hill 190, where a medevac jeep was going to pick him up. That night, the war was particularly busy and casualties were high, so no helicopters were available to pick Ray up. Since his wounds did not appear to be life-threatening, he could be transported by jeep instead. I remember falling over and over again in that rice paddy water as I helped carry Ray to the medevac point.

When Ray was injured, Eugene Bryant became our new point man. Bryant was a lanky man. He was like a cat with a sixth sense, a damn fine Marine who became a dear friend of mine. Once we got close to Hill 190, the Marines manning the perimeter needed to know it was our troops approaching so they wouldn't think we were the enemy and open fire. We contacted the radioman on Hill 190 and gave whatever that night's passwords were, and then the point man had to fire a green flare to let them know it was us. When fired, a flare is pretty much supposed to go straight up into the air. Bryant set off the flare by banging it off his knee, and instead of going straight up, it went right into Hill 190 and right into the brand-new beer tent the captain had built for us Marines.

Thankfully, no one was in it at the time, but it burned that sucker down to the ground. The captain was pissed, so he sent us back out on another ambush that night. Man, we were tired. We couldn't believe it.

What I came to realize was that he would have sent us back out on ambush no matter what. The only difference was this time he wasn't pleased with us because we'd accidently torched his new beer tent.

When I got back to Hill 190 the next morning, I went to clean my rifle like I always did and found that the barrel was completely filled with mud from falling in those rice paddies. The rifle was thick with it from the end of the muzzle to the beginning of the chamber. Had I pulled the trigger that night, I don't know what would have happened, but it wouldn't have been good.

I was bummed that Ray got hurt. I liked him a lot. He was a good guy and remains a friend of mine to this day. Although he was badly injured, he survived; he was totally disabled, though, and still walks with a cane.

On another night, we were going through a village during our first move. It was dark—very dark. We were making our way down a path past a row of trees on our left when suddenly our machine gunner, Brownie, turned and started firing. There were two enemy soldiers who'd come running out of a hooch, right in our direction. Brownie took care of the situation, killing both of them in a brutal blaze of firepower. It was over fast, and when we moved toward the dead bodies, I looked down and made eerie eye contact with the fresh corpses. They gazed up at me like two mangled, disfigured mannequins. When I took a closer look, they appeared to be young, just like us, perhaps eighteen or nineteen years old. They both had AK-47 rifles, so they were either Vietcong or maybe North Vietnamese Army soldiers and would have gladly killed us if they had the chance. Why they were there, I will never know. I often wondered if they were inside the hooch getting laid and were just rushing to get back to wherever they were supposed to be.

War is so brutal.

My squad spread out to sweep the area and make sure the place was secure, and, if possible, to up the body count. I walked past the hooch that I suspected those soldiers had run out of. I heard some movement from within, and I did what I was trained to do: I fired a half dozen rounds into the hooch. Something called me away suddenly—I don't recall what—but I never did check inside.

Once again, we were on the move. For some reason, I decided to throw a hand grenade past the hooch, out toward the dike. I pulled the pin, waited a few seconds, and then threw it. It didn't go nearly as far as I had expected it to. I was just a scrawny eighteen-year-old kid who had no practice throwing grenades. It landed in the water in the rice paddy on the other side of the dike, which absorbed most of the explosion, but it was very close to us—too close.

"Motherfucker! Did you throw that?" one of the guys called out.

Shit. I was two for two. First the snake and now the grenade.

I wasn't allowed to throw hand grenades after that.

Coming face-to-face with the enemy was what we'd trained for. Combat was what we were there to engage in. And to be successful at that, we had to be willing to do things others were not. Hard things, like staying awake all night or marching through those rice paddies. We carried stuff that would have been so much easier to leave behind, knowing that if the shit hit the fan, we'd be glad we had it. Enduring the pain was what it took to succeed—and I desperately wanted to succeed.

The Marine Corps was such a contrast to how I grew up. The rules were black-and-white. I had no trouble understanding that.

Looking back on it today, I can see that being a United States Marine was the first really positive thing I'd done in my life, the first thing that had real meaning. It taught me responsibility and gave me the backbone and dedication to see the things I had to do through to their conclusion. The Marine Corps also taught me that I had the right to be proud. It reinforced that a promise is sacred. If you say you're going to do something, you better do it. Nothing reinforced that like the Marine Corps. All you have in this world is your word. That's your value. If you establish a reputation for keeping your promises and for being as solid as your handshake, it will always serve you well. To this day, everything I do in business stems from these lessons. I still live by them. As a result, I've been able to accomplish much more than I had ever dreamed of doing.

And for the first time in my life, I was part of a team, if not a family. There was nothing we wouldn't do for one another, not then and not now. The guys I was in the Marines with treated me well, and I treated them well. And for sure the Marines I served with on Hill 190 were the best guys I've ever known. They treated each other with respect. Did that mean they were going to take your shit? No. Did that mean they wouldn't bust your balls every chance they got? No. But you know what? It was all in good fun, and it built a lifetime of camaraderie. Combat does that. It will bring you close really fast. I knew that

> Enduring the pain was what it took to succeed—and I desperately wanted to succeed.

> Looking back on it today, I can see that being a United States Marine was the first really positive thing I'd done in my life, the first thing that had real meaning.

from the word go. I would have taken a bullet for any of them, and they would have done the same for me.

Incredibly, Bryant spent most of his thirteen-month tour walking point. Walking point is by far the most dangerous position, and this Marine did it. I will forever respect him for doing that. He's my friend and my brother. I love him a lot.

> I would have taken a bullet for any of them, and they would have done the same for me.

When I share these stories, I can vividly see them in my mind like they happened yesterday. Perhaps, after all these years, I can't recall the exact details as well as I once did, but I can still see the two young boys and their mangled bodies from that night. I can smell the rice paddies and taste the horrible stench that hung in the thick air we breathed day in and day out.

Within a week of my arrival in Vietnam, I had begun to settle in, accepting this as my new reality and doing everything I could to stay alive. I did whatever job I was asked to do, including tail-end Charlie. It's probably the safest position in the squad when you're walking last, but it's also the creepiest. You're always looking over your shoulder in case somebody tries to sneak up on you. I carried the radio, too, which added twenty-five pounds to my already heavy pack. It was 1969 before there were cell phones, so the radio was our primary method of communication in the bush. It was a big, bulky thing with an eight-to-ten-foot antenna, and it was like carrying a sign that said, "Please shoot me first."

Every day I was learning how to find my place. It wasn't easy, but it was always interesting. I'd only been there a week, but it felt like I'd been there forever.

Light It Up

Sometimes the things that stick in your memory—that are planted there for life—aren't what you'd expect. Sure, I'll never forget the images of combat and gore. Those will forever be emblazoned in my mind. But there was one night that I remember that was terrifically different: the night the trees fell.

We'd set up an ambush in an old cemetery. Nothing like hiding in a graveyard to add a little creepiness to the situation, but Vietnamese cemeteries were particularly interesting, since they cover their dead in burial mounds, whereas we bury our dead underground. I was down low, stretched out next to a mound, as quiet and alert as I could be, trying like mad not to swat the mosquitoes that constantly attacked me. Another Marine in my squad was on the other side of the mound, but I couldn't see him. I couldn't see anyone else from my squad, for that matter. Just the dirt and the dark and a tinge of light from the moon. It was eerily quiet.

This particular cemetery came with a story, and I found myself thinking about it. A few months earlier, I was told a squad of eight Marines was set up here in ambush. They heard enemy activity all around, so they shot up a red flare to signal to the command post that they needed help—really badly, and really soon. The second that flare soared into the sky, a burst of intense gunfire erupted. Then, in a flash, it stopped. By the time the backup Marines reached the cemetery, having run seven klicks or so at a frantic pace, it was too late. (A klick, by the way, is one thousand meters/ one kilometer.) The bodies of all eight men lay scattered amid the mounds of interred Vietnamese.

That was the story of this cemetery—or at least the only one that mattered to me.

On this night, eleven of us lay in wait. Two other squads from Delta Company were out that night, too, one to my left, the other to my right. Both were about two or three klicks away. Rapid gunfire suddenly broke the silence. I heard the squad on my left shooting. Then I heard fierce gunfire from my right. Friendly fire? Vietcong? It didn't matter. Suddenly all that noise merged, blending from stereo into a cacophony of bullets buzzing and hissing as they flew by overhead. *Zzzzing!* The noise was everywhere and nowhere. It was utter mayhem. I didn't shoot—hell, I had no clue where or what to shoot at. I knew not to get up, though. Those bullets were zipping by way too close.

Then came the explosions. Someone had apparently called in artillery and mortars. It seemed like heavy artillery and/or mortars were landing a few hundred yards or so from where I was—directly in front of me. An intense flash, a loud boom, and then I saw the trees light up and fall—first one, then another. I'd see the flash, hear the boom, then feel the ground rattling with the shocking concussion from each explosion. I remember lying there watching all of this with my eyes as wide as could be as bullets flew over my head from the firefights going on to my left and right and thinking, *I wonder if this was anywhere close to the horror the French and English soldiers saw at Verdun during World War I.*

The graveyard grew hotter and hotter. I stared out, mesmer-
ized, as those tall trees fell like bowling pins. Some bounced up—
ripped from the ground—before tumbling, while others twisted
and shot out sideways as if they'd been kicked over at the bases of
their trunks. Some seemed to fall in slow motion.

Then, just as it had begun, it all stopped without notice. And it
ended with absolutely no casualties. I've never seen anything like
it, not before or since. I particularly think about that night whenever I'm at a Fourth of July fireworks display. I know that's not what
the fireworks are about, but I can't help going back to that night
in Vietnam.

As horrific as the Vietnam War was on most days, there were
occasional nights when the only combat we saw was a fight to stay
awake while lying in ambush in
those rice paddies. Waiting end-
lessly, quiet and still. While I
wasn't necessarily religious, at the
time I still thought of myself as a
Catholic. I believe that there is a way of the Universe, and there are
metaphysical things we don't know and can't possibly understand.
But whatever my beliefs, I knew for sure that there are no atheists
in a foxhole.

**I knew for sure that there
are no atheists in a foxhole.**

Some of my memories of being in Vietnam are, well . . . *sweet*.
One afternoon, two other Marines and I were sent to to find water
to fill the squad's canteens. Our entire company was involved in a
daytime operation, and it was hotter than four hoots of hell. When
we went into a village to get water, we came across a boy, maybe
ten years old, who was carrying a wooden tray held up with a strap
around his neck attached to each corner of the tray. He slowly
walked over to us and revealed a number of vanilla popsicles in
white wrappers insulated with a few sheets of burlap. We couldn't
believe our eyes. We traded cigarettes and C rations for this kid's

popsicles. The three of us put down our rifles, sat in the shade of a tree, and relaxed. Man, they were the best things I had ever tasted—homemade vanilla popsicles on a stifling afternoon in Vietnam. There weren't many moments like that during my time in the war, but I'm sure glad I had this one. The three of us sat there for a minute, and then one of the guys said, "What if these are poisoned?"

The other guy said, "Who gives a fuck?"

They were delicious. If this was the way we went out, then so be it.

When we got back to our platoon, no one in our squad believed us when we told them what had happened. They never once ran into a popsicle-toting kid anywhere in the bush. But I swear it happened. Funnily enough, we never ran into that kid again either.

While I may not have realized it at the time, our leaders, who were mostly tough sons of bitches, were protecting us—often from ourselves. I remember smoking a cigarette one early evening while sitting on top of a bunker. Staff Sergeant Long came over and asked if I worried about dying in Vietnam.

"No, I'm not worried."

"Get the fuck off that bunker, Parsons."

I didn't understand why he said that at the time, but looking back, it was obvious I was a sitting duck and didn't know any better. I was eighteen years old and a freshly minted combat Marine— and, in Staff Sergeant Long's eyes, an idiot. (Looking back, I agree with him.) What did I know? I thought I was smart, but boy, did I do some dumb things along the way. Like the time I cut the shields out of my flak jacket because it made it lighter and cooler to wear. Once again, Staff Sergeant Long asked me why I'd done that. When I told him, he handed me a brand-new flak jacket and told me to wear it without any alterations. Well, that jacket may well have saved my life. The concept of luck—the sheer randomness that determined whether you lived or died—really struck me in Vietnam. That thought just boggled my mind.

One night, I didn't go on ambush and instead stayed back on Hill 190 with a fellow Marine named Proctor. I was under the impression that I would walk first or second point for our sister squad. I'm not sure why Proctor was with me. After my normal squad moved out for that night's ambush, a Marine named Mitchell Morton, the normal point man for our sister squad, came over to me and said Proctor and I wouldn't be going with them that night after all. I later learned that that was because Morton needed to train another Marine to walk second point. I'd walked point only a few times myself, and I guess the squad leader, very smartly, wanted the more experienced Marine to do the training. Morton and the squad headed out to the same pagoda I'd been staked out in on my first night, the night Hunt was hurt. It wasn't far off— maybe thirty minutes, depending on how carefully you walked. But when Morton's squad got there, enemy soldiers were lurking in the dark, waiting in their own ambush.

An NVA machine gunner, sitting motionless and hidden deep in the dark pagoda, opened fire. The point man—whoever he happened to be that night—didn't stand a chance. Morton took six bullets in the chest, from close range. The guy behind him was shot through the hand. Morton made it onto the helicopter, but he died soon after in the field hospital.

Me, I was sitting back on Hill 190, safe as could be, listening to the gunfire in the distance and wondering what was happening. *That could have been me*, I've often thought. Maybe it should have been me and not Morton. Shit; who knows? Who could possibly make sense of any of this? Later, after recounting this story to Barry George and Doc Whitman, our corpsman, they both told me it didn't happen that way. They genuinely believe that. Maybe it didn't. Everybody's memory changes over time, but my memory is usually spot-on. The story as I told it is what I believe happened.

On another night, for whatever reason, our squad got to stay back again and didn't go out on ambush. Earlier in the day, one of the guys went for a haircut and came back with a fifth of Southern Comfort he'd shoplifted from the base exchange. Man, were we happy to see that! Even better, another guy received a canned ham from home. We got the idea to pour that booze all over the ham. We doused it and let it marinate before heating it up with C-4 plastic explosives. Cooking with C-4 was a talent. With a detonation cap, C-4 creates an explosion; without one, it just burns very hot. When the ham was cooked, we dove right in. Barry cut out pieces with a KA-BAR knife. We grabbed the large chunks with our hands and began to feast. I had never tasted anything so good. Somehow I managed to drop my portion, and it rolled down the hill and landed under concertina wire, making it very hard to get to. But I wasn't about to let that ham go to waste, so I turned to the guys and said, "I'm going after it. Whatever you do, don't shoot me!"

I made my way down the hill and shimmied under the wire until I could reach the chunk of ham. Once I had it in my hands, I worked myself out from under the wire and headed back up the hill. The ham was covered in dirt. I wiped off as much as I could, then poured water from my canteen over it before I chomped down on it, crunchy dirt and all. This is still one of my best memories ever. It was so good! To this day, whenever I prepare ham at my home, I *always* cook it in Southern Comfort. I call it Hill 190 ham.

When we weren't on an ambush or stalking the enemy, I liked to write letters home. They weren't long—mostly because I didn't have the time to write more—but I thought they would mean something to my parents.

Dear Mom and Dad,
I'm on ambush every night. It's really hard to stay awake
because we don't get much sleep. My life really depends on
me staying awake. If you could send me some NoDoz, I
would sure appreciate it.

Love,
Robert
P.S.: Don't worry.

That was pretty much the extent of the letters I wrote home. Thankfully, my family sent NoDoz once or twice, and it really helped, especially on those long nights in the paddies.

There Are No Coincidences

Eventually, I volunteered for the point team. There's no doubt that point for a rifle squad is the most dangerous position, and it's also where the most action is. The Marines who walk on the point team don't have to carry as much, so they can take quick action if needed. The first time I'd walked point, we had just entered a village. It was dusk, and the last light of the day was twinkling through the tree canopy above us. We were moving alongside a big overgrown hedge. I was the first man on the point team, so my job was to look for traps. I had my head down, searching for any signs of an explosive device. I was holding the main grip of my rifle, with the muzzle pointed toward the ground. I had my index finger next to the trigger but not on it. My thumb was on the safety. If something were to happen, I'd be able to quickly swing my rifle up, switch it off safe, and move my finger to the trigger, ready to rock and roll. As I led the squad around the hedgerow, there was suddenly a big commotion. Whatever was causing it was running through those hedges right toward me. I swung my rifle up like I'd prepared to do, and it came off safe; I put the butt of the rifle into my shoulder and was about to shoot when I realized the sounds were coming from a young boy carrying a bucket of water. I'm happy to say that, although I came whisker close, I didn't shoot him. I remember that he stopped and stood in front of me, maybe a foot away from the muzzle of my rifle. His eyes were as wide as saucers. My guess is that his mother sent him to get water much earlier, but he must have been goofing off with his buddies and was rushing home at the last minute. It almost cost him his life. To this day, I often think about that moment. I remember him like I saw him yesterday. There's one thing I know for sure: if he's alive today, he remembers me. And one other thing—I'm fairly certain he had a laundry problem when he got home that night.

Thirty days into my time in Vietnam, my squad was going through a village just as it was getting dark. This time I was walking second point, so my main job was to spot enemy shooters. Bryant was walking first point. We were following a trail through the village, and I remember thinking that everything seemed so quiet. Too quiet. And then, *BLAM!* Everything lit up.

How do I even describe a moment like this? One second you're fine, and the next you're exploding.

Something stung. I felt a huge slap, and then I felt nothing. My ears were ringing. I had no idea what happened. *Who was hurt?* Oh, shit—it was me. Bryant had stepped right over it, but I snagged a trip wire beside some low bushes. It was a Chicom, or at least I think that's what it was. I didn't actually hear it go off. I just heard ringing in my ears. When I used to light off firecrackers as a kid, sometimes

I wouldn't hear them either; I was too close to them. They would just make my ears vibrate. This was that times one thousand.

If I had stepped on something, I would have been blasted to pieces, or if the trap had been a Bouncing Betty, my head would have been blown off. But it wasn't anything like that. I felt a smack across my legs and arms, but it didn't knock me over because the explosive was set away from the trail.

I turned to George, who was behind me but far enough back so the explosion didn't touch him, and said, "Jesus Christ, it hurts."

And then I fell back. I was on the ground and going into shock. I remember that now, but for a long time this whole event was a blur. The explosion tore up my pants and my legs. I reached over with my left arm to stop the bleeding, but the bone from my elbow was sticking out. That's when I noticed there was blood every-where. George came over to help me, and Doc Whitman started bandaging me up. Doc gave me a shot of Morphine, which took effect immediately, then everything seemed surreal.

While I was lying there, a few of the other Marines in my squad got really pissed about what had happened. They took their Zippos to some nearby huts, and those hooches went up in flames. That's mainly what I remember.

George called for a medevac, but all the choppers were busy that night, and it was obvious that my wounds weren't life-threatening. The squad was told to carry me to a road, and the closest field hospital would send a jeep to get me, just like they did for Livesey weeks earlier. After a lot of stumbling and cursing, snorting and grunting, I was carried to the medevac point, where a jeep was waiting. Luckily for the Marines carrying me, I was skinny and didn't weigh a lot. Those Marines put me on a stretcher that was strapped to the back of the jeep.

I was lying there in the back of the jeep, floating from the shot of Morphine Doc gave me, when I heard the guys from my squad arguing over who was going to get my rubber lady. That was Vietnam talk for an air mattress, and having one was a real coup.

I wasn't really supposed to have a rubber lady, but she and I enjoyed a couple of well-deserved days together, back on Hill 190 when I had a chance to sleep. You see, sometime earlier I had been on a day patrol when somehow I caught my fatigues on a barbed-wire fence and tore them up. It was my only pair, and they were in rough shape, so I was sent back to headquarters in Da Nang to get a haircut and new fatigues. To get the new fatigues, the Marines at the supply building said I needed a requisition slip signed by the colonel and oh, by the way, the colonel wouldn't be around until the next week. I showed them the ripped up fatigues I was wearing and explained I had to return in the next hour to Hill 190. They said, "We can't help you. Sorry."

"Screw that," I muttered.

As me and my ripped up fatigues walked over to catch my truck back to the bush, I came upon some barracks. Partly out of curiosity, I pulled open a door and loved what I saw. No one was there. Just me. The place was full of everything you could imagine. I ducked inside, opened a locker, and found a brand-new set of fatigues. I took mine off and tried those on. Bingo—they fit. I replaced those new fatigues with my ripped up ones, hung them back up, and placed those old nasty fatigues back in the locker. I also grabbed a couple of cartons of choice cigarettes—Marlboros and Winstons. And then I spotted the grand prize: a gorgeous rubber lady. She was sprawled out on a cot, so I deflated her, tucked her under my arm with the other loot, and off I went. I remember the reaction I got when I returned to Hill 190 with my hair cut, new fatigues, cigarettes, and rubber lady.

"Where did you get all that?" asked one of my fellow Marines.

"Don't you worry about that. I got it," I said with a mischievous smile.

Now, as I lay wounded, my squad brothers were fighting over who'd get her while I wondered just how badly I was hurt. (I'll say it one more time just for the record: A rubber lady is an air mattress. It's not a blow-up doll. Really.)

The guy driving the medevac jeep and his companion were slightly inebriated or high as shit. And away we went. They kept the jeep's lights off and played country music, laughing and singing as we swerved down the bumpy back roads in the dark of night. I was tied down but still felt the Jeep bouncing all over the place. I was terrified. At least I think I was.

Before this night, I had started feeling oddly invincible. Memories of recent ambushes—so much war crammed into so few days—flowed through my head like a movie playing in fast-forward. I thought about the time we were on a day patrol and my platoon had surrounded a group of NVA soldiers we caught in a village during the day. We were exchanging gunfire, and the bullets were zipping all around when Bryant and I were ordered to run two cans of ammo to Brownie, our M60 machine gunner. That was the most powerful gun we had. When we took off running toward Brownie, an NVA machine gunner inside the village started shooting like crazy right at us. The dirt was flying up everywhere, and we dove behind a dike along a dry rice paddy. The shots kept coming, mostly going overhead, and I completely lost it: I started laughing uncontrollably, a big, hearty, loud-as-shit laugh. Bryant looked over at me and, amid the noise of war, shouted, "You're fuckin' nuts." After we got the ammo over to Brownie, I can't remember another thing about that day. But there I was, lying wounded on a stretcher, and for whatever reason, this was my thought.

When the medevac jeep finally arrived at the Navy field hospital, I was removed from the jeep. They cut all my new fatigues off, leaving me naked while they triaged me. Afterward, I could see that the war machine was busy that night. There were bodies on stretchers everywhere—wounded Marines all around me.

There was a huge tent at the field hospital that had really good air-conditioning. It was very cold inside, especially if you had just come out of the bush. I was put in a long line of other wounded Marines and was moved steadily closer and closer to what turned out to be an X-ray machine. Next to the X-ray machine were buckets of water. I wondered what they were for. It turned out that when each of us was placed on the X-ray machine, we'd bleed all over it. The buckets were there to wash the blood away.

The next thing I remember was waking up in a hospital bed the next morning. I had pissed all over it. One of the hospital corpsmen told me not to feel bad about it. It had been so busy the night before that they didn't have time to put a catheter in me. They quickly changed the sheets, and it was like it never happened. Maybe fifteen minutes later, a Marine Corps colonel came over to hand me a Purple Heart. He shook my hand, took a picture, and said, "Congratulations." It didn't feel like a moment I wanted to celebrate, but that's the way the military works. Later that day, I was transferred to the Air Force hospital in Da Nang. The picture taken that day is the only photo I have of my time in Vietnam.

Eventually, I was flown from Da Nang to the US Naval Hospital in Yokosuka, Japan. During the trip to Yokosuka, I was doped up on strong painkillers. When I woke up, I was surprised to see William Parker Jr. in the bed next to me. Parker, you'll recall, was the other napper who was with me when I missed my flight to Vietnam. He was also assigned to Delta Company, but he was in a different platoon. I learned that he'd taken a bullet right through his neck a week or so before I was injured. While I was recovering, Parker got his orders sending him back home.

I had been given morphine for the pain. To wean you off it, they decrease your doses pretty rapidly, making the withdrawal brutal.

I'd hear guys begging for a shot, especially at night. As for me? I suffered in silence. It was every bit as painful as being wounded. This went on for a few days, maybe more. Once I was on the other side, though, I never wanted to go through that again.

A few more weeks passed, and I got my orders to return to the war, but first I had to go to Okinawa. While I was recovering, the Navy had lost my payroll records, which meant they had no way to pay me—so they didn't. Everything happened based on that one document. No payroll record, no pay. It was as simple as that. I would say to some of the guys, "Why don't you loan me some cash so I can go off base?"

"You know, Parsons, we like you, brother. But not that much." I never got to go off base. I wrote my folks and asked them to send some money from home, and they managed to send a little bit of cash. That was a first.

I'd received multiple shrapnel wounds in both legs and my left elbow, but I would leave the hospital with all my limbs. Surgery repaired me, for the most part, though I will live the rest of my life with many small metal fragments in both of my legs. I tried to rest, but I was so used to sleeping in the dirt that the hospital bed was uncomfortable. It was way too soft. Even with all those tubes stuck in me, I would climb out of bed and stretch out on the linoleum floor, to the absolute dismay of the hospital staff. They continually put me back in bed, but I slept really well down there.

While I was at the staging and processing areas for Marines on their way to and from Vietnam at Camp Butler and then Camp Hansen in Okinawa, the doctors determined I wasn't ready to return to combat. The wound in my elbow was still open and not healing well, and my legs hadn't healed yet either. So they put me in a casualty company, where I was there to mend.

When my arm and legs were finally better, I went and talked to the surgeon. "Doc, I'm all healed up. I'm ready to go," I said.

"Parsons, you did your share, son. You don't need to go back into that meat grinder. If you want, I'll keep you here for the rest of your tour."

I thought about it for a minute. I knew he was making a kind gesture. God bless him for that. This was an opportunity most guys probably would have said yes to. But not me. I said, "Doc, I want to go. I want to be with the guys I served with."

"I understand . . . I *think*. Okay," he said. And then he put the papers through to send me back to the bush.

After about a week, my orders came through. I was set to leave the next day at 7:00 a.m. As luck would have it, my payroll records also showed up that same day, so they gave me $800 in back pay. It might as well have been $2 million to me. I mean, a beer was a buck, so I had money to have a hell of a party that last night.

"Go off base, have a good time. And be back at midnight. Be back at midnight. Be back at midnight." A Marine Sergeant who gave me my orders said it three times. I guess guys with a little extra money like to stay out late.

Armed with a wad of cash, I headed off base and had a blast. I hit every bar I could find. I lived it up. Boy, did I have a ball. I had no plan to be back by midnight, that's for sure. What were they going to do? Send me to Vietnam? I was already headed there, so I thought, *What the hell!*

It was around three in the morning, and I was looking for something else to do. I was walking down the streets of the village of Kin in Okinawa, looking for anything that was open. It was raining like hell, and I was dripping wet. Off in the distance, I noticed a person walking toward me; he was soaking wet too. We got to the point where we were about to pass each other and I thought, *Hey, that's . . . It couldn't be . . .* It was Sergeant Blackwell, the man whose life I saved from that chopper on my first night in the bush.

Was I seeing a ghost?

Blackwell had been badly wounded a few weeks before I was, and we all heard that he had died. I was sure of it. Yet here he stood, soaking wet on an empty, pitch-black street in Kin village. Man, I was happy to see him. Blackwell explained that he was now stationed in Okinawa, the result of a Marine rule that says anyone who's wounded three times doesn't have to return to combat. He was working in Marine Corps Intelligence (if you can imagine such a thing).

"You saved my life," Blackwell said.

"We were told you died!"

> "You saved my life," Blackwell said.

"Obviously that's not true. There's a lot of bullshit floating around. But you know, I'll never forget that you saved my life. I owe you."

I didn't respond, mostly because I didn't think he owed me a thing. I was just happy to see the guy alive.

He said he could get me a job in Okinawa with Headquarters Company. Among my other duties I would get to be a courier and ferry plans and intelligence and all sorts of critical information from Okinawa to Vietnam and back. It sounded terrific, though in the military you heard exaggerated promises and tall tales all the time, so I just thought he was being kind and that nothing would ever come of it.

Even so, I smiled and said, "Okay."

"When are you leaving?"

"I'm scheduled to leave at seven a.m. today."

It was 3:00 a.m. then, so that was only a few hours away.

"Oh, shit; I don't know if I can get it done."

I said, "Brother, don't even worry about it." And I meant it too. Frankly, I wanted to go back.

"I'll do what I can."

"Good to see you, brother," I said as I gave him a great big bear hug before heading back to my bunk for a little shut-eye.

When I returned to base, a military police officer was waiting for me. Of course he arrested me for breaking curfew. I explained that I was headed back to Vietnam in a few hours and hoped he'd be merciful to me.

"Get him the fuck out of here," the MP said. That was the way the Marine Corps executed an act of courtesy.

A couple of hours later, when I awoke at the barracks and fell out for morning formation with a hangover from hell, instead of being put on a plane back to Vietnam I had orders to report to Headquarters Company, right there in Okinawa.

"Parsons, I've got special orders for you. You're now stationed at 9th Marine Amphibious Brigade Headquarters."

I could hardly believe it. Blackwell had come through.

I don't think it was a coincidence that I ran into him that fateful night. I believe it was the handiwork of the guardian angel that watches over me. Had the Navy not lost my payroll records, had they not found them, had I not decided to go back, had I been on that street five minutes earlier or later, had I not broken curfew . . . I never would have bumped into Blackwell. Never. Yet there he was, walking in the rain just like me. I swear to God, I haven't embellished this story one bit.

Blackwell saved my life in many ways that night. He said to me afterward, "Now we're even."

Not even close, buddy.

I owed him so much more.

Request Denied

As a courier I traveled back and forth between Okinawa and Da Nang delivering orders, and I loved it. I carried the orders in a burlap bag, was armed with an M1911 pistol, and even managed to visit my pals in Delta Company. There was something that grounded me there. I didn't know what it was, but it calmed me. I loved the South Vietnamese. Whenever I was around them, I just relaxed. I loved their culture and the beautiful landscape. In a strange way, it felt like home to me.

When I was a courier, I used to go to Hill 327, also known as Freedom Hill, a former US Marine Corps, US Army, and Army of the Republic of Vietnam base southwest of Da Nang in central Vietnam. I also got to know where the South Korean contractors who worked there had a quonset hut set up for them where they served beer. I would go outside the fence that separated us from them and call out to the guys coming in and out of there, "Hey, Joe." For whatever reason, I used to call the guys Joe. None of them spoke English, or at least not very much. I would give them some money to buy me six beers and throw them over the fence; they always came through for me. The beer they tossed me was always ice-cold and just perfect.

I'd sit next to other Marines back on Freedom Hill, and they'd say things like, "Man, it's hot." I would never say anything. I'd just hand them an ice-cold beer.

"How the fuck did you get that?"

"I got it," I'd say as I tilted my head back and took a swig.

I volunteered to return to my combat unit two more times, but it was never approved.

I finally saw Blackwell again a couple of months after he got me my courier job. "Bob, this is goodbye," he said.

"Are you rotating home, brother?"

"No, I'm going back to Vietnam. I just put in for a transfer, and it came through. I'm going back to a rifle company. That, I understand. I don't understand all this. I need to be there."

I understood how he felt. "Good luck, Larry. I love you, brother."

"I love you too," he said. I would never talk to or see him again.

All the while, I kept track of the men in my former squad. They were then operating on Barrier Island, a big island off the coast of Vietnam that was densely jungled and riddled with tunnels. On one of my trips, I had the opportunity to visit the USS *Okinawa*, which was anchored just off Barrier Island. As fate would have it, my squad was on the ship taking a break from the combat they'd been engaged in on the island. When I heard they were on board, I couldn't wait to see them again.

When I got off the helicopter, the first thing I saw was four dead Marines in body bags. The bags were placed over their heads and came down to below their hips and sometimes their knees, so you could still see feet sticking out. It was a stark and dramatic reminder of the ongoing war. The bodies were going to be passengers on the helicopter back to Da Nang.

I finally got to see George and the guys, and they were not a happy lot. They were just waiting for this miserable war to be over. But at least they were glad to be on a ship and not back in the jungle on Barrier Island.

We said our hellos, and I blurted out, "Guys, I'm coming back. I've put in a request for transfer. I'm coming back, baby." And I meant it too.

They looked at me like I was nuts.

"Have you lost your fucking mind?" a Marine named Cook asked.

"If I was in your shoes, I wouldn't be coming back to this shit! What the fuck do you want to come back here for?" another Marine asked.

"I love you guys. I want to be with you," I said.

Cook looked at me and muttered, "Well, you're a fucking idiot."

That may have been true, but it didn't change how I felt.

I had already put in my transfer request. It was approved by everyone except the gunnery sergeant. When I returned to Okinawa, I was called in to see him. He was sitting at his desk, holding my transfer request.

"Parsons, what are you doing?" he asked in a slightly confused tone.

"I want to go back to my squad in Vietnam, sir." My response was very matter-of-fact.

"Why?"

"I want to be with the guys I served with," I explained.

The company gunny took a deep breath and said, "You've done your share, son."

"Sir, I just want to be with them," I repeated.

"Request denied." He tore up the transfer request in front of me.

And that was that. What I later realized was that if I were to have gone back somehow, it wouldn't have been with the same guys. I didn't want to be with just *some* squad over there; I wanted to be with *my* squad. However, the company gunny wasn't going to let me go back. When I was a courier, I saw mortar and rocket attacks, but I was never again in combat.

The war continued, and I still had time left on my enlistment. Months later, the unit I was stationed with in Okinawa was disbanded. Troops were either sent home or sent back to Vietnam. I was one of those going back to the bush. But I had only a few months left on my tour and didn't want to go back to some random unit.

On my way back to Vietnam, I first went through troop processing at Camp Butler. The place was overwhelmed, with some poor second lieutenant doing his best to handle the excessive workload. The only thing I could think of doing to help this poor bastard out was to jump in. I walked over and started talking to him, explaining that I had about three months left on my tour and could do anything. "It looks like you need some help. I'm a good worker. I can do all this stuff," I said.

"You've got the job," he replied.

My role was to put troops on planes that were going home and to process arriving troops to units in Vietnam. After working a spell in intelligence, I got to know who the hard-luck units were, such as the 9th Marines and certain other units. I would look at the fellas who were on their way to join combat units in Vietnam and know pretty much what was going to happen to them. They were all so clean-cut and eager, like guys I'd want to share a beer or play ball with.

As I processed each new Marine, it broke my heart to know what was waiting for them. These were just kids, young men who were as wide-eyed and enthusiastic as I had been when I arrived not so long ago. I was no longer that boy. I had changed in immeasurable ways. And I knew these boys would soon feel the same—if they lived long enough. I suppose everyone's fate is preordained in some way. Even so, I felt awful about knowing what was ahead for them.

Sometimes that troop processing job bothers me most of all. There was absolutely nothing I could do to change the fate of any of those Marines. To this day, especially when I visit the Vietnam Veterans Memorial wall in Washington, DC, I talk to them and tell them how truly sorry I am.

Eventually, my tour was up, and I rotated home. I boarded the plane and felt indescribable relief as I flew over the Pacific and made my way to El Toro Marine Corps Air Station in Southern California to be processed out of the Marine Corps.

The night before my discharge from Camp Pendleton and return to Baltimore, I was having a few beers when I ran into a Marine named Mike. I knew him from my time in infantry training before we headed out to war.

"*Psst*—Bob. I want to show you something," he whispered.

We walked over to the barracks and then to his bunk. Mike opened up his footlocker. He dug through some socks and pulled out a Brasso can, which normally contained soaked cotton pads used to polish brass. Inside this can was a small glass jar of formaldehyde. I looked a little closer and saw an ear and a finger floating in the liquid. I could see dirt under the fingernail and black hairs on the lobe of the severed ear.

I was speechless, my eyes wide, my mouth open. Just stunned.

"Brother, what the fuck are you doing with these?" I asked, admittedly a little shocked and horrified.

"I was sent out on an ambush on my last night there," he said. "We killed two NVA on that ambush."

Apparently, Mike had decided to bring back some body parts, so he cut the ears and some fingers off one of the dead NVA. He kept them wrapped up because he knew he was headed home. He traded a corpsman he met in Da Nang one finger and an ear for a bottle of formaldehyde so he could show his trophies to his father.

"Are you shitting me? You're home now, Mike. You can't get caught with this here. You're going to go to jail, buddy, or who knows what? This isn't okay," I said.

"Nah," Mike replied. "This is kind of cool. I'm always going to keep them as a souvenir."

A souvenir? I thought. *Did he really just say that?*

Mike held that little jar up as he spoke. I couldn't take my eyes off it—or the little black hairs on the earlobe or the dirt beneath the fingernail. Suddenly, everything that was so horrific about this nasty war washed over me—the pain, the noise, the suffering, the bones popping out of arms, the torn-apart faces, the evil. Yes, that was it. The evil of war—not of us, not of them, but of the whole damn thing. Evil. Most of us wanted nothing more than to rinse from our memories all we'd seen, and here this guy was keeping a finger and an ear in a jar to bring home as mementos, as if they were tiny replicas of the Eiffel Tower.

I could tell he was proud of what he'd done. That's how the war can turn your mind around. I never forgot it.

I Am a Veteran

*I stood up, I showed up, I stepped forward. I raised
my right hand, I stood in the gap, I walked in the fire.
I did not run, I did not hide, I did not dodge, I did
not evade. Consequently, I have nothing to prove, no
one to convince. Those who matter already know.
Those who don't never will.*

—Unknown

The late 1960s was a time when it was considered cool to burn
your draft card. Yet there were many of us who chose a different
path. We remained loyal to our country. There were many brave
men and women who fought and
did their duty when it was unpop-
ular to do so. God bless them.

> There were many brave
> men and women who
> fought and did their duty
> when it was unpopular to
> do so. God bless them.

My experience coming home
from Vietnam was hard—much
harder than I'd expected. Because
early on I had given myself up for

dead, I could hardly believe I was actually going home. That was my gut reaction when I found out I was headed stateside.

I had watched the demonstrations taking place in America on television while I was recuperating from my injuries, so I was aware of the division over the war and what protestors were doing. It was upsetting, to say the least. Although it wasn't happening where I was, it may as well have been, because it sure felt personal. I kept telling myself that their anger wouldn't be directed toward me or my brothers and sisters. I wanted to believe that would be true. I wanted to believe we'd be welcomed home as heroes, men and women who had fought for freedom. Having been there, that's surely the way we wanted to be seen. When I was released at El Toro Marine Corps Air Station, many of us were told that maybe we shouldn't wear our uniforms when we headed home. I wore mine, and everybody I knew wore theirs, but that's what was suggested to help us avoid any confrontations with the anti-war movement. You didn't even talk about being there because that's the way things were at that time. In retrospect, we should have spoken more about it, for so many reasons.

I remember feeling happy, if not a little relieved, as I was packing up my things. While I had desperately wanted to go back to serve with my squad, it wasn't meant to be. So I gave in to the idea that I had served my time and my country and now it was off to the next chapter.

Many Vietnam veterans will tell you that the hardest part of the war wasn't the combat, although that was no walk in the park. They'll tell you that the hardest part was coming home. Unfortunately, there was no hero's welcome, or any welcome at all for that matter. As expected, all too many of us were instead met by protestors with hostile signs and plenty of unsavory name-calling, which felt like a big "Fuck you." At first it made me bitter and resentful. The protestors' anger toward us was wrong and terribly misplaced. It doesn't matter whether they agreed or disagreed with the war; in my mind, we fought for their dumb asses and their right to express that view.

When I got back to Baltimore, my parents had a "Welcome Home" banner hanging over the front porch. Well, part of it was hanging; the other half had fallen down before I arrived. My parents had moved into that house right around the time I joined the Marine Corps, so I hadn't lived in it for long before leaving for Vietnam. It was a nice place—nicer than I remembered. My uncle had loaned them the money for the down payment.

Other than the location, not much had changed at home. My mother was still having her breakdowns, and Pop was always out. As for me? Well, I wanted to have some time when I could celebrate being back. I asked about the $3,000 I had won gambling and sent to them before leaving for Vietnam, but I knew it was long gone.

"Did you bring me anything?" Mom asked.

I didn't. I'd never even thought about buying her something over there. I was so happy to be alive and safely home that I thought she would be happy too. Even so, I spontaneously said, "I had these nice earrings for you, and I think someone stole them out of my bag."

"What did they look like?" she gleefully asked.

Christ. Now she had me. For a moment I thought about the finger and the ear my buddy was bringing home to his dad. Handing her *that* and saying, "Here you go, Mom. I got another jar for Dad too." Now that would have shaken Mom to her core. I didn't know how to answer, so I improvised and said, "I didn't spend a lot of time picking them out, but they were nice."

"I wish you hadn't lost them," she said in a disappointed tone.

"Mom, I didn't lose them. They were stolen." I didn't have the heart to tell her they'd never existed. I was afraid I would have let her down. Later that day, though, I heard Mom telling all our relatives about the earrings she *almost* had.

Deep down, I knew my time in Vietnam had rattled Mom. I can understand why. I was definitely different than when I left, and it quickly became obvious. While I was in Vietnam, I took a lot of pictures with a small camera I carried with me. I never got the film developed over there. I had planned to do that when I returned home. When Mom came across the rolls of film, she knew they were from my time in the war. She took a hammer to each roll and pulled the film out of the canisters to expose it, and then she poured milk on the film and threw it all in the trash. When I asked her why she did that, Mom said she didn't want me going to jail if there was something on there I could have been tried for. The My Lai massacre trials were happening right around that time. The My Lai massacre was the mass murder of unarmed South Vietnamese civilians by US Army troops in 1968. I assured her that I hadn't done anything like that, and she had nothing to worry about. Even so, her response was simply to say, "You never know."

Somehow, she made everything all about her while simultaneously dismissing my service to our country. But then again, it was always all about Mom. I thought about it afterward and came to the conclusion that she wasn't worried I'd be arrested so much as she didn't want to deal with my being indicted for something, especially a war crime. In her mind, everyone who went over to fight did horrific things. We certainly *saw* horrific things, but very few of us—and certainly no one in my squad—committed such atrocities as the My Lai massacre. Mom was mad as a hatter, and it wasn't her fault. She was made nuts. But I loved her deeply. She was my mom, my batshit crazy mom.

Settling back into civilian life was hard. There were many people I met along the way who were cruel about my time in Vietnam. To this day, those of us who served in the Vietnam War remain the only troops who fought for our country and were never welcomed home. It was brutal and just as jarring to experience in real life as it had been watching it on TV. When I look back, I can see that those protestors might have been right about the war, but they came after the wrong people for it. I don't have any hostility about it,

> **To this day, those of us who served in the Vietnam War remain the only troops who fought for our country and were never welcomed home.**

nor do I hold a grudge. Not because I don't feel outraged by it—I do. Many of the men I went to battle with feel the same way. However, I now know that hating anyone for that doesn't make things better, nor will it change the outcome. When you hate someone, it's like picking up hot coals with your bare hands and throwing it at them. Who does it burn first? *You.* It took me a little time to figure that out, but once I did, it was a burden I no longer needed to carry. I had plenty of other emotions to work through. And that would also take some time.

I spent the first week or two at home mostly knocking around with my buddies and drinking beer and the occasional whiskey. One time, I had so much to drink that the guys dropped me off in front of my house and I still got lost. I was pretty liquored up. I started walking and wound up in a different neighborhood trying to figure out where I was. A couple of hours must have passed when I began to sober up. It was only then that I finally found my house. I got drunk more than a few times during those first weeks. Was I self-medicating? Maybe. Did I need to blow off some steam? You bet.

It didn't take long before my mom started in on me about how she needed money, suggesting I should pay her rent and board.

I had just come back from the war; I didn't have much money, and everything I'd sent home had been gambled away. I got a job as a laborer at the number-two machine shop at Bethlehem Steel in Sparrows Point. They had these turret lathes that were just huge. The machines might have been twenty-five yards long, and they'd put these big, oblong steel beams in them. The lathes would mill them down smoothly into shafts for seagoing ships and ocean liners.

The lathes had a cutter that would go back and forth, spitting hot metal chips into these large pits underneath the machines as they sliced the steel. I was part of a team of laborers who would jump down into the pits and shovel the chips into big barrels, then cart them over to the collection area, lift them, and dump them. I did that for probably six months or so. By then, I was in great shape. Built like a bull. It was a tough job, but I didn't mind.

Eventually, I applied to become a machinist's apprentice at the same mill and got the job. My boss assigned me to work with a man named Roy. He ran one of the big turret lathes, and he was supposed to teach me and give me different tasks to do. Roy was an older guy who was bitter and mean. He would come into work pissed off at the company over whatever his grievance of the day was. However, he was in the union and had tenure, so no matter how horrible he acted, they couldn't fire him. Day after day, Roy would come in and set his lathe so it would never cut the metal. It would just move back and forth for his entire shift, essentially doing nothing. It didn't make a lot of sense to me, but that's the way it went.

Roy was probably one of the most persnickety people I had ever met. He barely spoke to me. No matter how many ways or times I tried to strike up a conversation, Roy would tell me to leave him alone. It was my job, though, to help him and hopefully to learn from him. Well, Roy taught me one very important lesson: I didn't want anything to do with him. He was a miserable man, someone I didn't want to be anything like. Ever.

Another thing Roy did for me was get me out of that steel mill. He was the reason I decided to go to college. The more time I spent with him, the more I knew I didn't want to end up a miserable old bastard like he was. I wanted to do something with my life, even if I wasn't sure what that was yet.

After about three months as a union machinist's apprentice, I was making decent money. Not a lot of money, but more than enough to get by. I saw an ad from the University of Baltimore that said they had a special deal for veterans. Basically, all I needed was a high school diploma and enough money to pay tuition and get set up for the semester. I wouldn't have to take an entrance exam, and my high school grades didn't matter. That was perfect for me.

Unfortunately, I was $300 short. I wasn't sure how quickly I could get the money together, or if I could get it at all. Then one day I was talking to my cousin Louis about my plan to go to college and mentioned that I was short on cash. He said, "I'll loan it to you."

That was the first time anyone had ever done something like that for me, and I never forgot his kindness. I was extremely grateful. With the full tuition in hand, I went to the University of Baltimore to register.

I was nineteen years old and would be the first member of my family to attend college. I went to the registrar's office, where I was told that I had to declare a major. I hadn't known I would need a major; I just thought you went to classes. I was clueless. The registrar sent me to the counselor's office, where he said they could help me decide. When I arrived, there was a long line down one hallway and into another. I didn't really want to stand in that line, so I went back to the registrar's office and asked if there was any way I could just pick my major. The registrar said yes and handed me a course booklet that listed the university's various majors. I opened the booklet and saw that the first major listed was accounting.

"What's this?" I asked the registrar.

"Are you good at math?" he asked.

"Yes, I am." Despite my horrible years as a student, I was always good with numbers. I probably owe that to my mom and her teaching me fractions and other facts and figures from the racing form.

"Are you interested in business?" he asked.

"Sure, yes. Why not?" I said.

"Well, you may want to major in accounting, then. If you don't like it, you can always change your major."

And so I decided to study accounting, literally because it was the first major listed in the course booklet. If I'd have opened it backward, I might have become a zoologist!

As it turned out, accounting was a fortuitous choice. I loved it. And I was good at it. From my first day in class, I focused all my attention on my studies—and, happily, studying was up my alley, because I had post-traumatic stress disorder, or PTSD, but didn't know it yet, so I liked doing stuff by myself. Whenever I heard the phrase *study groups*, I knew they weren't for me. I would spend countless hours doing my homework, never quitting until I completely understood it. As a result of my hard work, I got good grades for the first time in my life. That first semester, I was a little distracted by hanging out with my buddies and so forth, so I think I had a B in English and a C in sociology. But those were the worst grades I got in college.

While I was in Vietnam, the last thing I did when it was my turn to sleep during each night's ambush was to look up at the stars and think about how easy high school was compared to fighting in the war. Sometimes I wondered when my number would come up. But I always thought to myself, *If I live through this, when I get home I'm going to call Martha Ritterbusch.*

Maybe six months or so after I got home, I got her number and called. Whenever I phoned her house, her mom or dad would tell me she wasn't home. "Tell her Bob called," I'd say before hanging up. This happened three or four times without a return call. Martha later said that there was another guy named Bob who wanted to date her at the same time. She had zero interest in dating that Bob, so whenever I called, her folks thought I was him and told me she wasn't home. Finally, I called again. When her father answered the phone, he must've been tired of lying for Martha and made her come to the phone.

"Come and talk to this guy," he said.

When Martha said hello, I quickly blurted out, "Hi. This is Bob. I just got home from the military." And that's when she knew it was me. Later, Martha told me that a few months before I'd called, she had confided to some friends she and I would marry.

Martha was just as beautiful as I'd remembered. She looked like a Swedish-German bombshell, with long, fine blond hair and beautiful blue eyes. She was on the tall side, which I liked. I was two years older than Martha. Somehow, we figured out that I used to be her paperboy. Of course, back then she was just a goofy little girl. Not anymore. She had blossomed into a beautiful woman. I was smitten with her from hello.

Martha and I had been dating for around six months when she became pregnant with our son, Sean. When she told me the news, I wanted to marry her and start a family together. I immediately went to her father, Rob, to state my intentions. Rob was a good guy. He ran a grinder at Armco Steel, so we shared some common interests. Running the grinder was a really physical job. In many ways he was stronger than a bull—strong in mind and body, if not a little unpredictable. When I explained that Martha was pregnant and I wanted to marry her, he asked me just one question.

"Do you love her, Bob?"

"I do," I said.

"You know, you don't have to marry her if you don't want to," he offered.

"I want to marry her. I love your daughter. I won't let you down. I will support her and our family. I may not be the exact son-in-law you wanted, but I'll be a good one, this I promise you." I was sincere in my vow.

"All right, you can do it," her father said.

Just writing about this time in my life makes me emotional. This was when I had absolutely nothing. I was in my first year of college and just starting my life after serving in Vietnam. Martha's dad believed in me when he didn't have to, and that meant the world to me. As a result, I studied hard and worked my ass off. I buckled down even more so Martha and I could be together. I got serious about everything.

As I've said, when I came home, I was a totally different guy—the success machine had been built. I could do what I needed to do. Although I thought about it, I never reenlisted, mostly because of Martha and our soon-to-be-born son. I wouldn't have done that to our family. You could say that, given my upbringing, I shouldn't have succeeded. I'll tell you this: I did succeed because of it, and I worked hard for that success. Talking to my future father-in-law about marrying his pregnant daughter was the most difficult thing in the world for me, but I had that conversation anyway, and he was kind and accepting of me. I will never forget that.

> Talking to my future father-in-law about marrying his pregnant daughter was the most difficult thing in the world for me, but I had that conversation anyway, and he was kind and accepting of me. I will never forget that.

Rob taught me what it was to be a good guy. In some ways, he also showed me what it was to be a good husband and father. I didn't really have that with my dad. I respected and appreciated Rob a great deal for the influence he had on my life.

After we were married, Martha and I lived with her parents at their home in Baltimore. I didn't have a lot of money, so living with them was really our only choice. Their house had three levels, if you counted the basement. We lived in one of the upstairs bedrooms. When I married Martha, I didn't have a car or my driver's license. She didn't have her own car either. Sometimes we'd use her parents' vehicle, or we would walk. One afternoon we were taking a long stroll, talking for hours. We were probably a few miles away from her parents' place when I realized we were walking through a semi-industrial area. Suddenly, we were surrounded by a pack of wild dogs. There were either five or seven of them, I wasn't really sure. They were medium-sized and seemed to appear out of nowhere. Before I knew it, they were running at us. My Marine Corps instincts kicked right in. I was going to take those little bastards on one at a time. However, Martha, who was terrified, started to run. I reached out to steer her toward the steps of a closed corner store we happened to be next to at that moment. I was able to lift her onto a pedestal behind me, and then I fended off those dogs. They were snapping and snarling, showing all the teeth in their mouths. There was no doubt they were wild. If I hadn't grabbed Martha, I'm certain they would have eaten her alive. It was pretty intense for about five minutes. I was snarling back at them, occasionally taking a swing to keep them at bay. I somehow held them off without their attacking either of us. And just as suddenly as the dogs appeared, a man who looked like a vagrant showed up. It was Jimbo! What were the odds? Somehow, he was tight with the dogs. He called them, and they took off. That ended the whole ordeal. When I took Martha to be my wife, I made a promise that I wouldn't let anything happen to her. Not on my watch. If anyone was going to be bitten that day, you could bet your sweet ass it was going to be me.

Martha gave birth to our son, Robert Sean, on August 15, 1971. I was right outside the delivery room. I could hear a lot of what was happening, including Martha screaming, "That motherfucker!" Presumably, she was talking about me. The nurses later told me that was absolutely normal. I didn't take it personally. I just waited and waited, and finally, our son was here.

He was the cutest kid. I mean, he was just something else.

The first time I held my son, who we called Sean, was incredible. He was my little boy. Still is. I had already made a commitment that I would work as hard as I could to support my family. Thankfully, I wasn't plagued by alcohol, drugs, gambling, or any of the stuff I grew up surrounded by. I wasn't like that. I was pretty focused, and I planned to stay that way.

As happy as I felt, I didn't know how to be loving. Nobody had ever loved me as a kid, and this was one thing I couldn't figure out how to teach myself. I came from a family where my mom was cold and distant, and as it turned out, I was too. I didn't like to spend time with Sean the way I should have. It's my greatest regret to this day, one I continued to carry with me when my other two children, Marianne and Jessica, were born.

When Sean was a baby, we were still living with Martha's parents. Sometimes I'd be coming down the steps and Rob would be coming up, and he would reach into my stomach under my rib cage and pull just a little bit.

"What the hell are you doing?" I'd ask in agony.

"Just showing you I can do it," he'd say with a bit of a smile.

He had no problem with me that I was aware of, so it always caught me off guard when he'd get physical like that. I just thought,

I guess that's just what guys do. Maybe that's how he showed his love—or perhaps he was sending me a subtle message that if I hurt his daughter, he would hurt me too.

Martha's mother continuously badgered me to get another job. I looked every day, combing through newspapers and pounding the pavement. I wanted to do something that was accounting-related and that would build a future for me and my new family. I interviewed all the time. Everybody said the same thing: "Well, you seem okay. You seem sharp and you seem like you're going to work. But we're looking for experience."

One day I interviewed at the Williams and Wilkins Company, which was a medical publisher that was part of Waverly Press. When I went to interview, it was for a job as an accounts receivable clerk. It wasn't exactly what I wanted, but it was a foot in the door. After I finished the interview, the woman I'd met told me that they were looking for someone with experience. How was I supposed to get experience if I couldn't get hired?

"I understand that everybody wants experience. My dilemma is that I really want to work in the accounting field, and I don't have any experience yet, but I'm a fast learner and I'll work really hard. One day, somebody is going to give me a break—and when they do, they'll remember it as one of the best decisions they ever made, because I'm going to do nothing but work hard so they look good," I said.

> "One day, somebody is going to give me a break—and when they do, they'll remember it as one of the best decisions they ever made, because I'm going to do nothing but work hard so they look good,"

"Excuse me, can you wait a few moments?" the interviewer said before getting up and leaving.

I thought, *Well, I screwed that up pretty good.*

And then she came back and said, "When can you start?"

I guess I'd said the right thing after all. One thing was for sure—I was speaking from my heart. I was totally honest and transparent.

The first year there, I think I was making $2.35 an hour, which came to $94 a week. I busted my ass. My job was processing invoices in the accounts receivable department. I used to time myself on the different chores I did and keep track of any errors I made. I always tried to do better. In fact, I still do the same things for my businesses now.

A few months later, another accounting job opened up at Williams and Wilkins for an inventory control monitor. I interviewed and got that job, which meant a slight increase in pay. Whenever they needed anybody for overtime, I would take it. I didn't care what it was; I would do it.

Eventually, I saved enough money to buy my first car for $1,200. It was a Toyota Corolla. It had a stick shift, no radio, and no air-conditioning. It got really good mileage, but gas was cheap back then. I remember my father being a little upset with me because I bought a Japanese car. He was a World War II veteran, and that just didn't sit well with him. Either way, it was all I could afford. And it was a good little car. Boy, that thing ran and ran. It was hot as shit in the summer, but I didn't mind.

When I got the car, I didn't know how to drive, let alone handle a stick shift. I went to the DMV and applied for a learner's permit. I was twenty years old and still had to have somebody sign for me. Nobody would do it. My parents wouldn't. The in-laws wouldn't. So Howard, my brother-in-law at the time, said, "I'll sign for you." And he did.

I got my learner's permit, picked up the car, and learned how to work the clutch—sort of. I wasn't great at it, but I managed to get us home. I needed to practice so I could get better. Nobody would drive with me except for my wife, though, so I taught myself.

Eventually, I got pretty good. I could parallel park and do all the things I knew I'd need to master to get my license. On the big day, I asked my dad to go with me. He did, and I passed the test.

Martha and I eventually moved to our own place. Our first apartment in Baltimore was at the Goodnow Hill Apartments, near Sinclair Lane. There were some college guys living on the lower level and they'd throw knock-down, drag-out parties with blasting music. I could hardly hear myself think. They'd always invite me to the parties, and I'd go down for a bit, but truthfully, I didn't want to be there. Thankfully, Sean usually slept through the noise. It might not have been an ideal situation, but getting our own place was a step in the right direction.

16

Buying Our First Home

I loathe asking anyone for help with anything. Over the course of my life, there were a few times when people lent me a hand and it made a big difference. I never expected it, and I never forgot it. When Martha and I bought our first home in Baltimore, we had looked at house after house. The homes we could afford were row houses like the one I grew up in. Then we came upon a house on North Ellwood Avenue, not far from where I grew up. It was on a block that was full of bigger homes on larger lots. The basement was finished, the layout was great, and everything was just nice. I said to Martha, "This is it."

We talked to the real estate agent who explained that he already had two offers on the house, plus a third one coming in. If we wanted it, we'd have to move fast, and we'd have to make an offer they couldn't refuse. They were asking $10,000. I offered $11,000 to close, predicated on my getting credit. Lo and behold, they accepted my offer. To secure the bid, they wanted me to put $1,000 down as a deposit, which I did. When I spoke to the savings and loan bank, they said I needed to come up with 20 percent down to secure the loan. I only had $1,300 saved, but a thousand of that went toward the deposit, so I was more than a little short.

"Do you have the money?" the real estate agent asked.

"Yes. I have it in bonds," I said. I was bluffing, of course.

"You need to bring the money," he insisted.

"You'll have to trust me. I've got it." But I knew that wasn't true.

I'm not the kind of guy who usually gets stressed out, but this was one of those rare times when I did. I didn't know where I would find the remaining money. I had just quit smoking, but you'd better believe I started again that night. And then I went to work on getting the rest of the cash.

At the time, I was making $135 a week, supporting my wife and son. I always worked as many hours as I could. I had bought E bonds along the way, which I cashed in. When it came time to settle up, though, I was still short by $350. I couldn't go to my parents, because I knew they didn't have any money to spare. I went to my wife's parents, but they wouldn't loan me the money because my mother-in-law thought I'd overpaid for the house. Next I went to Rob Jr., my brother-in-law, who was a fireman. He wouldn't loan me the money either. No one would help me.

One day at work, I was standing by a filing cabinet when Jack Wilt, who to this day is a good friend of mine, asked if I was all right. I must have had a solemn look on my face.

"I don't know what I'm going to do. I'm short three hundred fifty dollars to close on this house I want for my family." I wasn't asking him for anything. I was just sharing why I was so glum.

> Jack always says that $350 was the best investment he ever made.

"I'll loan it to you," he said. No hesitation, no judgment.

"Brother, are you serious?" I was stunned by his offer.

It turned out that he was dead serious. He loaned me the money, and I was able to close on the house. Jack was a good guy who turned into a great friend. When I was in college and didn't have a car, he'd often give me a ride home. It was way out of his way, but he always offered, and I always took him up on it. He was just one of those guys who consistently stepped up, especially when no one else would. And I never forgot it. Fast forward to now, I send him $50,000 every year at Christmas, and have done so for many years as a token of my gratitude for showing up for me when no one else would. Jack always says that $350 was the best investment he ever made. He's such a good dude.

My mother-in-law was curious about how I got the money. I never told her. She thought I was out of my mind for spending as much as I did. I knew she was wrong. I was so happy because I knew we'd bought something special. It was perfect for our family. We moved in, scraped together whatever bits of furniture we could find, and made it our home.

Baltimore was a rough town. It was a tough, tough, tough place to live. At the time, it was the heroin capital of the country. It no longer felt like the place I wanted to raise my family. Even so, it was the only place we knew, and all our relatives were there. So where would we go?

Meanwhile, life went on. I left the University of Baltimore for a bit. My buddy Jack was going to Mount Saint Agnes, a Catholic college, so I decided to transfer there. I took a full load of classes at night, worked a full-time job during the day, and in my spare time ran a small business doing basic accounting and bookkeeping for some local companies. I'd study in between all that, which pretty much kept me busy 24-7. I was usually wiped but managed to keep going on adrenaline until there was just no more fuel in my tank.

As it turned out, I was good at math. *Really* good. When I was a kid, I fell asleep in math class because it was so boring to me.

It was just too easy. In college, however, I was exhausted in class because I was constantly working and going to school. My math professor was a nun. Unlike my teachers in grade school, she was an absolute angel. God put me there as one of her challenges, that's for sure. I tried to stay awake, but I just couldn't do it. She moved me to the front of the class, but that didn't work either, because sometimes I'd doze off and talk in my sleep. She even offered to buy me coffee, but caffeine has never worked for me. Even so, I nailed every test she gave me. Totally aced them.

Somehow, she knew I knew the material. She also knew I put in all the work I needed to. When my brother, Allan, was getting out of the Air Force, I went to her and said that I wanted to be there to welcome him home. Unfortunately, that was the same day she had scheduled our final exam. Between my service and his, it had been years since I'd seen my brother. I explained my predicament to her. I really wanted to be there when he got back so I could give him the hero's welcome I never received. I asked if it was okay if I didn't take the exam and if I still would get an A. She knew I would nail it if I did; I'd passed

> I'd never had a nun—or *any* teacher—be an advocate for me or treat me as well as she did.

every test that semester with flying colors. I was already getting an A, so I was hoping this wasn't a big ask. Much to my relief, she said it would be no problem. I was elated. I'd never had a nun—or *any* teacher—be an advocate for me or treat me as well as she did. It felt really good. I'll never forget her.

About a year after I enrolled, Mount Saint Agnes College was purchased by the University of Baltimore, and they merged. As a result, all the students went back to the University of Baltimore with full credit for the classes they had taken at Mount Saint Agnes. Somehow, even with my busy schedule, I finished college in four years by taking a full load each semester and every summer. I graduated magna cum laude from the University of Baltimore with a bachelor's degree in accountancy.

Next on my list was taking the CPA exam. To help me prepare, I took a CPA review course at night. I studied for several months. I would sit at my desk in our home, studying for hours on end, until I was so tired and sleep deprived that I had occasional small hallucinations. Quite teasingly, I told my wife I thought I saw a dragon walk across the desk. You know the feeling when you study so hard that you start to see things? That was where I was. When I finally took the exam, I didn't think I passed. But I did, and on the very first try. *Ka-boom, baby!*

> I learned that if you just keep going, that's when all your hard work starts to give back.

There are times when you've expended so much energy trying to reach your goals that you're running on fumes and you don't think you have anything else to give. I learned that if you just keep going, that's when all your hard work starts to give back.

Falling in Love with Computers

Once I passed the CPA exam, in addition to working my regular job, I opened my own practice. I had a modest clientele, mostly made up of small businesses such as local bars and pest control companies. In 1975, I became the controller for Commercial Credit Leasing Corporation, a subsidiary of Commercial Credit Corporation, and owned by Control Data. They leased fleets of cars to companies all over the country. Just before I started, they had purchased McCullagh Leasing, which became their fleet auto leasing division. They were always looking to buy other leasing companies, and it was my job to visit their prospective acquisitions and schedule the assets. For the most part, there were no personal computers, or PCs, then, and certainly not at the company I was now working for. It was the early days of computer technology. I had seen my first LCD calculator only a few years earlier. That calculator sold for $300 at the time. All it did was add, subtract, divide, and multiply. When my professor demonstrated his calculator, I could hardly believe my eyes. He pushed a few buttons and voilà! The math problem was solved. It was stunning. I had never seen anything like it. Not then, anyway.

One of my trips for the company was to Redwood City, California, to look at a luxury vehicle leasing business that specialized in exotic cars, including Ferraris, Lamborghinis, Mercedes, BMWs, and Rolls-Royces. When I finished up, I had twelve hours to kill before my flight out of San Francisco International. I started knocking around the area and found myself walking through the Stanford campus. Now, I've always loved a good bookstore; for me, they're happy, soulful places. Somehow, I found the Stanford bookstore and walked in. I was browsing through the aisles when I came upon the computer section. I pulled a book about programming in the BASIC computer language off the shelf. In college, I had taken a three-credit introductory course in data processing. Part of the curriculum was to write a simple program in FORTRAN. I remembered really enjoying that assignment. I've always liked solving puzzles, especially since my mind automatically sees everything as a problem looking for a solution. Getting a computer to do something I intended it to do was a powerful and incredibly satisfying experience.

Interesting, I thought. I bought the book and shoved it into my satchel.

With a lot of time left to kill, I drove to Fisherman's Wharf and walked around for a bit. I went into an art gallery that caught my attention. I was wearing a suit and tie, so I figured they wouldn't shoo me out the door. I looked presentable enough to be in there, or so I thought. The salesman offered me a glass of champagne. I should have known right then and there that I was out of my league.

"No, thank you," I said. "I don't want to buy anything; I'm just looking."

I stopped to admire a charcoal drawing of young Chinese children. One of the kids, a little girl, was reaching out to light the fuse of a big firecracker, while the others were covering their ears. Two of the children covered the ears of the younger kids too. To me, this piece was just perfect. I loved it. It was so vivid and inspiring. When I looked at it, I felt happy. It reminded me of my teenage years lighting off bottle rockets.

"How much is this?" I asked.

"Well, it's by an up-and-coming artist, Wai Ming, who swam to safety from a refugee boat. This is one of his first works," the salesman responded.

What I heard was, "Expensive."

I asked the price again.

"Ten thousand dollars," he said with a boatload of confidence.

He may as well have said $10 million, as the piece was way out of my price range. I thanked him for his time and headed to the airport to wait for my flight. For the rest of the day, I couldn't stop thinking about that piece.

At the airport, I opened my new book. I still had eight hours before my flight, which gave me not only enough time to read but also to start writing my first program. My idea was to write a simple program that would take a stream of cash flows, compare them against the amount that was invested, and tell you what the interest rate was. There's no formula for this. To find that information, you have to iterate and figure out how to get close. Interest rates were something I worked with all the time, so I thought it would be cool to have a tool like this, if only for myself. Of course, I didn't even own a computer, so I had no way of testing my program.

When I got back to the office, I started talking to one of the programmers in our company. Much to my surprise, he said the terminal in my office would run BASIC, the same language I was working in. What an incredible stroke of luck this would turn out to be.

While it took me a while to get the program to operate the way I wanted it to, I eventually got there. One of the company programmers was always lending me a hand, looking over my shoulder and mentoring me through the trial-and-error period. And then, *BAM*—it worked. Oh, baby. That was a beautiful feeling. I thought it was so cool. I spent a little time tweaking the program along the way, adding in amortization schedules, but for the most part, it was ready.

At one point, Commercial Credit decided to move their headquarters to Detroit. I flew from Baltimore to Michigan to see where I'd be living if I decided to stay with the company. When I checked into my motel, the clerk was sitting behind bulletproof glass. I had to use a tiny turnstile tray that was built into the lower portion of the glass divider to deal with him. After I put my payment on the tray, he took the money, dropped my key on the tray, and turned it back to me. When I got to my room, it had three deadbolts on the door. It didn't take much more than that experience to know I wasn't going to be moving my family there.

In 1978, I started working as a controller for Harford Metal Products. They made animal cages. Their parent company was Hazelton Labs, which conducted animal testing. When I realized what they were doing, I was disgusted. I didn't really care for the job; it was steady work, but the hours were long and the pay was just okay. A friend of mine had taken a job with a different group of companies owned by the Orscheln family in Moberly, Missouri, a little town not too far from Columbia. Moberly was smack-dab in the middle of the state. It was a rural community with corn and soybean fields everywhere. The company he worked for had a chain of farm and home stores throughout the Midwest. He called me to say they had an opening for a controller in the leasing division of the company, Third Century Leasing. At the time, they leased trucks and tractor trailers.

"Would you have any interest in this position?" he asked.

"I'd love to talk to the company about this opportunity," I said.

Shortly thereafter, the company flew me out to Missouri for an interview. The first time I saw Moberly, it reminded me of what Mayberry would probably be like if it were a real place. The town was picturesque and quiet. I thought it would be great to raise our kids there. By then we had two children, Sean and Marianne, and a dog named Sam.

With my experience I was more than qualified, so I was hopeful I would get the job. Sure enough, at the interview, they offered me the position, and I accepted.

Martha was thrilled. She immediately put our house on the market. She didn't want to use a real estate agent, so we listed it for sale by owner. Every penny counted, and this way we could save on the commission. I was thinking of listing it for $15,000. Martha suggested we try for $25,000. We did everything wrong, but that's how we handled it. On the day of our open house, it snowed. No one showed up to tour the place. Okay, one person did—but that was all we needed. They paid us our full asking price. *Ka-boom, baby!* Thank you, Martha. It was a great return on our investment. I couldn't wait to tell Martha's mother the good news, and maybe—just maybe—tell her that I might not have paid too much in the first place.

> We did everything wrong, but that's how we handled it.

We packed everything up with a moving company, loaded up our car with our kids and the dog, and drove from Baltimore to

Missouri. On our first night, we stopped in Terre Haute, Indiana, and checked into a Holiday Inn. I got one of the larger rooms with two beds. I can still see Marianne skipping around the room, jumping from bed to bed. She was so happy. We all were. Marianne kept asking, "Daddy, whose house is this?" It was such a precious moment, and a memory I think about all the time.

Project Freedom

When we arrived in Moberly in 1979, the US economy was pretty steady. By 1980, things were beginning to change. Interest rates soared to 20 percent, which meant many of our customers couldn't make their payments. We were repossessing trucks left and right. In fact, there were so many defaulted loans that I started helping out with repossessions of tractor trailers—not a lot of them, but enough to know I preferred accounting to repo work. The company looked like it might be heading for disaster. Business was drying up, and our customers couldn't pay their outstanding debt. I had just bought a new home and moved my family to the middle of the country. This didn't bode well for me.

I got along really well with the owner's son, Barry, who was the CEO. Our birthdays were just a few days apart, so not only were we both extremely driven to succeed but we were the same age. In fact, he's a dear friend of mine to this day. So when it looked like the business was going down, Barry came to me and said that we should shift away from trucks and start leasing copiers. In a very short time, Barry's idea took the company from the brink of bankruptcy to a new level of success. Working with copiers was the best decision he could have made. Compared to tractor trailers, copiers were much easier and a lot more profitable. Everybody wanted to use a copy machine. They were new and novel. They also cost only a few thousand dollars or so back then. Leasing made them more affordable, especially for companies in need of multiple copiers, so when it came time to collect, the lion's share of our clients would always pay. The real profit was in doing high volume.

By 1984, Third Century was doing great—so well, in fact, that LeaseAmerica, a middle-of-the-road leasing company that specialized in tractors, milling machines, and heavy road equipment, reached out to the owners to buy the company, but they weren't interested in selling. LeaseAmerica really had their eye on the copier leasing division we had built. When the owners said no, Lease-America contacted me on the sly to see if I would entertain leaving to start the same business for them. They were looking to expand into small-ticket vendor services—copiers mostly, which was an area I knew well. I was all in. After I told Barry that I was quitting, I was surprised that he didn't hold that decision against me.

I accepted the job with LeaseAmerica in 1984 and moved our family from Missouri to Cedar Rapids, Iowa. I would be starting their new copier division from scratch, which was part of the appeal of the job. Plus, in many ways, I would be my own boss, something I'd wanted for some time.

When we arrived in Cedar Rapids, it was like Gotham. Compared to Moberly, Cedar Rapids was the big city, with a little over 110,000 people residing there. Martha and I bought a nice house after making a small profit on our home in Missouri, where our daughter Jessica had been born in 1983. She was the sweetest little baby.

I worked at LeaseAmerica for a few years and was making more money than I had at my last job, but I wasn't raking in the dough. I managed all the legal work; I wrote contracts and handed them off to our attorney for a look, but he seldom made many changes. I streamlined everything, from the legal paperwork to the credit approval. I took all the documents you would need for a transaction and consolidated them into one document that had a guarantee, delivery details, and places to sign. It was easy, and it allowed us to make decisions in hours instead of weeks. I innovated that business like crazy, making it better and better—and more profitable.

> I innovated that business like crazy, making it better and better—and more profitable.

How? Simple: I hired incredibly sharp and attractive women who did all the selling over the phone. I taught them the leasing business in a couple of weeks. I called that Fat Bob's Leasing School, even though I wasn't fat at the time. It just had a nice ring to it.

When we went to our first leasing convention, we had a booth promoting our new LeaseAmerica vendor services division. Before we showed up, small-ticket leasing was always a predominantly male-driven business. Guys who worked at other leasing companies came over to our booth and just laughed at us because it was chock-full of females. By the time they realized they had been stabbed, their shoes were full of blood. Yep—those women walked all over the competition.

Eventually, the vendor services division became very profitable, and LeaseAmerica sold it to General Electric. I grew the business to include a dozen or so salespeople in just a couple of years. Even though we were LeaseAmerica's most profitable division, every time I approached Emmett Sherman, the CEO, to do my wage review, he would say, "I'll get to it." He always promised, but never did it. Emmett was a well-respected businessman who had been around for many years. He was also very old, lazy, and set in his ways. Every few months I'd ask for my review, but he kept ignoring me. He once said that if I persisted, he would never do it. It got to be two and then three years without a review, denying me a much-needed and well-deserved raise. This really got under my skin. What could I do about it? Not much from within the company, but it was because of his dismissal of my value that I started writing a new computer software program that could do family finances. I had the shell of it formed already, but now I was truly motivated to start digging in. I called it Project Freedom, because I wanted to be free of Emmett.

While living in Missouri, I bought my first computer, an Apple IIC. I switched from BASIC and taught myself the Pascal programming language, because it compiled and was faster. I studied the architecture of working in Pascal and got really good at it. I mean *really* good. Once I was proficient in Pascal, I sold my Apple and bought an IBM PC—and that changed everything for me. In fact, I still have that IBM computer in my office today. I put a silver nameplate on it that read "Cinderella." Why? From that day forward, I knew my life was going to be different. I didn't know the specifics, but you'd better believe I felt I was going places—and computers were the highways that would take me there.

> I put a silver nameplate on it that read "Cinderella." Why? From that day forward, I knew my life was going to be different.

It was right around then that I started writing a home accounting program that would work for any business that used a set of accounting books. The software was called MoneyCounts. At first it was buggy, but with patience and adjustments, it became less so, until it got to be pretty good. It wound up being way ahead of its time.

Back then, I had $15,000 in savings. I took that money and started a small business called Parsons Technology, through which I began selling my program using direct marketing, right to the consumer. I worked for LeaseAmerica during the day and ran Parsons Technology out of my basement at night. I was working around the clock and loved every minute of it.

I was buying small ads in various magazines to sell Money-Counts. I focused on publications such as *PC Magazine, Computer Shopper,* and others that were specifically focused on computer products. At first, I was selling the program for $99 to $129 but didn't get much action. Just a few sales. Was it the product or the pricing? I blasted through my $15,000 in no time.

The following year, I finally got a bonus from my job. I took that money and advances from three different credit cards and was able to scrape together $25,000 to keep my business afloat. I lowered my price to sixty-nine dollars and then to forty-nine dollars, but it still didn't work. No one was buying, and I lost all my money for the second year in a row. Undeterred, I kept working on the software, making it better with each pass. I also spent a lot of time looking at the ads the big boys were running in the magazines.

My father always told me that when you love something, it tells you all its secrets. As I worked more on the software, I learned a lot of stuff nobody else knew. This was valuable in every way. One of my best friends at the time was a guy named Dave Harvey. He and I would talk about my plans and what I believed the company could do. I liked Dave and wanted to cut him in on Parsons Technology. I thought it would be fun to work with a buddy.

> My father always told me that when you love something, it tells you all its secrets.

"Dave, I'm going to make you the best offer you'll ever get in your life. I'll sell you half of Parsons Technology for five thousand dollars," I said with a great big grin on my face.

"Let me think about it," he said.

Think about it? I was stunned. A week later, Dave came back and said he couldn't do it. I told him I understood, and we shook hands. In a way, I was relieved he said no. I had since realized that I never really wanted a business partner, and I've never had one since. I like to maintain full control of my businesses. I never made anyone an offer like that again.

In my third year of business, I received an unexpected call from a discount computer rag called *Computer Bargain Line*, out of Fort Dodge, Iowa. They had a catalogue with all kinds of computer deals—used stuff, new stuff, you name it. They sometimes ran reviews and articles, but mostly they just had a huge mailing list. They were able to send their magazine out to a lot of people free of charge, which was enough to keep their business going. Even then, I had a reputation for always doing whatever I said I would do, and I always paid my bills.

When *Computer Bargain Line* called, they said they could offer me the front cover of their magazine. They explained that they'd had a deal in place that fell through. That ad space normally cost $15,000, but they were willing to sell it to me for $5,000, as long as I could turn the ad around in five days.

I had nothing—no money and nowhere to turn to for it on such short notice. Even so, it was the outside front cover of the magazine. To me, it may as well have been *Time*. I was so excited and unwilling to let this opportunity pass that I said, "Cool, I'll do it."

I had never bought an ad from them before, so when they said I could adhere to their normal terms, I assumed it was sixty days, just like the other magazines. Nope—they wanted thirty days. Okay, it was going to be tight, but I was still willing to take the risk.

I went to a small ad firm to create an ad for MoneyCounts, only this time I dropped the price on the program all the way down to twelve bucks. We were going to blow this thing out the door. Back then, a lot of software was copy protected so you couldn't share the program, and some companies said their products could be used only by one person at a time. Our ad made it clear that our software wasn't copy protected and the consumer could share it with as many people as they wanted. In fact, they could do whatever the hell they wanted to; all they had to do was send me twelve bucks.

While I felt good about this approach and thought that it might work, I still had some doubts. The one thing I was certain of was that I had to do something different.

A week or so after the catalogue shipped, I started receiving orders. At first, there was a trickle of maybe five or six. That was the most orders I'd gotten from a single ad up to that point. But then, a few days later, our mailbox was stuffed with orders and our phone was ringing like crazy. We made $25,000 from that ad. It was clear that I was onto something. After that, I took that same ad and had it printed on flyers. I placed the flyers in envelopes, put stamps on them, and printed stickers with addresses from all the leads I had stockpiled. That effort netted a 30 percent response rate! I had never achieved that with any direct mailing piece before, and I haven't since. My family and I stuffed those envelopes together. Even my youngest daughter, Jessica, who was four years old, had a job. She was the dedicated mail carrier who would bring envelopes from one desk to another.

After that windfall, I realized it wasn't about small ads, it was about taking out big ads and making your product affordable. Period.

After that, I started reaching out to *Computer Shopper*, *Byte*, *PC Magazine*, and *PC World* to see who would give me credit so I could run a full-page ad in their magazines. They all got on board. I could hardly believe it. It was a long road and took a lot of hard work to get there, but things felt promising. And did those big ads work? You bet they did. In spades!

Eventually, MoneyCounts was competing with Andrew Tobias's Managing Your Money and Intuit's Quicken. And when that happened, I began experimenting with other approaches to advertising. I would buy a two-page spread, what the industry refers to as a centerfold. On the left side I'd compare all the other programs to ours, which I prominently featured in a full-page ad on the right side. I ate the others up—and then I beat them on price, features, you name it. I'd do whatever it took to make our product the superior deal. And I literally tripled my response rate by doing that. Now I had some real leverage with the magazines, which allowed me to negotiate better prices on the ads I was taking. They all worked with me.

In the meantime, I chose to stay at LeaseAmerica while I was growing Parsons Technology because I wanted to be sure I was able to make Parsons Technology work. I really wanted it to become a viable business. So, to ensure that outcome, I wrote faster, bigger versions of the program, updating them and creating new products with more memory and tools. MoneyCounts Plus needed 384 kilobytes of RAM, making it the flagship of our brand. I sold that program for forty-nine dollars and never missed a tick.

As we grew, I also formed a small customer service call center in my basement, hiring ladies from all over the neighborhood to work the phones. They didn't know anything about computers, but they could get a guy to buy. All they needed to hear was that they were on the phone with someone who had enough RAM to run our program. And they could sell while sitting there with their hair in curlers, just using their female charm. It worked every time.

"Hello, Frank. How are you today? I've got a question for you: How much RAM do you have on your computer?" they'd ask.

"512 K," the voice on the other end of the phone might say.

"Oooh, that's a lot of RAM. Do you ever think about how you're using that?"

Most would say no.

"Well, we have a special use for it that I think will be just perfect for you." And then, *ka-BOOM!* She would close the sale. The ladies would get ten dollars and I would pocket the remaining thirty-nine. It was a perfect setup for all of us. Plus, we were actually providing a great product to people who not only wanted it but needed it.

By October 1986, I'd started working on an income tax preparation program. I had the leasing division on autopilot, so it didn't require as much of my time or attention as it once did. Eventually, it became obvious that I couldn't develop more software and grow Parsons Technology while I was working for LeaseAmerica. I just didn't have enough time. So, I turned in my resignation. My boss was stunned. If I had stayed, I would have received a $50,000 bonus that year. I just needed to be on the payroll through December to make that happen. But I knew that if I stayed, I would never get the tax software done in time. Emmett was flabbergasted. He offered more money to keep me—much more money than I had been making. I still said no. He asked if I would consider working for them part-time. That's when I said I would need $300 an hour to do that. They countered with $200. It was an easy decision: My answer, again, was no. I didn't want to do it. It was time for me to go. I understood that, even if they didn't. There was simply no way I could grow Parsons Technology working part time.

On my last day at LeaseAmerica, Emmett said to me, "I learned a lot from you, Bob," and then he wished me luck. He never made any bones about my leaving the company. We both just marched on.

The day after I told my kids about my decision, my daughter Marianne came home from school crying.

"What's the matter, sweetheart?" I asked.

"I don't want to be poor," she declared.

"What are you talking about?" I asked, wiping away her tears.

A parent of one of her friends somehow heard I had quit my job and said I would never make it in the software business. "You might as well get used to having no money," he said to Marianne.

I took a deep breath and assured her that she had absolutely nothing to worry about, that we were going to be okay. "Hold your head up. Dad would never let you down." I meant it too. Remember the vow I had made when I was a young boy living in my parents' basement? My family would never want for anything. I never broke that promise, and I had no plans to then.

"You promise, Daddy?"

"Absolutely," I said as I wrapped my arms around her.

While I have a great relationship with my kids today, back then I wasn't actively involved in their lives. I was always so focused on providing for them, supporting them financially. Sadly, what they needed most I was incapable of giving. Sure, I occasionally spent time with all of them, but it wasn't much. Sometimes Sean and I played soccer with his buddies or went bowling together, but we didn't do much else. I just didn't have the time. I wanted to be better than my parents. And I tried.

> Remember the vow I had made when I was a young boy living in my parents' basement? My family would never want for anything. I never broke that promise, and I had no plans to then.

For example, there was a day back in the 1970s, when we were still living in Baltimore, when Sean and I found ourselves at the local mall. We went to the pet store to look at the puppies. That's when I bought our little Shetland sheepdog, Sam. We had Sam for fourteen years. He was such a good dog. When I brought him home, I sat Sean down and said, "I guess it's time to tell your mother."

"Let's not tell her, Dad."

"She's going to find out, so we may as well," I explained.

When we broke the news to Martha, she said, "So, you bought a dog. . . . The pet shop called to tell me!"

I was happy to spend that day with Sean and to be able to give him a new dog. I was also relieved that Martha was excited to welcome Sam into the family. I suppose Sam was a companion for my boy and his sisters during all those times when I wasn't.

Now, of course, I can see the impact my intense work ethic and my vow to always provide financially for my children had upon our family life, but after leaving LeaseAmerica, it was clear that my business required even more of my attention than ever before.

We had finally moved out of my basement and into a proper office space, and I needed to staff up some key positions. I reached out to the CFO of LeaseAmerica and mentioned I was looking for a controller. She immediately recommended Barbara Rechterman. Barb had joined LeaseAmerica in 1986. She worked in the accounting group and did the financial statements for my division. I liked her from the get-go. She's smart, direct, and a very hard worker—plus, she could tolerate me. She was a perfect choice.

I also worked with a woman at LeaseAmerica whose husband was an accountant for Life Investors, a financial services company in Cedar Rapids. LeaseAmerica was a subsidiary of that company. I needed someone to help us debug our tax package. Who better than an accountant? I reached out to the woman's husband, a fellow by the name of Mark Hartung, and asked if he wanted to earn some extra cash. It was around the holidays, so I thought that might be appealing.

"Heck yeah, I could use the money for presents," Mark said.

He came in and did the work for the season, and then he went his way and we went ours.

Later, when we were preparing to go into the next tax season, I reached out to Mark again and asked if he wanted to debug the latest tax package—only this time, I asked if he wanted to join our company. I made him a nice offer in the hope that he would come aboard. Leaving his steady job and paycheck was a risk, but much to my surprise, Mark said yes.

In the beginning, Mark did pretty much everything other than marketing and programming. He helped us build out our call center and dealt with disk duplication, shipping, security, you name it. He was even the guy who was called when the alarm went off in the middle of the night. At the time, we were duplicating our programs by inserting five-and-a-quarter-inch disks into a PC, one at a time. We didn't have a high-speed duplicator yet. We would eventually get one that could do hundreds of duplications in an hour, but in the meantime we were doing them the only way we could.

By this time, there were around a dozen or so people working for me. I would come to work early Monday morning and write code for the new tax software I was working on. I also operated the day-to-day business and would literally work for sixty hours straight. If the code was flowing for me, I would stay as long as it kept showing up so I could write new programs, fix bugs in the software, and keep the wheels turning. I would only know I needed to stop when I started hallucinating. If I started hearing voices or seeing colors or images or movement by the door when no one was there, it was time to go home and crash. When I woke up, I would run a few miles at the local high school track to get my adrenaline going and then I'd start all over again, working another sixty-hour shift. I never looked at the clock, and if I did, it wasn't to count the hours that had passed; it was to anticipate all the work I still had to do. I didn't want the clock to move. I never once thought, *How much time do I have left?* Instead, I would think, *Great! I've still got two days!* Time wasn't my friend unless I could figure out ways to stretch it out. I did this week in and week out for years. I loved running at that pace. It energized me in every way. I absolutely thrived on it. By February 1987, I'd finished the tax program, named it Personal Tax Edge, and released it for twenty-nine dollars. It was a dandy performer, and a really great program.

19

Big, Hairy, Audacious Goals

Parsons Technology became profitable in 1987, making $287,000, which was far more than I'd made at LeaseAmerica. Bringing in that kind of money was nice, but I never took it for granted. I was never cheap, but I always looked at how much money I had in the bank in terms of how many times it would cover my overhead. I always wanted to have three or four times the monthly overhead amount in case anything happened. And I always managed to do that.

The second year, we made $2.5 million, and $5 million the following year. We became direct competitors to Quicken and TurboTax, which only sold at retail stores. We didn't do that. We sold directly to the consumer. In essence, we had become a mail-order business that sold software. We took a very different distribution approach from that of any software company I had ever seen before, which was innovative and exciting.

By that fifth year, it was no longer about money; it was about passion and building the business. To do that, I had to throw myself all in. And I needed to continue building my team.

Tim Ruiz was another key hire for us. At the time, we had our flagship products, MoneyCounts and Personal Tax Edge, and we were in the process of developing our own legal product. However, much of the rest of the product development we did came to us through third parties, people who were external to the company but had written some piece of software for which we would become the marketing engine. Tim and Mark built that whole piece of the business out for us, creating a massive portfolio of additional products we would white label. Whenever we bought someone else's product, we would name it what we thought was right, and then we'd bring the product to market under our name and through our distribution channels. Having all these diverse products and finding the right customers for them helped increase our base.

> By that fifth year, it was no longer about money; it was about passion and building the business. To do that, I had to throw myself all in. And I needed to continue building my team.

Occasionally, I would get involved in a deal, like I did with QuickVerse, a program that was developed by Craig Rairdin that allowed you to search words or phrases from various versions of the Bible. This turned out to be a great product for Craig and for our company. We sold a slew of those programs.

As our company grew, we developed and increased our direct mail business. We sent out over one hundred million pieces of mail a year at our peak. In many ways, we were a proficient marketing company that happened to sell software. There wasn't much we couldn't sell if we wanted to. We'd created a formula and had numerous mailing lists that became so valuable that the product was almost irrelevant. We were constantly testing offers and direct mail pieces, utilizing our own lists and some other lists that we would rent every year.

Once we mastered the mailing piece of the equation, we took six of our inbound customer service people and experimented with outbound marketing by having them contact our customer base by phone. We didn't train anyone because it was all so new. We tasked them with selling a renewal for the tax package by explaining that we had sent them a couple of mail pieces and they might have missed our offer. We were calling because we were concerned that they didn't receive it—and we were. Man, that worked like a charm. We were so successful with those six callers that it was soon time to expand. We were definitely onto something big.

I charged our team with finding and bringing on fifty callers within three weeks. It's hard to find telemarketers, and even harder to find good ones. These types of requests, which I often made, were referred to around the water cooler as BHAGs—big, hairy, audacious goals—a term coined by Jim Collins and Jerry Porras. I would set BHAGs and hold my people to them.

As an incentive, we came up with a measurement device that based an employee's performance on the average of the group, not some arbitrary numbers. The group moved the average up or down. By doing this, we eliminated the idea that sales goals were random or that a specific product was hard to sell. The majority of the group loved it. Those who didn't weren't our best performers, and this weeded them out of sales.

There was a quality aspect to customer care as well as a selling aspect. In addition to problem-solving on those phone calls, we also needed to be selling. This shifted us from pure technical support question-and-answer exchanges with customers to more dynamic sales exchanges. All this led to significant growth for the company. We started to make a shift financially, too, because people no longer had to give us a credit card number or mail us a check. We had records of their prior payment methods, and this allowed us to take the calls to the next level. Whether it was upgrading to a newer version of a program or catering to their specific needs as a small business, we always had a way to upsell.

Parsons Technology eventually grew into a thousand-employee business with our own building. By that point, I was no longer writing code, or at least I was writing very little of it. Barb moved into product development and eventually became our chief technology officer, or CTO, responsible for all software development. Mark oversaw the call center and the manufacturing functions. Many others brought their talents to the job each and every day. People in Iowa are good, hardworking people. It was a great place to have a call center and run a business.

> People in Iowa are good, hardworking people. It was a great place to have a call center and run a business.

For the most part, I'm a hands-off leader. The only time I want to be involved in something is if I'm really interested in it, especially when it comes to creating advertising and marketing plans, pricing, and certain kinds of product development. Otherwise, I trust my team to do their thing. I always tried to hire the best of the best and tried not to get in their way unless I had to. Look, nobody's perfect, and if you expect your employees to be perfect, you won't have any employees; so I got really skilled at understanding where my employees were weak and then giving them the tools to improve. If they still didn't cut it, I would let them go. As I've grown older, I've learned that pleasing everyone is impossible, so I don't even try.

As we grew, so did technology. We had started as a shrink-wrap software company selling a few thousand SKUs including a successful church software division that dominated that segment of the market, with licenses for just about every translation of the Bible, allowing users to look at the same scripture from four different translations side by side. We had successful tax and financial programs. We had MoneyCounts and MoneyPlans, another program for financial planning. Bring Back was a program that allowed users to retrieve deleted material. Announcements was an invitation program that allowed you to create all types of invitations. And we had many, many more products. We were flying high.

Once the company was solid and steady, I began taking a little time off. It was then that I took up golf. When my brother, Allan, and I were younger, Pop used to bring us with him to Clifton Park, an inner-city golf course in Baltimore. He let us hit a few balls on the range, and then he'd give each of us a saltshaker. There were rabbits all around that course, and Pop said if we wanted to catch a rabbit, we had to put salt on its tail. We were just little guys at the time, so we'd chase them. It was better than a video game. We spent hours trying to get salt on their tails. We never did. Years later my dad confessed that the saltshaker ploy was just to keep us busy while he hit buckets of balls.

My father was a scratch golfer. He had many trophies, which my mother destroyed whenever she got angry with him. Pop golfed for most of his life, at least until he wasn't able to anymore. Allan and my dad were very close, and when he came back from the Air Force, Allan took up golf as a way to spend time with my dad. He also became a really good golfer. I, on the other hand, was a late bloomer.

Although I enjoyed golf, I hadn't played in a long time, because all I did was work during my days at Parsons Technology. When I started to get out on the links more often, I invited a few of the guys from the company. At first we were terrible, but the more we played, the better we all got, and the more I fell in love with the game. I would play golf every Wednesday afternoon and Thursday morning with some of my top executives. On Wednesday, we would leave the office in time to get in eighteen holes. On Thursdays, we'd be the first group out of the block and then hightail it back to the office. Sometimes we'd play on Saturdays and Sundays too. If we went to a trade show, we rarely saw the inside of the convention center, but we surely found ourselves on a golf course somewhere, having a good time and betting on every shot. It was a lot of fun, and eventually I improved. I never cared too much about my game, at least not then. I just liked having something enjoyable to do with my friends.

But back to business. Parsons Technology was a reliable earner and had been for many years. We had grown into a much larger company than I could have imagined. At the same time, the internet was starting to evolve too. The business was quickly changing, and I was ready to do something else, so I thought it might be time to sell the company. We hired a consulting firm to represent us in the sale. I wasn't sure how much it was worth or how to go about finding the right buyer, but I was smart enough to find people who could help. Martha and I decided that if we received an offer over $48 million, we'd make the deal. We never told anyone that this was our number, but anything over that would be good.

> Martha and I decided that if we received an offer over $48 million, we'd make the deal. We never told anyone that this was our number, but anything over that would be good.

When word got out that we were interested in selling, various suitors came to check us out. H&R Block came by, took a look, and said they weren't interested. People from the Tribune Company, which owned the *Chicago Tribune* and other newspapers, also checked us out. The Tribune guys were old and stodgy, and as they were walking through our creative area, they spotted an invitation to a party on the screen of one of our employees' computers. It read "Stop by and hump the host."

"Hump the host?" one of the fellas from the Tribune asked. "Obviously, it's something for the church software division."

"Yes, that's it," I said. Much later I talked to the employee and strongly suggested he get a screensaver—pronto.

But in the end, the Tribune Company wasn't our buyer either.

In September 1994, I completed a deal with Intuit to purchase Parsons Technology. Their initial offer was $60 million. Although that was well over the $48 million floor Martha and I had set, I knew enough about negotiating to tell them I was insulted by such a low number. We went back and forth until we came to an agreement at $64 million. If you looked at everything I had personally put into the business over time, it would come to around $40,000, so it was a pretty good return on my investment. I also thought it was a fair deal all the way around. After I sold the company, Barb stayed on and became the copresident with our CFO, Scott Porter. Everyone won. Those are the best deals.

We had become a genuine threat to Intuit's business, and it was easier for them to buy Parsons Technology than it was to compete with us. When the deal was complete, I threw a party for our employees and my friends and family. Dave Harvey was there. I walked up, put my arm around him, and said, "Dave, do you remember when I offered you half the company for five grand?"

"Yeah," he said.

"Do you ever think about that decision?" I asked.

"I think about it all the time."

When we sold Parsons Technology, Martha and I had been married for twenty-three years. After the deal closed, I guess you could say she'd finally had enough. I'll say this about Martha: during our twenty-three years of marriage, she was a wonderful mother to our children and a wonderful wife to me. There's no way I could have asked for any more from her. She did the absolute best she could. But being with me, given my severe PTSD, was more than she could deal with. I was absolutely the reason for the divorce.

My second marriage, to a woman named Lisa, came a few years after that divorce. I loved that girl from the get-go. By then, I had moved to Scottsdale, Arizona, and I met her there. While I was married to Lisa, I began noticing that I was becoming inexplicably emotional and unpredictable. I knew the marriage wasn't meant to last. And I was right.

About two years into our marriage, she left me. I was devastated. I would lie in bed at night and cry myself to sleep. I know that doesn't sound like something a combat Marine would do, but it's how I handled that breakup. This went on for a week or two, until I walked into a local Barnes and Noble bookstore. The manager announced that they were closing for the night. I was the last man standing. I was still looking at books on how to survive divorce. Finally, I went up to the register and handed a book to the cashier behind the counter. When I looked up, I noticed he was right around my age.

"Do you have a discount card?" the clerk asked.

I couldn't answer. I just started to cry.

"Oh, don't worry, sir. I'll just give the discount to you anyway." I think he felt bad for me, but not for the real reason I was crying.

I got the discount, paid for the book, grabbed the shopping bag, and made a straight line to my car, where I cried some more. And then . . . I started laughing. I stopped and thought about my situation for a moment, and it all just seemed absurdly hilarious. Here I was, making a few million dollars a year, and the salesclerk thought I was worried about a discount. For whatever reason, that turned everything around for me. From that day forward, I never looked back. I knew I would find the right woman and someday learn to give the love I was capable of giving.

> From that day forward, I never looked back. I knew I would find the right woman and someday learn to give the love I was capable of giving.

20

There Is No Such Thing as Bad News

In retrospect, I'm certain that if we'd held on to Parsons Technology long enough, we might have gotten a billion dollars or more for it, but I was very satisfied with our eventual deal. The one thing I agreed to that was kind of stupid was a two-year noncompete, which they defined as not working for anybody. It was pretty strict. They withheld $4 million from the purchase price to ensure that I complied. One of the top executives from Intuit, Bill Campbell, said they weren't going to watch me that closely but made it clear they would keep an eye on me. As long as I didn't do anything that could hurt their company, they would look the other way. Even so, I agreed to the noncompete. I had given them my word and would do what I said I'd do.

It wasn't really a hard decision. I wasn't interested in the company anymore. Just as I had wanted to go back and serve with the guys in my original company in the war, my interest was in being with my team, not a different group of people doing the same thing. That's exactly how I felt when I closed the deal. Besides, I had never had time off; I figured it would give me a chance to think about what I wanted to do next.

As a going-away present, Intuit gave me an around-the-world golf trip, including flights on the *Concorde*, which was really their way of getting me out of their hair. Little did they know that I hadn't intended to become a pain for them anyway, but I gladly accepted the trip. Since the trip was for just one person, I went by myself. As fate would have it, I met a beautiful woman on the flight over who had recently gotten divorced. Let's just say we got to know each other fairly quickly.

When I came home, a woman I had been seeing back in Arizona started to unpack my suitcase.

"What's this half box of condoms doing in your bag, Bob?" she asked, holding up the box and waving it in the air with great fury.

I didn't know what to say, so I blurted out, "I'm holding them for a guy I met on the trip named Freddy. He was traveling with his mother. He met a girl and asked me to hold the condoms for him."

I had barely finished the sentence before she said, "If I've ever heard anything that sounded like a lie, it's this. Let me get this straight: You're holding a box of condoms for some guy named Freddy who didn't want his mother to know he was fucking some girl? This is a lie. Call Freddy."

"I don't have his number," I mumbled. I stood there shuffling my feet and avoiding all eye contact.

"All I want is the truth. It won't be a problem, Bob. Just tell me the truth," she said.

"Really? It won't be a problem? Okay. I met this girl—" I started to explain when I noticed a lamp flying toward me. I ducked just as it shot by my head. Then she threw something else. And that, as you might imagine, was the end of that relationship.

The next morning, my buddy Earl was at my house watching football when the doorbell rang.

"I'll get it," Earl said.

A minute or two later I heard him call out, "Bob, you better come out here."

There was a cake on the stoop for me with the feet of a stuffed teddy bear I had bought for this woman sticking out of it. After pulling the rest of the bear from inside the cake, Earl got a fork and shamelessly dug in.

"This is pretty good cake," he said.

I had to laugh. What else could I do except get a fork and dive in too?

I spent the next two years playing golf with my buddies, dating, and having a good ol' time. Everyone kept telling me I would get really good at golf if I played more, but I didn't get any better—or at least not a lot better. I actually play better today than I did then, but I look at the game differently now.

Anyhow, it had been twenty years since my trip to San Francisco, but I got the urge to find that charcoal drawing I'd fallen in love with on that fateful day at Fisherman's Wharf. The piece had so much meaning to me. Now that I could afford to buy it, I thought it would look great in my new home. I had never forgotten it. There was one problem, though: I discovered that it was now hanging in a museum. The artist, Wai Ming, had become world-renowned. So, I bought a signed lithograph of the original piece. I keep it in my bedroom and look at it very gratefully every day. Whenever I even glance at it, I feel happy and at peace.

My father used to say that whenever he thought about what I'd done with Parsons Technology, he would have to pinch himself. I know he was proud of me and all that I'd accomplished. Even so, when I told him I'd sold the company, he asked how much I got for it.

"Sixty-four million," I said.

"It sounds like you gave it away," he sniped.

I was beside myself. I wasn't expecting that answer from him. I was hoping for something a little more supportive and enthusiastic. But it did teach me a valuable lesson. From that day forward, I don't tell anyone numbers they don't have to know. In retrospect, I should have said, "Dad, that's for me to know. But be assured, I did okay."

As it turned out, Intuit had no plans for keeping Parsons Technology. They bought it to kill those products that competed with them, and that's exactly what they did. They eventually sold the company to someone else, who sold it again. Ultimately, Parsons Technology ceased to exist. Everyone who owned it down the line screwed it up a little more than the previous owners. That's what happens when you bring in level B managers who don't have an entrepreneurial spirit. I watched it disintegrate from afar, and it made me sad. At the end of the day, I had made my choice to sell, but it's a hard thing to watch someone else drive your company into the ground through inept business decisions. It taught me a lot—lessons I wouldn't have learned without watching our company's growth and its eventual demise after I sold it. I would carry those invaluable experiences with me as I went forward.

> **From that day forward, I don't tell anyone numbers they don't have to know.**

Here's what I know for sure: the success or failure of any business revolves around the leader. To be successful, a leader needs to be doing something they really like to do. They need to know more about their business than their competition knows about their own. Remember, when times are good, anyone can make a buck. Your measure is taken by how you deal with adversity, how you solve problems, how you hang in there, and how you react. The way you do those things will determine how successful you'll be.

> **Here's what I know for sure: the success or failure of any business revolves around the leader. To be successful, a leader needs to be doing something they really like to do.**

I never turn away from a problem. If I become aware of something going awry, I'm on it. There's no such thing as bad news in business. It doesn't really matter if you want to hear it or not. All news is good to know. When people tell me something can't be done, I always respond with, "The moment you say you can't do it, you're right. You don't want to be right about this. Keep trying."

One of my personal pet peeves in business is the withholding of information. If someone keeps critical information from me (and I don't care why), you can be sure I'm going to have words with them, and believe me, they will remember those words.

Never minimize damage. Don't hide it. Bring it forward. I usually don't care about who did what. Most problems occur by accident, so I don't care about that. What I do care about is fixing the situation—fast. That's important. Good news is nice to hear, but bad news is *essential* to hear.

Knowing bad news quickly is critical. Why? So you can do something about it. Adversity is opportunity, especially for a small company, which can move swiftly and use the news to its advantage. Adversity shows you where you need to fix things, where you need to improve. When you do that, there's usually an opportunity you can take advantage of in some way.

And the most important thing to remember is the quality of the product—how well it does what it's supposed to do and how good a deal it is for the customer. Is the product functional? Innovative? Fun? All of these things played into the success of Parsons Technology when I was at the helm.

Now, hear me on this: when an entrepreneur is more concerned about making money than delivering a great product, they're doomed. You need to care about your company, your people, and your product. Within any organization, there are two groups of

> Good news is nice to hear, but bad news is *essential* to hear.

people you must focus on: your employees and your customers. The most important group is your employees. You need to create enthusiasm among your team members, because they're the people who are interacting with your customers day in and day out. If they're happy with their job, their pay, and how they're treated, and they believe in what the company is doing, they'll be excited about your products. They'll be full of enthusiasm. And what do we know about enthusiasm? *It's contagious.* We all want to be where enthusiasm is. Employees transfer enthusiasm to customers if they're in the right position and do their job. And when that happens, customers instill enthusiasm in other prospective buyers by spreading the word on your behalf. That carries much greater weight than any ad.

Parsons Technology also taught me a lot about managing people while creating a successful business. Your goals should be to operate better and more efficiently each and every day, in some small way. Just get better every day. The Japanese call this *kaizen*, which means "change for better." It's all about small, daily improvements that translate over time into huge gains. I didn't know this term when we were first building Parsons Technology, but once I read about it, I understood the purpose and the principle. When we were just a fledgling company, all I had was my family and my work. Although I was burning the candle at both ends, those were some of the happiest times in my life. There's nothing better than watching everything move in unison toward a common goal.

> Within any organization, there are two groups of people you must focus on: your employees and your customers. The most important group is your employees.

Finally, if you screw up—and you will—be honest about it. If you've got a problem, be honest about it. And if the media is onto your problem, well, take it from me: be honest about that too . . . then exaggerate the problem a small amount. Why exaggerate? Because the media is so used to everybody minimizing stories and blowing smoke up their ass. These guys are there to ferret out the truth, and you don't stand a chance of keeping it from them. So the best thing to do is level with them and then exaggerate, making the problem seem a little worse than it is. When the media digs in and finds out that it's not as bad as you claimed, they'll move on to something or someone else.

Ready, Set, GoDaddy

During my two-year sabbatical, I had a lot of time to think about my next move. I spent it enjoying the financial freedom I now had and the beautiful weather in Scottsdale, which was an upgrade from Iowa's weather, that's for sure. But the time off was relatively short-lived. I'm a guy who needs to be busy, to pour myself into my work. It gives me meaning, purpose—a reason to get up every morning.

When the sabbatical ended, there were two things I knew for certain. Number one, my golf game hadn't gotten much better. Number two, I needed to get back to work. I had about $38 million to play with and knew I wanted to do something involving the internet. I didn't know exactly what that would be, so I hired a number of very sharp people to work with me and help me find an interesting niche.

We called the new company Jomax Technologies, named for a road I passed every day on the way to work. The name of the company wasn't that important at the time, because we weren't really doing anything yet. Our people had business cards, but whenever someone asked what they did, they'd have to say, "We don't know yet. We're trying to figure that out."

We tried a lot of things, like selling hardware, building intranets and extranets, and developing educational software. None of it worked. What did work was building websites. The only problem I saw with this direction was that websites didn't scale at that time. We started writing software and eventually developed a program that helped people build their own website. We called it Website Complete. Now, remember, this was long before everybody had websites. It was when they were just becoming popular. At the time, our approach was groundbreaking. Instead of charging people a fee of $5,000 to $10,000 to build them a starter site, depending on what they wanted, we provided them easy-to-use software for a small fee so they could build their own website. This ultimately morphed into Website Tonight. The idea was that customers could build their own website in one night.

By this time, Barbara Rechterman had joined us to run the engineering team. She'd stayed with Parsons Technology for three years after I sold it and had just left them when the opportunity with us came up. Parsons Technology was undergoing massive lay-offs, and she had the good fortune and foresight to put herself on that list. Three weeks later, Barb and I connected. She came down to see me in Arizona.

I offered her a job right away. I couldn't tell her exactly what this new adventure would entail, but she said she understood that I was a visionary and there was no doubt we would eventually get to where we wanted to be. Barb trusted me, and I her. We love each other like siblings. And, occasionally, we'd fight like siblings too—but we were usually able to make some great decisions as a result of that tension. Some people misunderstood my gruff ways. Not Barb. She appreciated being challenged to reach new levels.

Barb always told me I was the biggest risk-taker she knew. She'd never met anybody who took risks like I did. But I don't think the choices I make are nearly as risky as she sees them. They're always calculated. And, to be certain, I usually work on things I like to do. I don't do anything I don't like to do. As I've said before, one thing I know for sure is, when you love something, it tells you all its secrets—and those are the things that make the biggest difference.

We got the website software completed in late 1997. It was right around then that we decided to change the name of the company. We needed something better than Jomax Technologies. It was too forgettable. We spent two or three days going down several paths trying to conjure up that new name, and after a couple of hours on the third night, I suggested Big Daddy. Taken. Fat Daddy. Taken. Then I remembered that America Online used the word *go* as the operative word for their customers to execute various commands. So I blurted out to Barb, "What about *Go* Daddy?" She checked to see if that was available, and lo and behold, it was. We instantly bought the domain name. The next day when I came into work, I told the employees I had a new name for the company: GoDaddy.com.

"That's a shitty name," someone said. But it stuck.

Now that we had a name, we needed a logo. The artist who created it for me is a dear friend of mine from Cedar Rapids. She did a bunch of sample logos, but none of them were right. Then she pulled out one she'd drawn while playing with her little girl. It was a line drawing of a guy who looked very remotely like me, with messy orange hair and sunglasses. For whatever reason, he also had a star on the side of his head. That was it. I loved it. It felt happy and it felt right.

At the time, a company called Network Solutions dominated the domain registration market. They were the Goliath in the industry. The companies that were selling domain names back then were all run by engineers, and most were not good businesspeople. Their websites were hard to navigate. We knew we could do better, so we applied to become a domain registrar. The software necessary for us to do that took a year to code and $1 million to build. We sold our first domain name in November 2000. I think it went for eight dollars. It felt as if we were off to a great start. Even so, the world's attention was still focused on dot-coms. At the time, the dot-com boom was in full swing. Companies that didn't even have products were paying stupid, crazy prices for advertising. Tech start-ups, for instance, were paying $200 to $300 per customer acquisition when the customers they acquired were worth just a few dollars. I was convinced that advertising should cost two dollars, not $200. I couldn't do that, though, so ad sellers wouldn't even talk to me. In the beginning, we just didn't buy any ads. Everything the other companies were doing was a cash burn—blazing other people's money. And yet banks and venture capitalists were investing wildly in all those dot-com start-ups. Even though most weren't making any profit, they had these insane, overinflated valuations. It didn't make any sense. We were going through a ton of cash, too, though our cash burn was entirely my money. And my money wasn't unlimited.

Social media didn't exist yet either. The internet was just getting going. We were treading water, and the prospect of sinking was beginning to look real. When I started the company, I had somewhere around $38 million. I gauged how I was doing by how much cash I had. When I started the company, I remember thinking, *I won't worry about it until I get down to thirty million dollars.* And then I lowered that number to $25 million, then $20 million, $18 million, and then to $15 million, and then to $12 million, $10 million, then $8 million. In early 2001, I was down to $6 million left in the bank and decided to shut the company down. We were making progress in the market, sharing the space with Dotster and

Enom, but we weren't nearly as large as Network Solutions, who still dominated the industry. We were bleeding cash at a rate that would have left me penniless if I'd allowed it to continue.

> In early 2001, I was down to $6 million left in the bank and decided to shut the company down.

Early on, I had moved our headquarters to a nice, high-end office space. What a waste of money that turned out to be. So I bought a ranch house in Scottsdale. I wanted to move the company into the house, but the city said it was only zoned for residential use and ranching. Okay, fine; I put up a sign that said "The GoDaddy Ranch" and moved the company there anyway. Never had a problem.

My neighbors, who bred horses, came over one time. "You're not making porn in here, are you?" one old rancher asked.

I said, "No, sir. Come on in." I showed them all the computers and walked them around. The only women in the place were Barb and a programmer named Angel, who was pregnant at the time. I never had an issue with the neighbors after that.

I'd learned a long time ago to keep my own counsel. Whenever I have a big decision to make, I didn't discuss it with anybody. I think about it but always keep it to myself. As cash was running low, I planned to shut the company down but decided to go away for a week to think about how I was going to pay the employees a severance and how I was going to pay the creditors without going bankrupt. Bankruptcy was never an option. Thankfully, we had zero debt because I was completely funded by cash, my cash. I've always operated that way. No partners, no debt. My no-partner rule was simple; I just never wanted one. I never met anybody who was

> Thankfully, we had zero debt because I was completely funded by cash, my cash.

like-minded enough, who thought the way I thought or did business the way I did. Besides, what would a partner do for me? I can problem-solve anything. It might take me a while, and I may mess up a couple of times, but eventually I'll get it right.

So I booked a room at a resort that had just opened and got on a plane and flew to Hawaii. I remember thinking about how I was going to do things. I just needed a break, to let go for a while. And as the week went on, I started feeling like I didn't really want to walk away from the business after all. My epiphany happened when I was waiting for my car at the hotel valet station. The guy who was parking cars came over to me. He looked to be about my age. (I was fifty then.) He was walking along and throwing the keys up in the air, as happy as could be.

"Hi, how you doing, Mr. Parsons? Good day, isn't it?" The guy was so happy. I remember thinking, *This guy might be the richest guy in the world*, but since he was parking cars, he probably didn't have much money; he was just happy as a lark. I had $6 million in the bank, and I was miserable.

What's wrong with this picture?

So I stood there and thought about it for a moment. The happiest times in my life were always when I was broke. What difference did it make if I went broke again? Why worry? Why not hold on to this business? What's the worse that can happen to me if the business failed? I could park cars. I could be happy doing that.

> The happiest times in my life were always when I was broke. What difference did it make if I went broke again? Why worry? Why not hold on to this business?

So I decided to go back home and not shutter the company. If the ship went down, I would go down with it.

I wish I could tell you I did things differently. I didn't.

Life is really all about timing. Sometimes it's good; sometimes it's bad. As luck would have it, ours was about to change. In fact, our luck was about to become phenomenal. A few months went by, and then the dot-com crash happened. That's when GoDaddy was really born. It's true, what they say: one door closes and another opens. The dot-com crash *made* GoDaddy, just like COVID-19 would later help create Parsons Xtreme Golf, or PXG (more on that to come).

When the crash happened, if you were a dot-com, your name was mud. Luckily, I never borrowed any money. I had cash in the bank—certainly enough to continue operations. I scaled back on personnel and other expenses, but since I'd bought the ranch with cash, there was no rent. I wasn't in a bad situation like most of the other dot-com companies.

> A few months went by, and then the dot-com crash happened. That's when GoDaddy was really born.

Every week for a while, one or two companies we were doing business with just vanished. We'd send them checks and they'd return them. They weren't accepting mail. I was one of the few who was still paying their bills. I'll never stiff anybody. I just don't do that. So, though we couldn't get anyone to work with us on advertising before the dot-com bust, all of a sudden, people were standing in line to give me advertising or sell it to me for a song. *BAM!* That's when we started running ads. Now that all the dot-com noise was gone, our products started resonating with people, and we started taking orders.

By October 2001, we'd turned the corner. We became cash-flow positive. Note that in January, February, and March, when I was thinking of shutting things down, I was so close to succeeding. The Chinese have a saying: "The temptation to quit will be greatest just before you are about to succeed." And that's true; success is often found on the brink of failure. I hung in there, and right at the wire we pulled it out. We never missed a month after that. Never.

> The Chinese have a saying: "The temptation to quit will be greatest just before you are about to succeed."

GoDaddy started making money from that point onward. We grew so fast that we were busting at the seams at the ranch, so we rented some office space in northern Scottsdale and moved the operation there. Things were going along pretty well—that is, until I came into work one day to find everyone running around screaming and crying. "We lost all our data," someone said. A programmer made a mistake and deleted it, then wrote over it, and there were no backups. I've noticed that when that sort of thing happens, people panic. One of my gifts is that I don't panic. I also don't get really euphoric about anything. I just stay pretty much in the middle of the road. It keeps me levelheaded, especially in a crisis.

I got everybody together and said, "Here we go . . ." Within thirty minutes, I had us all moving in the right direction. We went to the zone file, combed through it, looked at the domains we'd registered, and created the backup. After being offline for about two weeks, we finally recovered all the data. When we opened again, we reconfigured our software and our systems, putting in double and triple redundancy, and nothing even remotely close to that ever happened again. We did everything we could to ensure that we never put ourselves back in that situation.

To be honest, I never knew that we could be in that situation until we were. Of course, that wasn't a great thing, but we survived it. After that, GoDaddy continued to grow. By 2004, we had about a 16 percent market share worldwide, which wasn't bad, but it wasn't moving as much as I wished. I couldn't figure out why we weren't gaining more market share. There certainly were companies that were in a far worse place than we were. Their prices were higher. Their service was shit. Their websites were terrible. Their customer policies were brutal. And yet, they were still writing a lot of business. Why wasn't that business coming to us? That was a question I couldn't seem to resolve on my own.

I hired a market research firm to help me figure out our next steps. They went through their gyrations, and then they told me the obvious: "People aren't doing business with you because they don't know you exist. Since you're only advertising on the internet and they aren't using the internet for that purpose, they aren't reachable that way." The consultants said we needed to try traditional media—television, radio, magazines, that sort of thing. It made sense to me, so I listened to them. This was close to August of 2004. I remember thinking that the Super Bowl was right around the corner. I had a $10 million war chest built up already. Unlike the other dot-coms who couldn't handle the demand a Super Bowl ad would bring, I knew our systems were solid and could absorb whatever traffic came our way. As a precaution, Barb and the engineering team made sure the website and all our systems could deal with the potential traffic. At the time, that was a pretty tall order, since our company was still small and our site hadn't been getting what we might get with a Super Bowl ad.

When I decided to run a Super Bowl ad, everything in my gut told me it was the right time to do it. Up until then, the dot-coms that advertised during the Super Bowl weren't viable—to say the least. But we weren't like those companies. We were selling domain names and website software, which was about as exciting as a cup of sawdust. My dilemma was figuring out how to tell people about us in thirty seconds and get them to pay attention. Everything was telling me it wasn't possible, because people watching the Super

Bowl at home are basically at a social event. They're busy talking to their friends, and many of them are enjoying alcoholic beverages. If our commercial was going to gain anybody's attention, it had to be different—something people would talk about.

I thought about an ad I once saw that I thought was hilarious. In the commercial, a guy is sitting at a bar, holding an empty bottle of Mike's Hard Limeade. He sticks his tongue into the bottle to get the last few drops, swirling it around rather suggestively in the process. Three beautiful women are sitting across from him at the bar watching this, and one of them says, "I'd like one of those." That ad really struck me as funny and quite memorable, and I knew people would be talking about it around the watercooler. That's when I decided I had to find the team in charge of marketing for Mike's.

I reached out to the Ad Store, the firm that created that commercial, and talked with them about doing an ad for GoDaddy that would be just a little outrageous. I told them, "Bad advertising, which is boring and inoffensive, is like a fat guy at a party. He doesn't offend anybody, he smiles a lot, but he doesn't get any action." We needed to create something that would get people talking—I mean *really* get their attention.

> "Bad advertising is like a fat guy at a party. He doesn't offend anybody, he smiles a lot, but he doesn't get any action."

I had an idea. You see, the previous Super Bowl was the one with the infamous Justin Timberlake–Janet Jackson wardrobe malfunction during the halftime show. "What if we spoof it?" I asked, tossing it out there like a hot potato.

They loved it.

They did a search for our first official GoDaddy Girl, only she wasn't called a GoDaddy Girl yet. The media would come up with the *GoDaddy Girl* name later. They told me they were going to do a casting call with around five hundred women for the spot. I had a clear idea of who I wanted.

"I want a brunette; I want her well-endowed, and I want GoDaddy.com right across her endowment," I said with a Cheshire cat grin. Hate me if you want to, but I knew that's where the boys were going to be looking.

The very last woman they saw was the one who got the job. Her name was Candice Michelle. The team from the Ad Store called me and said, "Bob, we just found the perfect girl."

The good news was that Candice was all in on our concept. She was more than willing to play the part.

The agency created an ad that spoofed the review process for Super Bowl ads. It took place in what appeared to be a courtroom setting. As Candice's character is pleading her case, one of the little straps pops from her tank top and she catches it. For fun, we put "Salem, Massachusetts" on the screen as the court's location.

We got our storyboards approved, shot the commercial, and submitted it to the Fox Sports Standards and Practices department for approval. It was denied. They flat-out rejected it. So, we replaced many of the close-ups with scenes from the back or from a distance. Candice's cleavage was blurred. We got it to a place where Fox Standards and Practices finally approved it a week before the Super Bowl.

When we got our approval, someone from the network called to congratulate me and offer me the opportunity to buy a second slot. I was interested, but I needed more information. It was the commercial break right before the two-minute warning, which seemed like a good idea to me. They made me a nice deal, although I was concerned about getting another ad done in time. When I shared my concern, the person from FOX suggested we run the same ad twice. That was a great idea; it had already been approved, so there would be no issue whatsoever. Or so I thought.

Super Bowl XXXIX was going to be a big workday for us. I planned to spend the day in my office eating popcorn and drinking ginger ale, watching the game and our servers. The Patriots were playing the Eagles, and I knew it would be a good game. I hoped this particular Super Bowl Sunday would be epic for us.

After the first ad ran, the building shook with people who flocked to our website. I'd never seen anything like it, and man, I loved every minute. The servers were strained, but they held.

When it was time for the second ad, the Eagles were on the one-yard line, ready to score. If they did, they would take the lead. All eyes were glued to the television. I couldn't believe we had gotten this lucky, especially when they went to commercial at the two-minute warning. We waited for our ad to come on. And waited. Instead, they aired an ad for *The Simpsons*, with one of the characters, Bart or Homer, stabbing a baby! We weren't sure why our ad wasn't running, so we waited some more. We figured it would be the next ad, but it never aired. We didn't know what was happening.

I got ahold of the president of Fox Sports and asked, "What happened?"

"Your ad was out of tenor with the rest of the ads. We had to pull it. Call me tomorrow and let me know what you want."

My staff was livid. They were up in arms, stomping around saying this wasn't right. Not me. I turned to Warren Adelman our COO, and said, "Could we be this lucky?"

At the time, I had an active blog, so I sat down and started writing about what had happened. Pulling an ad during the Super Bowl after it had been approved and had already run once just wasn't something that was done. I'm not sure it had ever happened before in the history of television. Well, my blog post about the ad getting dropped and what ran in its place got picked up everywhere. I was interviewed by Bill O'Reilly, CNN, and others. I was doing interviews from dawn to dusk for almost a week. One after the other, after the other, after the other. And it wasn't just me being interviewed—Candice was doing the rounds too. She was on the *Today* show, *Tomorrow Coast to Coast*, and *The Howard Stern Show*. When she did *Howard Stern*, I said, "Candice, you get in front of that Super Soaker, you're done."

"I won't, Bob."

Sure enough, Howard tried, but Candice kept her word.

The story was picked up by TV stations, radio stations, and newspapers. The best part? They all explained what we did—that we registered domain names and created websites. The advertising value of that exposure was worth well over $20 million. And as a result, our market share went from 16 percent to 25 percent! And it stayed there.

In the meantime, I worked out a deal with the network. Of course I didn't have to pay for the ad that didn't run. The rest of the settlement remains confidential. It turned out to be a great deal for all of us.

When I was done negotiating with the network, I set my sights on the NFL. We were on a conference call with the League and Fox. Even though the NFL was blameless for what had happened, they kept asking me if we had a deal. I kept thinking, *I'd better ask for something else while I have the chance.* But I couldn't think of what the hell to ask for, so I finally said, "Give me two game balls from every Super Bowl."

"Done." They couldn't get the word out fast enough.

Whenever those balls arrived, I put them in a big round dog bed in my office. It got to the point where I had quite a few. Eventually, they stopped sending them—which was a good thing, since I could never really figure out what to do with them. In the end, I was happy with the deal, and I think they were too.

GoDaddy continued to run Super Bowl ads for years. The media often asked why I kept running the ads after what had happened the first time around. I would pose the question right back to them by saying, "If you did an ad like this and you had a result that almost doubled your business, would you do it again?"

Of course they would.

And I did.

We took something (domain names and web hosting) that was as exciting as saw dust and made it fun. Year after year, people actually looked forward to our ads. How many companies do you hear that about?

The GoDaddy Girl

As I mentioned earlier, it was the media who coined the term *GoDaddy Girl*. I didn't do that. They came up with it when they said we'd developed a new standard for network indecency, which was ridiculous. There was nothing indecent about that first ad, or any that followed. Sure enough, for years, whenever another company—like Dentyne, Bob's Big Boy, or Carl's Jr.—ran a spicy ad, they used to show my original Super Bowl ad right alongside it, describing the new ads as being GoDaddy-esque. Man, that was a beautiful thing. We got even more exposure from other people's ads! I couldn't believe that was happening.

We wanted to do another Super Bowl ad in 2006, but I'd parted ways with the agency we used for the first one. Not because I wasn't happy with them; I was. It was just that we could save a small fortune on the ads if we did them in-house. This gave birth to a new department within our company that we called GoDaddy Productions, run by Will Sliger. It made perfect sense, as I knew we could easily be advertising all year long, and not just once a year for the big game.

I tasked Barb with creating our television strategy, from production to advertising. We just went in and figured it out. One thing we completely understood was that television ads were expensive to buy. Barb was now dealing with the networks and cable providers, purchasing all our ad time directly. That involved getting a really good feel for what was performing or not performing, and for what criteria and methodology should be used to measure whether something was working or not.

Over the course of the year, I figured out that there were two steps to creating an ad that got noticed. First, you create an ad that won't be approved by Standards and Practices. Second, you produce a different ad—one that teases the *real* ad without giving it all away. This other ad will always get approved. What you create by doing this is excitement, interest, and mystery around the first ad—and around your company. If you're successful, people will visit your website to gain access to the real ad, the one they weren't allowed to see on network television.

> I figured out that there were two steps to creating an ad that got noticed. First, you create an ad that won't be approved by Standards and Practices. Second, you produce a different ad—one that teases the *real* ad without giving it all away. This other ad will always get approved.

After the success of the first commercial, I also thought it was time to find a new woman to become the face of our company. She had to be young, smart, accomplished, good-looking—and somewhat known.

I was in Alaska with a group of friends, and some locals were showing us the territory. One night, the name Danica Patrick came up. This was right after she led the Indy 500 for several laps, making her the first woman to ever do that. Even the locals, who lived in the most remote part of Alaska with no electricity, knew who Danica was. She was quickly becoming a racing sensation for her skill, talent, and, yes, looks. When I got back to Arizona, I reached out to her. As it turned out, she was living in Scottsdale too. At the time, I didn't know that. It wouldn't have made a difference if she lived somewhere else, but it was convenient that she was in our backyard. Before we met, I wanted to make sure she wouldn't have any issues with doing our ads. She had done a photo shoot for *FHM* that was provocative, and after seeing that ad, I said, "Let's hire her." It was, as they say, the start of a beautiful business relationship. It was truly wonderful and we worked together for ten years.

When I signed Danica, part of the deal was that we would also sponsor her race car. The cost of that wasn't for the faint of heart. It was a few million dollars a year, but it was worth it. Everyone knew who she was and, by proxy, who we were.

The first time I actually met Danica was in Chicago. She had just switched from Bobby Rahal's racing team to Michael Andretti's team. There was a lot of media coverage, with all the sponsors unveiling their racers' cars. Danica drove her Indy car through downtown Chicago. At the time, we were an associate sponsor. Motorola was her primary sponsor, and they were in the middle of a three-year deal when we came on board. When that deal expired, we became her primary sponsor—putting GoDaddy front and center on her Indy car.

During those years, Danica and I forged a really great relationship. We both believed the other was more important. I always said she was the most important person in the picture and usually thanked God for her. At the same time, she would say the exact same thing about me. Our mutual respect created one of the most unique and beneficial business relationships I'd ever had. I was grateful for Danica, and she for GoDaddy.

Over the years, I used to take long motorcycle trips. Whenever I stopped for gas, I always met the most interesting people. One thing about a gas station is that you'll find a cross section of people from every socioeconomic level there. Gassing up your tank is a good opportunity to just talk to people. Whenever I would stop, I'd always say, "Excuse me, can I ask you a few questions? Have you ever heard of a company called GoDaddy.com?"

Invariably, they would bring up Danica Patrick.

Sometimes I would flip the question around and ask, "Have you ever heard of a celebrity by the name of Danica Patrick?"

Sure enough, they would eventually bring up GoDaddy.

It didn't matter where I was or who I was talking to; everyone equated the two brands. We had become synonymous. It was perfect, because we both benefited. We had the mindshare of both brands.

Sometimes I would go to her races. People would stop and ask me if I was a big racing fan. I wasn't, really. I was a Danica Patrick fan. If she had been an ice-skater or a ballerina, I would have sponsored that endeavor instead. Lucky for me, she was the only female Indy race car driver at the time, and I enjoyed the racetrack more than the ballet.

> Exciting things were happening, creating growth and awareness.

One time, my brother and I were watching a race together. For a while, especially during her NASCAR tenure, Danica would wreck out. My brother thought I had to pay for the cars when she crashed. He turned to me, stone-faced, and said, "Robert, you need to talk to her about not wrecking every car she drives."

I just had to laugh. That was my brother. Man, I loved him so.

In the end, Danica did thirteen Super Bowl commercials for GoDaddy. We always ran the creative by her, explaining the theme and vision for each commercial and what was going to happen.

If she was in town and available, I would take her and her then-husband to dinner, order a nice bottle of wine, and lay it all out for her approval. It was a magical time for both of us. We were both in such a great flow. Exciting things were happening, creating growth and awareness.

There were more than a few times when Danica took the hit for using her sexuality in some of the ads. She was always clear that she would do only what she was comfortable with. In fact, there were a few ads we pitched that she said no to. And that was fine by me; I respected her integrity and always went back to the team to find a different path forward. She got wonderful exposure, made a good living, became more popular because of the ads, and raised her brand profile and awareness to a place where other opportunities followed—other jobs, other sponsors. I was proud of her and the success she achieved and even prouder to have her as our spokesperson for so many years.

It's been wonderful to see Danica branch out into her own business ventures. I'd like to think she learned a thing or two about marketing from when we worked together. I also hope I left a good impression on her from the many long conversations we had about business over the years. I think we both appreciated the other's directness. Her fearlessness as a driver was awesome. Her willingness to be bold, especially while building her brand, is to be admired. We were and are kindred spirits in many ways. I will always look back on those years with great fondness and appreciation.

Everyone Wins

That period when you're tipping toward great success is such an exciting time in companies. I'd been through it with Parsons Technology, and now I could feel it happening with GoDaddy too. From the time of our first Super Bowl commercial onward, GoDaddy always had people pursuing us for acquisition. By 2005, we were the largest ICANN-accredited registrar on the internet. (ICANN stands for Internet Corporation for Assigned Names and Numbers.) Then in April 2006, things really heated up. That was around the time we announced our plan to go public. I had hired Lehman Brothers to manage the initial stock offering. We were looking to raise over $100 million and to significantly increase the value of the company. We went through the motions, jumped through all the hoops, filed the appropriate paperwork, and were moving forward as if this were the right next step. However, the closer we got to the date, the more I thought it was a bad idea and potentially a bad deal. I was suddenly going to have all this reporting and bureaucratic stuff to do, and, frankly, there wasn't enough money involved to invite that headache. So many people who'd had nothing to do with building our company were standing in line with their hands out. I don't like partners, and for the most part, I don't take loans to operate my businesses. It was my money, my rules.

Before anyone knew my latest thinking on the subject, the Lehman team came to me and said they had bad news. They were going to have to give a haircut to our stock price. They said it like it was a joke. I didn't find it funny. Not one bit. So I responded the only way I knew how: honestly and to the point.

"Well, I've got some worse news. I'm not going public."

"Oh, you're teasing," they said, half laughing, half panicked.

"No. I'm as serious as a heart attack." And I was.

They couldn't believe it.

Our lead attorney, who had handled the initial public offerings, or IPOs, of a lot of companies, said that in his entire career, mine was the only company he had ever dealt with that had backed out of an IPO. Much later, he also said that my decision was right as rain.

On August 8, I officially pulled the plug. I didn't make too many friends by doing that, but that was fine by me. I wasn't looking to make friends.

After that, several other companies came to us and made offers, but I never felt like it was the right offer or the right time. I was having fun. I would know when it was time to cash in my chips. There was still a lot of work to do and a lot of good times to have.

Something that was always important to me, whether it was at Parsons Technology or GoDaddy, was creating an environment where people wanted to come to

> Something that was always important to me, whether it was at Parsons Technology or GoDaddy, was creating an environment where people wanted to come to work, and we were creative in the ways we achieved that.

work, and we were creative in the ways we achieved that. As the company changed and grew, I did my best not to lose that family feeling we'd had in the beginning. I think it's inevitable when you grow a company to a large number of employees that the feeling of the place will be different from the feeling when just a dozen people were working. That's to be expected. Even so, there were many times when I would go out on a motorcycle ride in the evening and stop in to visit the team members working the night shift at one of our customer service call centers. I'd go into the building, say hello to them all, shake their hands, and see what they were doing.

One of the most important things I learned over the years was how to create a call center that was a blast to work at. Here was my inspiration: I had my teeth cleaned by a girlfriend of mine who was a dental hygienist.

"Hey, Bob, we just got nitrous oxide; you ought to try it. I'll goose it a little for you," she said.

Holy smokes! She had me on the roof.

When you're disconnected from the nitrous, you come right down, but you feel good for the rest of the day. I left the dentist's office and went back to work. When I got there, I walked through the call center like I always did. It just seemed a little dingy and sad. It didn't feel like a very exciting or happy place to be.

I turned to one of the supervisors and asked, "How come the place seems so dim and unhappy?"

"It seems like it always does," he said with a shrug.

"I'll tell you what. Let's spend a thousand bucks and have a contest for both the web board and for the people on the phones. And make it fun."

So he did, and sales went up $8,000 that day.

The web board cleared twice, meaning there were no outstanding questions from people who posted on our site. As far as I knew, we had never cleared the web board before. But on this day, we cleared it two times in about six hours. I had learned that these types of incentives worked during my time at Parsons Technology. Tech support and the call center at Parsons held contests all the time. We always tried to have fun. Back then, I'd offer an extra dollar or two if the customer calling in bought an additional product. GoDaddy took things up a notch. Maybe two. Eventually I started doing all sorts of things to keep

> "I'll tell you what. Let's spend a thousand bucks and have a contest for both the web board and for the people on the phones. And make it fun."

the place lively and our team inspired. We'd hold hourly contests. Daily contests. Weekly contests. Monthly contests. I would even pay their rent or mortgages for a year. I'd throw out unexpected big cash payments, trips, cars, motorcycles, all sorts of stuff. I put people in a cash machine and blew fifty-dollar bills at them. They could have whatever they could catch. It was always fun.

As a result, a couple of things happened. We learned that the best way to sell in a call center is to deliver incredible service. When you call for service nowadays, what are you expecting? No service, right? Or mediocre service at best. But if you reach somebody who's excited, enthusiastic, and friendly, and they help you feel good about the experience and the company, then what happens is you want to return the favor. It's the principle of reciprocity. So, following this principle, we would never sell products to somebody who didn't need them—and if we did and they brought it up to us, they would immediately get their money back. It got to the point where people would say, "GoDaddy has got the best service of any software company." And we did.

Sometimes we'd take the incentives outside the office too. I've been known for throwing some great parties over the years. I'll tell you, there were some doozies. I used to rent the baseball stadium

ipage214 FIRE IN THE HOLE

where the Arizona Diamondbacks play and invite our entire company. It was the only place big enough for our events. I'd have everybody in the company come, and we'd entertain them like they'd never been entertained before. Aside from hiring well-known musical acts, I would also give away a few million dollars to our employees during the party. I had so much fun doing it that I never

> We learned that the best way to sell in a call center is to deliver incredible service.

wanted to stop—so I'd give away another million and a half to keep the atmosphere exciting. Employees loved it. The media? Not as much. There were times during the recession, around 2008, when the press would attend and ask if I thought it was right to host such extravagant events when so many people were out of work. I said, "Absolutely. Spending money is going to get us out of this recession. The easiest thing for me to do would be to pocket the profits, but I think it's better to spend the money and share it with our people at GoDaddy. When I do, that money is going to be spent in the local economy, so you should be encouraging me to do this."

I never felt like the media had it in for me. It was just their job to ask those types of questions. As we expanded, I learned how to work with them, and they were always pretty good to us. There was no doubt that they could see how happy our employees were, especially when they attended those events. What they didn't know was why I did those types of promotions. First, I wanted to acknowledge and give back to the people who'd helped us reach such a tremendous level of success. Second, I did it to keep that momentum. There's an old saying: "Happy wife, happy life." Well, the business equivalent is "A happy employee is a productive employee." If you take care of your employees, they will take care of your customers.

One of the most valuable lessons we learned about customer service at GoDaddy was that people liked using the internet for education, recreation, social media, shopping, research, those sorts of things. But when it came to solving problems, people much prefer to talk to other people, other human beings. If you know that, why would you simply post a bunch of FAQs— frequently asked questions—and avoid talking to your customers? We believed in speaking with our customers as much as possible, and that was a huge difference in our model, and ultimately a difference-maker in our success. All our service was soft touch. When somebody bought a domain name from us, we were the only company that would call to thank them. Maybe you received one of those calls over the years. Once we had their time and attention, we'd explain

> **We believed in speaking with our customers as much as possible, and that was a huge difference in our model, and ultimately a difference-maker in our success.**

how to set up their domain or website. That turned them into a customer forever. About once a year, we'd call to just ask them how they were doing and if there was anything we could help with. Customers loved it.

Those practices were some of our aces in the hole. We had excellent customer service, the widest array of products, and better pricing than anybody else. Okay—now I'm going to let you in on our trade secret. The reason we did all of that was because I'd noticed that when people decided to launch a website, they always purchased the domain name first. Internally, I called domain names the "tickets to the ballpark." The ballpark consisted of secure sockets layer (SSL) certificates, websites, software, and all sorts of other things we eventually sold to them, which became very profitable for us. SSL certificates encrypt what you send from your computer and decrypt it on the other end so it can't be intercepted in the middle. They confirm that your site is really your site and not a clone of your site. They were an endless river of cash flow.

It was through a company called GeoTrust that I got involved in the secure certificate business. I approached the company about reselling for them. They agreed, and we made a deal. Shortly thereafter, I noticed that one of my competitors was selling the same product for less than my costs. I called GeoTrust and asked, "What's happening here?"

Instead of offering an explanation, they were actually rude to me. They said, "Well, that's the deal. We expect you to honor it."

"Really?" I said, knowing someone can't make you sell their product, and I quit doing it. I went ahead and found somebody who had a root certificate for sale instead. A root certificate assures the right to have a secure certificate, though it still needs software to be written around it. No problem. We got into that business, creating our own secure certificates and selling them for a song. We became one of the top issuers of secure certificates in the world. As the saying goes, "Pigs get fat and hogs get slaughtered."

Another thing we took very seriously was privacy. It used to be that when you bought a domain name, your name and address were published for everyone to see. That's just how it was done back in the day. One afternoon, I got a call from a woman who wanted to delete her domain name. At the time, I would never let employees delete domain names unless I signed off on the request because I just didn't want to deal with the fallout if it was done in error. I got on the phone with the woman, and she explained that she'd bought a domain name through us and wanted to delete both her domain name and her website, effective immediately. While she was talking, I quickly looked at her website, and it was terrific. I couldn't understand why she wanted to shut it down, so I asked for her reasons. She explained that she had a stalker and was concerned about having her address published anywhere.

That stopped me cold in my tracks. I had never considered something like that would be an issue. I asked if I could think about it and call her back. There had to be a way to keep her website up and running without exposing her name and location. It made sense for all sorts of reasons, but especially for her privacy and safety. I didn't want her to become any more of a victim than she already was, so I called her back with an idea: I would create a vehicle that would shield her personal information. But until I could do that, I would transfer her domain information to myself. That way, her personal information would be nowhere anyone else could find it. There would be nothing connecting her to the site. I assured her that she could trust me on this. She agreed, and we got to work. I called our in-house counsel, Christine Jones, and together we created domains by proxy. We kept personal information private for a small fee. If somebody wanted to send a message to the owner of a specific domain name, they would send it to a certain code in the ICANN record that we maintained, and we would then forward it to the person it was intended for. It was a double-blind process; no one knew who was sending or receiving the message. For years, we were the only company that offered this protection.

We had a lot of customers who were domainers, which means they bought and sold domains for a profit. Some companies wouldn't do business with them. I did. I said, "Come to us." They could do their own deals, and we'd be the warehouse. I ran the table; I didn't play the game. We had a department that would reach out to domainers and offer them all sorts of products as a way of creating every possible channel of income. It took a lot of smart people working together to brainstorm all these ideas and turn them into income for us. I certainly didn't do all this alone. You're as good as the company you keep, and I had the very best team in the business.

By 2011, GoDaddy had grown to over six thousand employees and became a behemoth. I began to think that it might be kind of fun to do something else. It was time to start getting ready to move on. I signed a deal with Frank Quattrone and his company, Qatalyst Partners, to represent us. Frank was the best in the business. He began his career with Morgan Stanley in 1977, has advised technology companies since 1981, and headed the global technology groups for Morgan Stanley, Deutsche Bank, and Credit Suisse before cofounding Qatalyst. Frank and his teams have advised on more than 600 mergers and acquisitions, with an aggregate transaction value of over $1 trillion, and on more than 350 financings that raised over $65 billion for technology companies worldwide. He was the perfect person for the job.

> You're as good as the company you keep, and I had the very best team in the business.

After a few false starts that were mostly due to my being difficult to deal with, Frank and Qatalyst guided that baby right down the flight path and finally landed the plane. We sold 71 percent of the company to three private equity firms, KKR, Silver Lake, and TCV. Frank and his team knocked it out of the park. So did I. I wound up with $2.3 billion in cash and stock and retained 29 percent of GoDaddy. With that deal, I also created thirty-six millionaires among my employees. *Thirty-six of them!*

To me, considering the way I grew up, $2.3 billion is quite a stack of cash. I never dreamed I would accomplish that. Over the years, I also paid well over $900 million in income tax—and despite the fact that I never received a thank-you note, I was honored to do so. For the record, I am audited by the state and federal government nearly every year—and there are almost never any adjustments. If there are, they're usually in my favor, meaning I overpaid.

When I left GoDaddy, we had a 70 percent market share of worldwide domain names. We had a lot of fun reaching that height while becoming a true disruptor in the industry. Something I'm extremely proud of is the role I played in developing the internet. I get no credit for it, but when it comes to domain names, I democratized them by making them available to everybody. Everyday people who never would have dreamed of such a thing before we made the opportunity available to them were able to have websites. Compared to everyone else, we moved so many domain names, and the internet moved right along with us. My troops and I were responsible for that—and in the process, we helped to create a lot of wealth for people too. But the monetary gain isn't something I feel as proud of as I do about the many motivated employees and staff members we had at our organization. When you put your people first, success follows, and everyone wins. Period.

> When you put your people first, success follows, and everyone wins. Period.

Meeting the Love of My Life

While there was a period when I was out having a lot of fun, I had gotten to a point in my life where I grew tired of dating. Being single takes a lot of energy, and I just needed a break. For a while it was just me and Max and Chief, my two border terriers. I loved those dogs to pieces. They were my best buddies, and they never complained about a thing. No matter what the situation was, they were always glad to see me.

Occasionally, I would go out with some friends to a club or bar. I'd stay for a bit, but I'd always head home early. Although I may have enjoyed that scene in the past, it was no longer my thing. Truth be told, I never really cared about being in a bar. I once dated three women in a row, all of whom had a drinking problem. Then it occurred to me I'd met all of them in bars. If that was who I was destined to meet and date there, I decided not to put myself in that position anymore. Okay, occasionally, I might have stopped in for a beer, but I no longer wanted to hang out there. One thing I was absolutely clear on: if you were looking for trouble, you could always find it in a bar.

From time to time, I would meet my buddies for dinner, then come home, where the dogs would be eagerly awaiting me, their tails wagging. And when I didn't go out, I'd fry up a batch of ground beef in a pan, pour a can of pork and beans on top, add some maple syrup and brown sugar, and I was ready to go. If I let it sit for a couple of days, it was even better. Man, it tasted good. Max and Chief loved it too. I could watch whatever I wanted on television or dive into a good book, and no one bothered me. I could get into bed and blow a four-second fart. You know it's wicked when the dogs leave the room! Anyway, I always had a good laugh, and then I'd go right to sleep.

A few months into my dating sabbatical, my friend John started calling me incessantly. He's a notorious matchmaker. When I'd see his number come up on my phone, I would send it right to voicemail. I just wasn't interested in whoever he had in mind for me. But one day, I decided to answer his call.

"Bobby, I got a girl for you," he said, full of excitement.

"John, I'm not dating," I emphatically responded.

"No, no, Bobby, you've got to meet this girl while she's available."

Admittedly, I was a little intrigued, because I'd never heard him so confident about anyone. "Okay, John. Tell me what you want me to do."

"Just call her. Her name is Renee," he said.

So I did. Renee and I spoke for a while, and I enjoyed our conversation. Before hanging up, we agreed to go out on a date to meet. She picked a nice restaurant with a bar. I had a pretty steadfast rule about meeting for a drink on the first date. If things went well, we

> On the night of our first date, I called to say I was running fifteen minutes late. Not the best way to start off, except for one thing: Renee said she was running forty-five minutes late. I liked her already!

could move on to dinner. If they didn't, well, that was just fine. I was a little nervous, but I honestly didn't care if Renee looked like Broom Hilda when she arrived. I'm not the type of man who would bolt.

On the night of our first date, I called to say I was running fifteen minutes late. Not the best way to start off, except for one thing: Renee said she was running forty-five minutes late. I liked her already!

I arrived at the restaurant and promptly found a seat at the bar with a perfect view of the entrance. And then I waited. And waited. When Renee walked through the door, I recognized her right away based on what she said she'd be wearing—a lovely brown dress and flats.

Most of us have an idea of who we think our other half will be when we settle down. We have something in our mind's eye about the way they'll look, dress, speak—the way they'll present themselves to the world. Very seldom does that image come true. When Renee came through the door, I couldn't believe it. She was my vision to a T. I nearly fell off my bar stool. I was smitten. I couldn't talk. She had no frame of reference, but I was being incredibly quiet, mostly because I was tongue-tied. Every time I tried to speak, it was like I had a mouth full of marbles. We ordered a couple of cocktails, and eventually I loosened up a bit. By the second drink, I asked Renee if she'd like to have dinner. She said she would love to.

"I have to make a phone call," I told her. "I'll be back in fifteen minutes." The call was business-related and couldn't wait. When I got up, I turned to her and said, "Order us both dinner. I'll be back before it's served."

As I was walking away, she called out, "Wait a minute. What do you like? Do you have any allergies?"

"I like everything," I replied. "And no, I have no allergies."

Renee ordered salmon for herself and short ribs for me. She could have ordered me a salad with dressing on the side and I would have been happy, because the food didn't matter. Her company was all I needed. We talked for hours, and I loved it. She was everything I was hoping for. We left the restaurant and went to a coffee shop that was open late, where we talked even more about life and our interests, getting to know each other.

> She could have ordered me a salad with dressing on the side and I would have been happy, because the food didn't matter. Her company was all I needed.

We really hit it off. At first I thought she might be too young for me. The next day, I told Nima, my executive assistant at the time, that I had met the most wonderful woman. The only concern I had was that I thought she was probably too young.

"How old do you think she is?" Nima asked.

"I'd guess she's in her early twenties," I said.

"What's her name?"

I gave Nima her name and went on with my day. By five o'clock, Nima came into my office and said, "Bob, I've got some great news. Renee is thirty-nine!"

Well, that made things a lot easier. We started dating and spending time together over the next several months. I was very up-front about not wanting to get married. I had all but quit dating, yet here I was, smitten as a kitten. Renee was indeed one fine woman. I liked everything about her. But I don't ever think of things as forever, because forever is a long time. I was enjoying our near-term relationship. I didn't want to screw it up. At the same time, I wasn't looking for something serious. I know that must have frustrated Renee.

As we continued to see each other, things were going well—
or at least I thought so. Renee, on the other hand, wanted to get
married. She wasn't demanding it by any means, but she was clear
about her intentions. Unfortunately, I wasn't in the same place she
was, and I didn't want to stand in her way, so we broke up. All the
while, we kept in touch, though we didn't see each other much
after that.

A few months later, I was riding my motorcycle when I was hit
by a car. Now, understand, when it comes to motorcycles, I'm like
a cat. I've got nine lives. Every time I've been hit or gone down with
my bike, I've walked away. This time, I was thrown from the bike.
It went up in the air and landed on top of me, and I couldn't get
out from under it. Luckily, I was wearing jeans, but the tailpipes
were so hot that they burned my legs right through the denim. My
leg was smoking. Two guys rushed over and lifted the bike off me.

"Thank you, brother," I said to one of the guys.

The man who hit me came over and handed me his card and
insurance information.

"Get out of here," I said. I didn't want his money. I didn't want
whatever insurance he had, so I sent him on his way. No police
report, no claim.

He hightailed it out of there like the Road Runner. I hoped he
appreciated being set free and would be more careful in the future.

I was still able to walk away from this crash like all the others, but this time, I was hurt. I called my office and asked them
to come get my motorcycle and me. I went in to work the rest
of the day. As each hour passed, though, I experienced more and
more pain. My leg was swelling, and the discomfort was becoming
unbearable. My daughter Marianne, who is a physician's assistant
but also worked with me, insisted I go to the hospital. I went to the
Mayo Clinic to get checked out. On the way, for whatever reason,
I called Renee to tell her what had happened.

I got to the hospital and they immediately packed my leg in ice to reduce the swelling. I looked up from my bed and saw Renee standing there. She was dressed to the nines. Man, I was so happy to see her. When the doctors released me, Renee came home with me and took care of me—and we haven't been apart since. I had a change of heart after that. I knew she was the woman I wanted to spend the rest of my life with. I was done being a knucklehead. This was my relationship to screw up, and I wasn't about to let that happen.

> I knew she was the woman I wanted to spend the rest of my life with.

I started to plan my proposal after that. I went to the jeweler to look at rings. As I admired the bigger diamonds, I said to the jeweler, "I think this may be too big."

"Trust me, Bob. It won't be a problem," he said with a wide, toothy grin.

I hemmed and hawed, worried that she might not like such a large stone.

"I don't know. I don't think she's going to want it," I insisted.

"I've been doing this a long time, and I've never met a bride who thought her stone was too big. I've never heard of it!" he said with a laugh. "Trust me, it won't be a problem."

I bought the ring, had it set, and was going to hide it for a few months.

I had met a popular chef in the jewelry store that day and he'd seen that I'd bought the ring, sure enough, a few weeks later Marianne, my daughter, overheard the chef telling some people that I had bought a ring and was going to propose. Marianne called me to confirm. I told her that what she'd heard was correct, and then I called the jeweler and requested that he ask the chef to keep the news under his hat. I explained that I wasn't sure when I was going to propose. I thought it might be in a few months. He completely understood and assured me that mum was the word.

The more I thought about it, the sooner I wanted to ask Renee for her hand in marriage. I was ready within a week of buying the ring. Renee is a wonderful woman. I didn't deserve her—not then, not now—and she didn't deserve me, for vastly different reasons. She deserved better. I was a lucky man to have this woman in my life. What was I waiting for?

A week later, I told Renee we were going to the botanical gardens outside Phoenix. I took her on the back of my motorcycle. We were zipping around when I realized I had burned out the clutch. As I figured out how to manipulate the burned out clutch, Renee was a sport and hung in there with me.

> Renee is a wonderful woman. I didn't deserve her—not then, not now.

When we finally arrived at the botanical garden, Renee removed her helmet. She was wearing a leather motorcycle jacket and her hair was a sexy mess. The attendants had a special location set up for me at the top of a long staircase. We didn't run into another soul because I'd bought out the gardens for complete privacy.

"I think they want to ask me for a donation," I said, trying to throw off any suspicions she may have had.

"It must be a big donation," she said.

We walked up the steps and arrived at the table. She sat down first, then I sat. We had a few sips of champagne, and then I took out the engagement ring, dropped to one knee, and popped the question. She said yes! And she made me the happiest man in the world.

With that, it was time to plan our big day. I really wanted a Southern wedding. My mom wouldn't fly; by this time she was in her eighties, so we had to plan the event somewhere she could get to by car. Renee and I picked Charlottesville, Virginia, because it wasn't that far from Baltimore. Renee decided on Keswick Hall, an iconic resort in the Virginia countryside, as the venue. We worked with the very talented Kristin Newman, from Charleston, South Carolina. She had a stellar reputation for planning extraordinary Southern weddings. We liked her right away. She was wonderful to work with, and she planned the most beautiful ceremony and reception. We took our vows in front of two hundred or so of our closest family and friends. I was in this for the long haul. I'd known it from the day I met Renee, even if it took my heart and my head a little time to catch up with each other.

Renee is the most consistently happy woman I've ever met. I never get tired of looking at her. I don't care how she's dressed or if she's losing her cookies; I love every bit of her. But I especially love what's inside this woman. The fact that she's gorgeous is a bonus.

I believe the key to making relationships work is to be happy. If you want a great relationship, find someone who's happy on their own. I once read about a psychiatrist who has a 95 percent

> I believe the key to making relationships work is to be happy. If you want a great relationship, find someone who's happy on their own.

accuracy rate in predicting whether relationships will be successful. The definition of success is that they stay together after they get married. He takes about an hour to talk to couples, and somehow he knows the probable outcome of the relationship. He looks for any signs of contempt. If he spots anything suspicious on either side, he knows the relationship is bound to fail.

Another factor that can impact the outcome of a relationship is when one partner looks to the other for their own happiness. I don't need a doctor to tell me that's a sign the relationship could wane. It certainly won't be the happiest relationship. The fact is, happiness comes and goes—especially if you're waiting for someone else to provide it. A much better path is to find happiness on your own. Be fulfilled by who you are without needing or depending on someone else. I've always been a pretty happy guy. When I met Renee, she was also happy. The chances of us being happy in our relationship were therefore really good. Don't put your happiness on the other person. It's impossible to be happy that way. You're responsible for your own happiness. It's all you. And if you're not happy, maybe you need to talk to someone who can help you get through whatever is keeping you from finding happiness within. Happiness is a choice; it's a decision we can all make. I know you've heard that many times before, so it's not just me telling you. I genuinely believe we all have the capacity to be happy; we just need to decide to be.

> **Happiness is a choice; it's a decision we can all make.**

Okay, maybe you're thinking I'm happy because I've achieved great success in life. And while that may be partially true, I'm happier now than I have ever been. Even when I struggled with PTSD, I was often still somewhat happy, or at least content. I never wanted to focus on my PTSD. If I had allowed myself to do that, I would have been miserable. Instead, I began to focus on everything outside myself. I love helping people, doing things for people whether I know them or not. I've tried to remain humble in my ways because I know I'm no better than anyone else. I like lifting people up. That makes me happy. And it's a genuine happiness that doesn't leave me the next day. It's the kind of happiness that fuels me to keep doing the things that fill my bucket. Giving to others is really a selfish act. Why? Because in the process, it makes you feel really good.

Happiness and longevity are arguably two of the most sought-after objectives in life. Many years ago, I read an article about Kirk Douglas in which he shared his secret to a happy existence. He said having a purpose for being is what helped him live a long life. He endured a helicopter crash and a stroke, but despite those setbacks, he believed he had more work to do in the world before leaving it. His words inspired me. The more I thought about what he said, the more I realized that he was right.

After reading that article, I took a two-week trip to Zambia. I was staying in huts with dirt floors, no AC, and no modern conveniences. During the day, the tsetse flies were up my nose and in my ears, eyes, and mouth. In some ways, I felt like I was back in the bush in Vietnam. For a moment, I was miserable. But then I remembered what Kirk Douglas said in the article and began to focus outside myself—outside my discomfort—and I repurposed my energy toward helping our guides pack up camp and load the truck. Suddenly, I found myself having a great time—all because of the shift in my mindset. I learned many times throughout my life that, especially in business, the thing that determines how well you succeed is how you think. That's a source of your strength—or weakness. As you think, so shall you be.

So the next time you're stranded in an airport because you missed your flight, why not be happy about the opportunity? By using this valuable tool, you can turn any situation around. Start thinking about the other passengers. Who can you assist? Use the time to call a relative or an old friend you haven't connected with for a while and lift them up somehow. You know what? If you do this, everything changes. Everything! This one little tip—this thing you have total control over—can absolutely change your life, yet few know about it, and even fewer use it. The more you do this, the stronger your desire to keep on doing it becomes. Before you know it, these acts of kindness will become automatic. In the process, you'll lift yourself up, and then *BAM!* You'll suddenly become a happy person because you've changed the way you think and act. I may be oversimplifying this, but I'm here to tell you it works for me. And if it works for me, I promise, it will work for you too.

25

Can I Have a Hug and a Kiss?

By now you understand that my relationship with my parents had a profound effect on me. Although my dad wasn't a bad guy, he wasn't a great father. He never abused me, at least not physically, but there's no doubt I was neglected. The crossfire and hostility between my parents were hard to take. I have some fond memories of him, but mostly those didn't come until I was much older and better able to understand his struggles. In many ways, I grew up to be like my dad—and in many ways, thankfully, I didn't. Despite everything, I always had a lot of respect for my father. He had his faults, but he was my dad, and I loved him.

I was fifty-three when my father passed. He died from doing nothing. Here's what I mean: over the years, he suffered a number of heart attacks, but he never did anything the doctors told him to do. After his second heart attack, the cardiologist told him he needed to have bypass surgery within the month. He never told anybody. And, of course, he never got the bypass. A year and a half went by, and it happened again. The same cardiologist said he had warned him over a year ago that this would happen. Like me, though, Pop kept his own counsel.

I always thought that because I wasn't very close with him, I would be able to handle it when he died. But when that day came, I was devastated. And I was shocked by my reaction to losing him.

On the day Dad passed away, he was in hospice at my sister Beverly's home in Baltimore. He had been suffering from dementia for some time. Before they placed Dad in hospice, the doctors gave us some difficult choices to make. They said they could put feeding tubes in him, but they would have to keep him strapped down. Or we could do nothing.

Nothing.

I knew there was no way I would ever let our dad spend his final days strapped to a bed, helpless and scared. That wasn't going to happen. After some dialogue, the doctors suspected he'd be gone by the first morning at my sister's. But he hung in there and lived for five days. I went to Beverly's apartment each of those days to visit with him. I'd talk to him sometimes, but he never responded. The hospice workers did what they could to keep my dad comfortable until his body just quit.

After he took his last breath, the coroner had taken his body away, and everyone had left Beverly's apartment, I stayed back. I went into the bedroom, shut the door, and lay in his bed. I could feel him next to me. And I cried and cried. I knew he wasn't there, but I could still feel him. Oh God, I could feel him. That's how I said my final goodbye to my daddy.

Dad was hard to please. Nothing was good enough. At least, that's how I felt.

Even so, I sure miss him.

My mom lived to be ninety-four years old. Somehow, she became addicted to Nexium, taking three or four pills every couple of hours. She wouldn't stop, and the medication destroyed her gut. By the time we placed her in hospice, she probably weighed seventy pounds. And then, she just died.

As lacking as both of my parents were, I still loved them. Allan once called me and said, "I pity the fool who doesn't love his mommy."

"That's not me, brother," I said. And I meant it.

A year after Mom passed, I was at our home in Hawaii. Around three in the morning, I woke up from the most vivid dream. Even as I sit here writing this now, I feel as if it just happened. In my dream, I walked into a room. I didn't recognize where it was, but it felt like home. Mom was lying on a couch. When she saw me, she got up, walked over to me, and said, "Robert, can I have a hug and a kiss?"

> "Robert, can I have a hug and a kiss?"

I said, "Sure you can, Mom."

She leaned in, hugged me, gave me a kiss on the cheek, and said, "I love you." And then she did it again. She said, "Can I have another hug and a kiss?"

"Of course you can, Mom," I said.

She looked at me quietly for a moment, and then she hugged me and gave me another kiss, once again saying, "I love you."

In the dream, I looked down and then back up, only to find that she was gone.

I awoke, and it felt so real. Somehow I expected her to be there. Later that morning, my brother called me and asked, "Do you know what day today is?"

I didn't.

"It's Mom's birthday."

I choked back my tears and said, "You know, I saw her last night."

That was the most loving moment I'd ever had with my mother. I believe she came back to put things right, if only in a small way. I'd like to believe this is exactly what happened that night.

I love you too, Mommy.

26

It's Not What I Did During Vietnam, It's What the War Did to Me

As I've already shared, when I came home from Vietnam, I was a changed man—in some ways for good, and in other ways, not so good. On one hand, there's no doubt that everything I've ever accomplished I owe to the Marine Corps. First, I learned that many things are black-and-white; there is no gray. One of my favorite takeaways from boot camp is "Pretty clean is dirty." I hear that in my mind most every day, even now.

Mother Green (a common nickname for the Marine Corps) also taught me responsibility and the importance of discipline in order to achieve much more than I dared to dream possible. I'm not talking about discipline in the form of punishment, although there was plenty of that; rather, I mean the kind of discipline that teaches you if you have a job to do, you don't have to like doing it—you just have to do it. Marines absolutely need to count on

> There's no doubt that everything I've ever accomplished I owe to the Marine Corps.

each other in order to function as a unit. It's a sacred commitment you make to each other. And come hell or high water, you must do whatever it takes to honor that commitment.

Finally, the Marine Corps taught me to believe in myself. It also taught me that I had a right to be proud.

On the other hand, not all the changes that took place served me well. As I got older, it became evident that a lot of damage was done, and it was taking a toll on nearly everything in my life. Suddenly, I didn't like being around groups of people—large or small. Everyone seemed so different from me, especially those who hadn't seen combat, which was just about everybody. I rarely identified with anyone, no matter what group I was with. I never felt like I belonged, or even that I wanted to belong. I wrestled with depression, had a quick temper, and was usually, if not always, on edge. I was often described—accurately—as one of the most intense people anybody around me had ever met.

Like a lot of vets, I managed it as best I could. I pushed the unpleasant memories and dark feelings deep down whenever they started to rear up. I learned to bury myself in my work. And that, more than anything, drove me hard and kept me going.

When I came back from the war, nobody paid any attention to post-traumatic stress disorder. At the time, few people even knew what it was. But it's been around since antiquity; it was called shell shock, war neurosis, and battle fatigue, and then someone named it Vietnam veterans' disorder. All these terms limited the condition to people who'd fought in wars, even though anyone can develop PTSD from experiencing or witnessing traumatic, shocking, scary, or dangerous events, such as natural disasters, physical or sexual assault, abuse, neglect, severe illness, loss, and more. It wasn't until 1980 that PTSD was added to the American Psychiatric Association's *Diagnostic and Statistical Manual of Mental Disorders*, and the World Health Organization didn't include it in the *International Statistical Classification of Diseases and Related Health Problems* until 1992! So, yeah, you can see why no one really told me I had PTSD in those early years. There were so many of us suffering in silence, with no explanation, nowhere to turn, and few resources to help.

> There were so many of us suffering in silence, with no explanation, nowhere to turn, and few resources to help.

As the years slipped by, I eventually became aware of the term *PTSD*. I kept telling myself I couldn't or shouldn't have it. After all, I didn't see that much combat—just a month. But now I know that one month of combat, certainly for me, was more than enough. My life became so much more difficult than it should have been—not just for me but also, sadly and regrettably, for those around me.

Today, I'm certain that my PTSD had an impact on my marriage to Martha, and on our three children as well. Back then, I wasn't aware of just how much it affected my relationships. While I was married to my second wife, Lisa, I started to become more conscious of my unpredictable and inexplicable emotional behavior. I may have come home from the war in 1970, but it wasn't until 1990—twenty years later—that I realized I had severe PTSD.

My realization was triggered by Iraq's invasion of Kuwait and the first Gulf War. Something about seeing our troops out in the field set me off in a very unexpected way. I was forty by then, and even tried to reenlist in the Marines Corps, but of course they wouldn't take me. They said I was too old. And I probably was. However, it didn't stop me from wanting to go.

> I may have come home from the war in 1970, but it wasn't until 1990–twenty years later–that I realized I had severe PTSD.

Then I heard George H. W. Bush say something to the effect of, "This will not be another Vietnam" when he was speaking about the troops coming home from the Gulf War. Those words, especially coming from our president, made my blood boil. They also brought on one of my worst bouts of PTSD.

Suddenly, horrific and traumatic memories from Vietnam began to bubble up. Unexpectedly, all that Vietnam horror, so much of which I had kept buried deep inside, surfaced. It just snuck up and whacked me. I'd be at a cocktail party and *wham*— I'd get a flashback of an NVA getting aerated by machine-gun fire, our point man hitting a trap and having his legs blown out from under him, or Ermal Hunt struggling to touch the eye that didn't exist anymore with a hand that was no longer there. This was not the kind of stuff I could talk about with anyone, so I tried to bury it . . . again.

It didn't work.

I would be at a movie and suddenly find myself weeping. That wasn't me. I'm not the crying type. But I began to cry more often, for no apparent reason. It was a reaction I couldn't attribute to anything going on around me.

Even worse, out of nowhere, I'd snap at those closest to me, especially my kids. It got to the point where I didn't want to go anywhere. I didn't want to do anything. I just wanted to get loaded, which only seemed to exacerbate my feelings. I was mad at the world, which wasn't a great state to be in while I was running Parsons Technology and raising three children. They deserved better— so much more than I was capable of giving to them at the time.

> PTSD is a wide-ranging, debilitating, and all-too-real disease. Symptoms usually set in within three months of the traumatic incident, but sometimes PTSD can take years to rear its head. Mine was a slow build.

PTSD is a wide-ranging, debilitating, and all-too-real disease. Symptoms usually set in within three months of the traumatic incident, but sometimes PTSD can take years to rear its head. Mine was a slow build.

When you suffer from PTSD, it interferes with relationships, work, and your everyday life. In addition to that feeling of not belonging no matter who you're with, it can create extreme mental anguish and an inability to control your emotions.

Many veterans never consider that they've been traumatized on such a deep level. Just as I did, they may think, *I didn't see enough action. I don't have to deal with that. I don't have PTSD*. But that isn't the case. You don't need to see a lot of action to have been deeply affected. The delay in experiencing symptoms also added to the denial for me.

PTSD is often accompanied by depression and anxiety disorders. Many Vietnam veterans turned to hard drugs, such as heroin, to try to escape these inexplicable feelings, which only intensified the symptoms. We all know of such stories. I knew men who turned to drugs to ease their pain. And I knew too many who lost their battle against drugs. In the end, it wasn't the drugs that killed them, not really. It was the lasting effects of war.

If you've been through a traumatic event or experience, it's completely normal to feel some of these symptoms for a few weeks. When the symptoms last more than a month and begin to seriously impact your ability to function (and aren't due to substance abuse, medical illness, or anything other than the event itself), it may very well be PTSD.

To be diagnosed with PTSD, you must have these symptoms for at least a month:

1. At least one reexperiencing symptom:
   a. Flashbacks (reliving the trauma over and over), often with accompanying physical symptoms, such as sweating or a racing heart rate

      b. Bad dreams

      c. Frightening thoughts

2. At least one avoidance symptom:

      a. Staying away from places, events, or objects that are reminders of the traumatic experience

      b. Avoiding thoughts or feelings related to the traumatic event

3. At least two arousal and reactivity symptoms:

      a. Being easily startled

      b. Feeling tense or on edge

      c. Experiencing difficulty sleeping

      d. Having angry outbursts

4. At least two cognition and mood symptoms:

      a. Trouble remembering key facts of the traumatic event

      b. Negative thoughts about oneself or the world

      c. Distorted feelings, such as guilt or blame

      d. Loss of interest in previously enjoyable activities

I checked almost every box. And I wasn't alone.

After doing some research, I was intrigued but not surprised that, according to the National Center for PTSD, around 6 percent of the US population will experience PTSD at some point in their lives. The US Department of Veterans Affairs estimates about twelve million adults in the United States experience PTSD each year. Interestingly, women are more prone to develop PTSD than men, and some experts believe you can be genetically predisposed to developing it. There have been many studies that looked at veterans from different wars and evaluated their rates of PTSD. For example, it is believed that 11 to 20 percent of veterans who served in Operations Iraqi Freedom and Enduring Freedom and approximately 12 percent of Gulf War veterans have endured PTSD in a given year. According to the US Department of Veterans Affairs, it was originally believed that around 15 percent of Vietnam War veterans had been diagnosed with PTSD in the late 1980s. A subsequent review by the National Vietnam Veterans Readjustment Study, estimated that the number is closer to 30 percent. As General William Tecumseh Sherman famously noted during an address to the graduating class of the Michigan Military Academy in 1879, "War is hell."

As General William Tecumseh Sherman famously noted during an address to the graduating class of the Michigan Military Academy in 1879, "War is hell."

Although my war was long over, mentally I was still there. So many veterans of war feel this way, but especially my brothers and sisters who served in Vietnam. Over the years, I've read a number of historical books that describe something called "seeing the elephant." The most prominent use of war elephants was by Hannibal, who marched across the Alps with thirty-seven such imposing animals. But war elephants had been used in India for centuries before they ever made an appearance on European battlefields. The Achaemenid Empire (also called the First Persian Empire) was the first Western empire to use imported Indian war elephants. Alexander the Great encountered them when he fought the Persian army at the Battle of Gaugamela in 331 BC. I've often thought about what it must have been like for those guys on the front line as they came face-to-face with those enormous and fierce creatures. They were tough soldiers, but I imagine it must have been terrifying. I believe that's why being face-to-face with the enemy on the front lines for the first time is often referred to as seeing the elephant. For some, it's considered a laudable rite of passage—but it's also a big step backward, because once you see the elephant, it will never leave you alone. No matter what you're doing or what you're thinking about, the elephant will always be lurking. And that's how I felt for so long. The elephant infiltrated everything—my parenting, my relationships, my work. It would take me more than twenty years to begin to figure this out, and many more to do something about it. I certainly didn't understand it at the time.

It's been reported that during the Second World War, the average number of combat days a soldier saw was between ten and twenty. In Vietnam, the average number of combat days was 250—on a single tour. The number of days for the Marine Corps and many Army units was probably higher because of where they were in the country. Even though I was in Vietnam for just a month, I saw my share. But I'm no hero. I didn't see anywhere near what a lot of my brothers and sisters did, and many of them have suffered with a great deal of grief and agony. As I said, because many veterans are unaware of the root causes or what to do about PTSD, they treat themselves with isolation, drugs, and alcohol. Some even attempt suicide—and all too many die by suicide.

> It's been reported that during the Second World War, the average number of combat days a soldier saw was between ten and twenty. In Vietnam, the average number of combat days was 250—on a single tour.

But it's not helpful to resort to these things, especially when the angel inside you is longing to be released. Those who've seen the elephant aren't the same people on the inside as they are on the outside. They're not the edgy, temperamental, or closed-off people they appear to be. When all that is stripped away, others can see the angel within; but that can only happen when the elephant is finally gone.

For me, one of the most difficult aspects of post-traumatic stress disorder was the cruel trick it played: I always thought that I should be able to handle it, to cope with it on my own. My deeply ingrained belief in self-reliance made me think that even more. But as my PTSD got worse, I began to suffer crippling nightmares and occasional flashbacks, and then I would beat myself up for not being able to stuff those demons back into the mental cages I'd kept them in for so long. It was debilitating. And yes, I once even thought about killing myself. It felt so bleak, so empty. After thinking about it for ten minutes, though, I thought, *That's not me.* And I never really contemplated taking my life again—at least, not very often.

Eventually, my PTSD got bad enough that I realized it was something I simply couldn't fix by myself. I found a psychologist near where I was living in Cedar Rapids. He was retired from the Navy. Once a week, I would see this counselor; we'd talk, and within minutes I would be crying like a baby. I began opening up about so many things I'd never dealt with. I was angry about how returning Vietnam vets were treated. I had never spoken about the things I saw in the war. I had never talked about the guilt I felt over surviving when others were killed, or the guilt I felt over some of what I did—some of what we all did—during that nasty war. All those demons were lurking, and if I hadn't confronted them, who knows what would have happened. I might have drunk myself to death or emotionally withered away.

I also realized that it wasn't just the war that had led me there; it was also my past, my childhood and upbringing. I began delving into all that, too, trying to heal the broken little boy who still lived inside me. It was around this time that I attended the inner-child workshop where I wrote myself the letters you read in the beginning of this book. Like everything else I'd done in my life, I knew this would require hard work—perhaps some of the hardest work I'd ever done. But I was willing to do it to get through the darkness I was living in and move toward the light. I didn't want to be angry all the time. I didn't want to hurt the people I loved. If I were going to conquer this beast, it would take a level of perseverance that matched what had gotten me through all the life events that brought me to this place.

I would often ask myself why I felt this way and why I was now being triggered. I never had a problem watching war movies or documentaries on the Vietnam War. I was always okay with the action. It was the stories of coming home that really tore me apart. I just couldn't watch those scenes.

I. Could. Not. Fucking. Watch.

If it wasn't enough to be knee-deep in that shit war, rejecting us when we came home was even worse. None of us deserved that. It wasn't fair. And by now you know my feelings about fairness.

Of course, today we know that PTSD is real, and, thankfully, it's treatable. New and exciting methods of addressing PTSD are becoming available all the time—but more on that later.

I continued my journey to healing by occasionally getting together with the Marines I served with in Vietnam. I knew that if I was feeling this way, many of my brothers must be too. I linked up with some of them on the internet and found others with the help of the Marine Corps. I often wondered what happened to Larry Blackwell. After all, that man more than likely saved my

> Of course, today we know that PTSD is real, and, thankfully, it's treatable.

life, both physically and for sure mentally. Through some contacts at the Marine Corps, I was able to track down his sister and learned that after Larry returned from Vietnam, he became addicted to heroin. His sister told me that Larry tried so hard to quit heroin, but he just couldn't do it and overdosed in 1993. This broke my heart. If I had known sooner, I would have done anything to help him. After learning about Larry, I called Barry George, my squad leader in Vietnam, and told him what had happened to Larry. I was crying like a baby the whole time. Barry told me, "Bob, you have to get it through your head: the heroin didn't kill him. That fucking war did."

After I heard that, I had a strong desire to connect with more of my brothers. I once went to a get-together we had in Gulfport, Mississippi. Just being around other Marines who'd done the same things I had and knew firsthand what I knew made such a difference. It was a breath of fresh air and a relief. Being together was beneficial for all of us. Simply acknowledging our PTSD took away some of the stigma that had surrounded it for so long. Finally having a name to give to those feelings also helped us begin to heal. It started to make a difference—not a big one, but it was movement in the right direction and a positive first step toward being happier.

Initially, counseling helped me begin to get through my PTSD. Over the course of several months, I poked around in some dark places to try to get my psyche settled. The hell and irony of having PTSD is that I might not have been as successful as I am now without it. For whatever reason, it worked differently on me. Sure, it was debilitating at times, but I learned to repurpose that energy and use it as fuel in my business, relentlessly burying myself in work. That commitment paid off in many ways, but there was also a steep price to pay. It took a toll on the people and relationships I cherished more than anything. Even if I didn't realize it in the moment, I have to admit that today. Therapy helped, and being with the guys helped, but that never got me to where I felt like my old self. And that was what I was searching for.

As I began to feel better about myself and to understand what I was struggling with, I desperately wanted to reconnect with my children, who were young adults by then. I'm often asked about my biggest regrets in life—if I have any. I always respond the same way: "Just one." You see, I'd missed out on so much of my kids' lives while they were growing up because I was always working. I missed their childhoods, or at least a large part of them. I look back and wish I'd been around to watch them grow, to help them when they stumbled, to be there for them when they needed me—and to create enough trust between us so they would know they could always bring their problems to me. But that horse had left the barn early on. And perhaps it was a mixed blessing for them, because my having PTSD meant I wasn't always the nicest person to be around. I had a hard edge. Of course, at the time, I didn't realize it was PTSD that was wreaking all that havoc; I just thought that was the way I was. I had no frame of reference, especially when it came to being a present parent. I should have known better. I wasn't aware that there was an issue that could be fixed. It wasn't until I wrote this book that I realized my absence might have been a lucky break for the kids in some ways. It was better for them that I wasn't around. But as I learned from my own journey toward self-discovery, every day is an opportunity to start over, and I was determined to make up for lost time.

One of the most memorable, loving, and soul-touching experiences I had happened exactly when it shouldn't have. Let me explain. My youngest daughter, Jessica, graduated high school in 2001. Unsure of how to celebrate her accomplishment, I asked, "What can your dad do for you?"

"Dad, I'd like to spend time with you. Let's take a trip together. It can be anyplace, as long as it's outside the country. I want to go someplace new, see other people, and learn about another culture."

My answer was an immediate "Absolutely."

I planned an epic trip to Italy for the two of us. First we went to Rome to see the Colosseum, the Vatican, and other historical sights. Our next stop was Florence, where we hired a driver named Joseph to show us around. Jessica asked him about restaurants we should try while we were there, and he suggested a Michelin-rated place that was supposed to be the third-best restaurant in the world.

Third best? Okay, that sounded good to me.

Jessica wanted to buy a new dress for our dinner, so I took her to the Armani store and let her pick out something special to wear. She looked like a princess. I wore a suit and tie, and she was dressed to the nines. We were so excited for our big night. When we arrived at the restaurant, it was very nice. I wouldn't say the staff was especially cordial, but the restaurant was beautiful. We were seated, and we did our best to take in this experience. After quite a while, the waiter finally came over to take our drink order.

"I'd like a Bellini, please," Jessica said.

"We don't serve Bellinis," the waiter huffed.

"Why not?" Jessica asked.

"Because we don't. May I suggest champagne?" The waiter seemed annoyed.

Jessica said okay.

"Make it two," I chimed in.

He brought our champagne, placed it on the table, and asked if we were ready to order. He was abrupt and curt, as if we were somehow an inconvenience to him. This wasn't what I'd been expecting at all. But we were there, and this was Jessica's night, so I decided to roll with it.

"What would you like?" the waiter asked Jessica.

"I would just like some calamari, please."

"Not possible. We don't serve it this way."

"Well, how about you give me some spaghetti with calamari, but don't put any pasta on the plate?"

"Not possible."

"Why not?"

"That would make the chef very mad."

Those were the waiter's exact words. By this time I was thinking, *The chef isn't the only one who will be angry.* Jessica leaned back, folded her arms, and didn't say another word. I could see she was taken aback and quite disappointed. We were supposed to be sharing a great experience at the third-best restaurant in the world. It was obvious why they weren't number one. The whole experience was the complete opposite of what we'd expected. It was the meanest restaurant I'd ever stepped foot in, and I'd had it with the rude attitude and dismissiveness.

"Excuse me. Let me jump in here. Brother, we're from America. We're used to more accommodating service when we eat out. Obviously, your restaurant isn't that way, so maybe it's best we get our check and leave."

"Very well," he said without hesitation. Then he stormed away.

Within minutes, the owner of the restaurant came over and asked what the problem was. She appeared to be a lovely woman who looked to be in her mid-seventies. I explained the situation to her, thinking she would surely understand. I told her we'd asked for the check and thought it was best for us to leave.

"That is a very good idea," she sniped, and then she too stormed away. She returned a few minutes later with our check. When she handed it to me, there was no charge for our drinks.

We got up and left.

Our driver was nowhere to be found. Of course, he thought we'd be in the restaurant for a few hours, so I couldn't fault him. Jessica and I decided a walk might do us some good. I knew she was disappointed, and so was I. We didn't say a lot for the first block, but then my little girl reached over, put her arm around me, and said, "I love you, Daddy."

Jessica had said she loved me before, but not often. I knew she loved me, yet it was so nice to hear. That was one of the best things that had ever happened to me. I'll never forget it; it meant so much. I looked at Jessica and said, "I love you too, darling."

We finally got ahold of the driver, who took us to his favorite casual family-style restaurant. It wasn't Michelin-starred or fancy, and that was fine by us. We were overdressed to beat the band, but we ended up having the absolute time of our lives that night. They treated Jessica and me like we were royalty. The restaurant played loud music, encouraged dancing, and served up some of the best Italian food we had all that week.

As the night came to an end, Jessica said, "Daddy, this has been so much fun. Thank you."

"I'm here to take care of you, sweetheart," I said. And I meant it. My job is to protect her, and all my children. In many ways, I'm their United States Marine too.

That trip to Italy definitely brought us closer. It also showed us both that being with the ones you love is about being together, not about where you eat. I'll never forget this experience or the time we shared in Italy.

When I'd moved to Arizona after selling Parsons Technology, I hadn't asked any of my three kids to move there with me. That evening in Italy, Jessica said there was something she wanted to tell me, but she didn't want to say it that night. She said it could wait until the next morning. Of course, I immediately thought she was in crisis. And then I thought, *No matter what she tells me, I'll assure her that I'll be by her side.* The next morning at breakfast, I took a deep breath and said, "Jessica, you can tell me anything. Whatever it is, it'll be okay."

> Being with the ones you love is about being together, not about where you eat.

"Dad, I want to move to Arizona. I want to live with you."

I let out a huge sigh of relief and said, "That's it?" I was thrilled—and of course I said yes. Every house I'd owned since her mother and I had divorced had a sunflower-themed bedroom ready for Jessica. She loved sunflowers, and I wanted her to always feel at home. I wouldn't do anything to disrupt that.

Today, my children are grown, and I'm happy to say that I've got a good relationship with each of them. All three eventually moved to Arizona at one time or another. Martha even bought a house there. Marianne and Sean still live in Scottsdale. Sean runs our PXG rental division, and Marianne is now a full-time mom and a part-time physician's assistant. Jessica lives in Portland, Oregon, with her family. She's an accomplished chef and, like her sister, a wonderful mother. Jessica has two boys, and Marianne has two boys and a girl. Sean has a son and a daughter. He works hard to be a good father, the father I never was. I couldn't be happier to see all my children thriving. I learned to let them live their lives and make their own choices. No matter the circumstance, I'm just here to reinforce and protect.

The more healing and work I did to manage my PTSD, the more I wanted to keep healing. In the fall of 2016, I tried a novel and incredibly easy form of neurofeedback provided by a company called Cereset. At the time, Jessica had been in a car accident. She was T-boned and had post-traumatic stress disorder from the collision. It was during a visit to my allergist's office that I was flipping through a magazine in the waiting room and saw an ad for Cereset. I was intrigued, so I called on behalf of my daughter, and then for myself. It changed both of our lives for the better. Those treatments helped me a lot, and completely cured her PTSD.

Cereset uses a proven technology that's noninvasive and highly effective. When your brain is out of balance or stuck, you don't feel right, and it's impossible to function at your highest level. That's exactly how the effects of PTSD made me feel. Cereset helps the brain free and heal itself, leading to higher levels of well-being and balance. I felt a big shift from these treatments and began telling everyone I knew about Cereset's novel approach.

Another treatment I turned to and swear by is a stellate ganglion block, also called an SGB block. And the combination of

Cereset and an SGB block? Whoa, baby. That's the ticket. The SGB block involves the injection of a numbing medication into a bundle of nerves located in the side of your neck. It's a low-risk procedure that has been performed since 1925 and that today is done by a doctor with ultrasound guidance. Here's how it works: A part of the sympathetic nervous system called the stellate ganglion works in tandem with the amygdala, the part of the brain that handles the fight-or-flight response and our emotions. Researchers believe that the numbing agent helps reduce nerve growth factor levels, which then decreases norepinephrine levels in the brain and calms the elevated sympathetic nervous system activity brought on by PTSD. The procedure can relieve symptoms in as little as thirty minutes, and for some, the relief lasts for years. For others, the effects are equally remarkable but temporary, requiring additional shots. Much like rebooting your computer when it freezes, an SGB block "reboots" the sympathetic nervous system, mostly (and sometimes completely) returning it to its pre-trauma state. The results can be astounding.

Traditional treatments for PTSD can take anywhere from months to years to work and have success rates of less than 40 percent. Overall SGB success rates have averaged between 70 and 75 percent over the first nine years of use, and results begin with the very first shot. This is very promising, and a game changer when it comes to treating PTSD.

An SGB block is not a cure for PTSD, but it can help control symptoms for a sustained period. And you don't need to be a veteran to get an SGB block; if you suffer from PTSD from trauma or other events in your life, it may be a viable option to help relieve your symptoms. It's groundbreaking, effective, and can help you get back on your feet. It did for me.

You know, I've talked a lot about the impact my PTSD had on my loved ones. In many cases, marriages end because of it. I think that's true for my first two marriages. And I'm sure there are those I've worked with over the years who perhaps didn't know or understand what I was struggling with and just saw me as a gruff, unpredictable, way-too-intense guy. They wouldn't be wrong. I was. I didn't mean to be. It wasn't my intention. But until I could seek treatment, everyone around me suffered from my pain.

> **In any relationship, it's important to take care of your own mental health first. You have to set boundaries and work to understand and accept that your loved one's behavior isn't about you.**

While writing this book, I asked my wife, Renee, if she would describe her experience of being married to me and whether she had any advice for someone who loves a person with PTSD. This was a hard question for me but an important one. Her answer was so relevant that I thought I would share it with you just in case you're in a similar position:

> *In any relationship, it's important to take care of your own mental health first. You have to set boundaries and work to understand and accept that your loved one's behavior isn't about you. If you don't, it's easy to get sucked into thinking you're doing something—or everything—wrong; that you're an awful person, a selfish person; that you aren't thoughtful or _____ (fill in the blank). If you have the benefit of knowing the person you love is suffering from PTSD, learn to protect yourself and seek your own ways of coping. If, through that, you decide to stay with the person, how can you help them? At the end of the day, you have to first help yourself. When you're in a good place, you can help others, including that person. But that person also needs to be willing, ready, and wanting to do the work, because you can't do it for them.*

I was finally willing to do the work when I realized I was suffering from PTSD. It was only then that I sought answers—and solutions. I kept searching because I wanted to get better for myself and for my relationships. If you're suffering from PTSD, this is what you also need to do. Find something that works. There are options out there; a one-size-fits-all solution doesn't exist, but you don't need to suffer anymore.

There is one other thing that helps my PTSD, and that's visiting the Vietnam Veterans Memorial in Washington, DC. When we came back from the war, it seemed only right that Vietnam veterans should have their own place of remembrance, but it wasn't going to happen. Our government was never going to honor the lost souls who fought in that war. In order for us to have a proper memorial, we had to build it ourselves. We did so without government funds, not that any would have been available for us. The Vietnam Veterans Memorial, also called "The Wall", was unveiled in November of 1982. It's a 486-foot-long black granite wall that displays the names of the over fifty-eight thousand men and women who lost their lives in the Vietnam War. It looks like a scar in the earth—a perfect memorial for that war. Standing in front of that wall, you can't help but get a strong sense of the thousands upon thousands of young Americans who fought and died in that enormous, horrific, nasty war.

Whenever I'm in DC, I always make it a point to go by "The Wall." And when I do, I go there at midnight. The reason I do this is because I'm usually the only one there at that time, and if I want to talk to the wall, I can. In the darkness of night, I stand right up next to the wall. I tear up. And I listen. I listen to those over fifty-eight thousand names of our brothers and sisters on the wall as they whisper what America couldn't bring itself to say to us so very long ago. They whisper, "Thanks for all you did. Welcome home."

If you think you're experiencing symptoms of PTSD, there is help. And if you're a veteran of war, you know it's never easy to be brave, but I'm asking you to step up and be brave one more time. For us veterans, as proud as we are, it often isn't easy to admit that we need help with PTSD. But this is what needs to happen if we're to make progress. To begin your journey to a better life, please call the Semper Fi and America's Fund at 760-725-3680. Semper Fi and America's Fund is an organization that cares for our nation's critically wounded, ill, and injured service members, veterans, and military families. It was started in 2003 by military nurses who volunteered to provide bedside support to those who were wounded or injured while serving in Iraq and Afghanistan. The Fund, as it's now known, is still operated by those same military nurses and includes a nationwide staff of patriotic veterans, community members, and volunteers.

If you don't want to make the call for yourself, for God's sake, make it for your family and for your fellow veterans.

There's no doubt that many who served during the Vietnam War saw far more action than I did. As I've said, I'm no hero, that's for sure—but I wanted to lay all this out for you so you could see that if I had significant PTSD, there's a good chance you might too. I've had the feeling of finally coming home, and it's a wonderful feeling indeed. Now it's your turn to experience that. You deserve to come home too. So

> And a special message from all of us who served in the Vietnam War: "Welcome Home."

please, pick up your phone and make that call. The Semper Fi and America's Fund is waiting to help put you on the road to overcoming PTSD. God bless you, Semper Fi. And a special message from all of us who served in the Vietnam War: "Welcome Home."

27

You're a Mess

While I was at GoDaddy, I began investing in other businesses. In 2012, I created a company called YAM Worldwide to over-see those new endeavors. YAM would become the home of my entrepreneurship operations in the fields of power sports, golf, real estate, marketing, and philanthropy.

The name YAM is an acronym for a saying that we used a lot growing up in Baltimore: "You're a mess." It was more a term of endearment than an insult. It wasn't meant to be derogatory at all. When I thought about a name for this company, I immediately thought, *Yeah, YAM.* No apologies, no regrets.

When we were launching, a mutual friend introduced me to a woman named Anne O'Moore. She was an attorney by trade, but when we met she was ready to make a change. I liked her right away and asked her to become my special counsel. She's tough but fair, and I'm her only client. She helps with family matters, business ventures, and anything else that may come up. It's funny to think that I've gotten to a place in my life where I need a lawyer like Anne, especially for family matters. When I was growing up, the only family matter to resolve was figuring out how I was going to get to the bag with the bread in it before all the bread was gone.

Steve Gabbay was also referred to me by another mutual friend. He joined us as the CFO of our business office around the same time as Anne, just prior to the GoDaddy deal in 2011. I never much liked the term "family office," because I run businesses. Family offices are typically investment vehicles and not places where companies are run—and I wanted to run businesses that made a difference. We operate 100 percent of anything we invest in. Remember—no partners for me.

Steve spent most of his time operating the various businesses I owned then, including my motorcycle dealerships. I bought my first motorcycle dealership in 2008. It was a BMW, Ducati, Triumph, and Vespa dealership in Scottsdale. As you may recall, 2008 was a rough year for the economy. Luxury brands suffered in the wake of the financial crisis, but that made it a good time for me to acquire additional dealerships at bargain prices. I purchased a Honda dealership for a few hundred thousand and a Kawasaki dealership for around the same price. Passion is a wonderful driver for success.

At the time, I loved riding motorcycles, taking many long trips of a thousand miles or more. In fact, you could say I'm very enthusiastic about motorcycles and the people who ride them. There was a time when I thought about riding a motorcycle down the Ho Chi Minh Trail, but as I became

Passion is a wonderful driver for success.

more and more aware of what that would involve, the idea faded out. I still think about that trip every so often, and it makes me smile. You see, despite everything I experienced during the war, Vietnam holds a very special place in my heart. It's such a beautiful country, and its people are very welcoming and kind. I went back to Vietnam once after the war to give a keynote speech at a golf conference. From the moment I landed, I had this indescribable sensation of being home.

Anyway, when it came to my motorcycle trips, I most often rode with my buddy Ian Kenny. He's a piece of work, which meant Ian and I got along great. Unfortunately, he can't ride any longer due to a sleigh accident he had while visiting family in New Hampshire. The sleigh flipped and he landed on a large rock, breaking his back. After that, he just didn't want to ride motorcycles anymore. Since then, I haven't found anyone I really want to take those long trips with. I'd occasionally take a day trip with some friends, perhaps riding from Phoenix to Las Vegas, where we would watch a boxing match, stay overnight, and come home early the next day. But the days of those long, beautiful adventures are sadly over for me.

Throughout the years, I've been involved in seven motorcycle accidents, but as I mentioned earlier, I was able to walk away from all of them. I guess you could say I was lucky. These days, I don't get on bikes much, but I still love them and have a collection of beautiful motorcycles that are mostly all black.

In 2015, I bought Hacienda Harley and renamed it Harley-Davidson of Scottsdale, which is now the largest Harley-Davidson dealership in the world. The 150,000-square-foot site takes the motorcycle retail experience to new heights by including a lingerie boutique, a tattoo and piercing parlor, a barber shop, an arcade, a movie theater, and a wedding chapel. We also have several other multibrand dealerships, all of which operate under the name Go AZ Motorcycles.

As it turned out, motorcycles were a tough way to make a living, so we kept diversifying our portfolio, including opening Spooky Fast Customs, which creates customized motorcycle designs and fabrications. Today, Gina Marra is the CEO of YAM Powersports, our motorsports division, and she does a hell of a job. I never worry about those businesses. She's smart and sharp, and she runs a tight ship.

At the same time that our motorcycle businesses were growing into YAM Powersports, we were adding even more businesses to our larger YAM portfolio. Because I owned the real estate where our Harley-Davidson dealership is in Scottsdale, plus all the property where our offices are located, but didn't yet own any investment real estate, I decided that as soon as the GoDaddy deal closed, that was an area for further expansion.

Again, Steve Gabbay was right by my side in these many pursuits. He was charged with building out our real estate portfolio, hedge fund, and a few other investments, all of which were in their infancy when he came on board. As with Barb, he and I challenge each other in the best ways.

By 2012, I'd bought our first commercial investment property with a focus on outdoor strip malls, neighborhood centers, and some larger power centers. In 2015, I established Sneaky Big Studios, a fifteen-thousand-square-foot world-class production facility offering cutting-edge technology in video and audio production, live broadcasting, and postproduction.

I guess if you were on the outside looking in at that time, you might have thought, *YAM, Bob*. But I really wasn't a mess. I may have had a clearer direction or a more singular focus at other times in my career, but this was my time to test-build things and let anything that couldn't stand go with the wind. I knew in time I would find the perfect business to focus my attention on and sink my teeth into. The fun was in figuring out what that was.

28

This Is How You Play the Game

After building two tech companies, I knew I wanted to do something other than software development and the many other things I did at GoDaddy. I wanted to do something that involved what I'm truly passionate about now. I already owned several successful motorcycle dealerships, yet I still wanted to do more. For some time, I'd been contemplating buying a professional football team or a golf course. I was looking for an investment that tapped into activities I really loved, and football and golf were at the top of that list. They're both legacy investments—or at least that's how owning an NFL franchise was once explained to me. I was seriously thinking about buying one of several NFL teams, figuring that the worse a team had performed over the past few years, the better the deal would be. At the same time, I'd developed a love for golf that had its roots way back in my Parsons Technology days.

I love how the Universe has a way of bringing the right people and opportunities into our lives at exactly the right time. Early one Saturday morning in April 2013, I called Steve and said, "Hey, it's

Bob. I'm up at the Golf Club Scottsdale. [That's right—there was no "of" in the club name.] It's really nice. We should buy it."

I had mentioned wanting to buy a golf club once or twice to Steve but never pursued it until that day. When I told him about this club, he said he hadn't heard it was for sale. I was aware of some talk about the family who owned it putting it on the market, and I suggested Steve and I make a few calls to see what we could find out.

> I love how the Universe has a way of bringing the right people and opportunities into our lives at exactly the right time.

By Monday, we were both fishing for any information we could find. We learned that the club had struggled financially over the years. With a keen eye toward at least breaking even, the absentee owners had created reciprocal arrangements with other clubs and hotels all over the valley, which includes Scottsdale, Phoenix, Paradise Valley, and many other communities. This meant that a member who'd paid to join and continued to pay monthly dues often found themselves on the golf course with a player who'd paid only a daily fee. Worse yet, because of heavy play from outside sources, members sometimes couldn't even play the course. Many members weren't utilizing the clubhouse, carts, or other services either, which meant there was no substantial additional income.

A few years earlier, Crown Golf Properties, a company based in Chicago that owned the course, had tried to sell it to an outside group, but the membership revolted and the deal fell apart. Then, in late March of 2013, Crown sent out a letter to their membership letting them know that they were going to sell and giving the members the right of first refusal to buy the club for $100,000 plus a $3 million line of credit to support its operations for a couple of years. Crown fully anticipated that this would never turn into a purchase.

As Steve and I started to feel things out, I smelled a once-in-a-lifetime opportunity. According to the right-of-first-refusal agreement, the club members had to hold a vote within three months to determine whether they were going to buy or not, and they needed to secure the approval of at least 50 percent of the group on their plan, whatever that plan may be. Interestingly, Crown had decided to send the letter to the membership just as the winter season was ending and many of the members weren't in Arizona. A significant percentage of the members were people who came to Arizona for the winter months and returned to their other homes around April or May to avoid Arizona's scorching-hot summer. Crown's strategy on waiting until this time to make the offer ensured that it would be a herculean task for the members to buy the club, and one that would likely fail. This opened up the opportunity for the owners to auction the club for significantly more money after the deal they made the members expired.

Membership was very divided. The club had opened in 2004 and went through several iterations over the years, including an attempt to make it a men-only club. When the Golf Club Scottsdale first opened, they charged $110,000 for an equity membership. After the recession hit in 2008, they created a new non-equity membership with a lower initiation fee of $25,000. They also dropped the initiation fee for an equity membership to $55,000. This created a class system consisting of two groups of members who likely wouldn't agree with one another on anything. Some joined for the promise of X; others joined for the frugality of Y. It was going to be very hard to get both classes of membership to vote together, regardless of the reason. If the membership was going to buy the club, that would mean making some very serious decisions about what was going to happen with membership dues, assessments, debt assumed by each member, deposits, and equity, among other considerations.

The more exploring we did, the more opportunity I saw. I told Steve we needed to go play the course. Within a week of that first call, we were on the fifth hole, looking out into undisturbed desert as far as the eye could see.

"We're going to buy this place," I said to Steve.

Later that day Steve and I went to lunch with Lyle Anderson, a well-known developer who is responsible for numerous golf and residential properties around the world. He built Desert Mountain Golf Club in Scottsdale and Superstition Mountain Golf and Country Club in Gold Canyon, Arizona, among others. He's one of the groundbreaking visionaries who understood the appeal a golf community has for home buyers. He and a partner owned 235 acres of land adjacent to the Golf Club Scottsdale. He was the logical buyer for the club so he could build a community that came with a golf amenity. As we ate lunch, Lyle began to walk us through why we needed to wait for the members to clear the purchase. He told us that once that had happened, the owners could bring it to market and we could participate in whatever auction they held. It also turned out that Lyle had a long-standing relationship with Crown Golf Properties that allowed for a significant number of memberships to come with the houses he planned to build.

I didn't agree with Lyle's thinking—at least, not as far as what we wanted to do. So, I asked Steve to call Dave Fairman, who was then the president of Crown Golf, and invite him to come see us so we could talk about buying the club. When Dave came to Scottsdale, he told us what was happening as far as the members, their right of first refusal, and the associated process. I offered him $7 million on the spot. He told us the same thing Lyle had—that no one from outside the club membership could buy it yet, and we would have to wait until Crown brought it to market in the back half of the year if we were still interested.

After Dave returned to Chicago, Steve and I talked for days about workarounds. We were trying to figure out a way to get in before the club was put up for sale on the open market. We also felt we weren't being given the whole story. By the end of April, it occurred to me that there was a way to get on with buying the club—but first we would have to join as equity members. Interestingly enough, both Lyle and Dave told us not to join the club. I called Steve and said, "I've got it. We *have* to join. That's how we're going to get this thing. Meet me at the club first thing tomorrow."

Steve then said to me, "But everybody told us not to join the club."

I replied, "Trust me—that's exactly why we have to join. Joining the club is how we're going to get this deal done."

The following morning, Steve and I met with Sharon Carry, the club's membership sales director, and told her we would like to join. Remember, there were two types of memberships. One came with no equity rights; the other came with full equity rights. We wanted to be able to voice our opinions and have a hand in controlling the club's outcome, so I said, quickly and emphatically, "We'll each take the fifty-five-thousand-dollar membership."

Sharon hadn't sold a $55,000 membership in the past five years. We were the only two idiots who'd decided to buy them at that price. She explained that the membership process was very selective. They looked at each potential member's background and vetted them thoroughly through their sophisticated process. I wasn't worried about that.

We filled out the applications on the spot. I listed the various clubs I'd been a member at, past and present. Steve had never been a member of a golf club, so he didn't list any on his application. When Sharon asked about it, he said, "I hope that's okay."

"Oh, that's no problem at all," she replied.

We wrote our checks, and voilà! We became the newest members of the club, with full equity rights and access to all the membership information. The "sophisticated" membership vetting process took less than an hour.

It didn't take long to discover that there was now a newly formed acquisition committee. They were actively having meetings about the sale when we joined. We reached out, introduced ourselves, and offered to help, explaining that we could assist in development plans and such. They completely shut us out. They wouldn't let us be involved in anything that was going on as far as the process was concerned. They were a tight-knit group who had been together for a number of years, and they wanted to control everything. They didn't want anybody else to get into the mix, especially new members.

I spent time getting to know other members, walking around and introducing myself. On occasion, I would meet someone who would divulge that they weren't a member of the club at all. They were members of a reciprocal club or guests at a local hotel. I remember thinking, *Who are these people, and why are they here?* It didn't feel right to me, especially as a paying member.

Time was ticking down on the deadline to formulate a plan and execute a vote. All the while, I was on the outside looking in, a place I wasn't comfortable with and certainly not where I wanted to be. We couldn't get any information from the club's acquisition committee or from Crown Golf because we weren't buyers or committee members.

Eventually, they sent out a plan detailing what they were proposing to do. Their strategy was wildly complicated. It was four or five pages long and impossible to figure out or understand. For the most part, their plan turned everyone's deposit into equity and called for raising dues. Not too many members were going to approve that.

After work each day, Steve and I would head down to the basement in our office, where I have a golf simulator. We would think, talk, explore, and strategize about how we could buy the club, all while we practiced hitting golf balls. I didn't want to get into a bidding war. There had to be a better way in.

This went on for days, until one night I said, "I've got an idea. Let's put together a different plan." I figured that if the committee wouldn't let us be a part of their plan, I would put out a plan of my own. And as full-equity members, Steve and I had access to the addresses and emails of all the other members. A few days later, I set up a website and named it thebobparsonsplan.com. Once that was active, I sent an email to the entire membership that said, "I've got a better idea." On a single page, I laid out what I was proposing.

First, I was willing to guarantee half their deposit—meaning I would refund half of their initiation fee if they decided to leave the club—and I promised that dues wouldn't go up by more than ten percent a year. I was very careful to state that we, the members, would be buying the club. I said I would put up the $100,000 purchase price and guarantee the necessary $3 million line of credit and all liabilities. That way, the members would have the backing required to make the deal with Crown. I disclosed the changes I would make to the operation of the club, the physical improvements I planned for the clubhouse, the new equipment I would purchase, and more—all without any assessment to the membership. To make this work, there had to be a simultaneous transaction once the deal closed: all the members had to do was automatically transfer ownership to me for the exact same price they paid to Crown. At the end of my email, I said I was available to discuss the matter with anyone who had questions. It was simple, clean, and effective.

It definitely got the members talking. Those who had $25,000 memberships were thrilled because someone was willing to put money into the club, and those who had $110,000 memberships thought it was great because they could get a portion of their deposit back if they chose to leave. Our plan couldn't have been more different from the one proposed by the acquisition committee. Best of all, it was easy to understand.

I've always believed in the value of keeping things simple. Simple is better than complicated. Give people what they want and allow them to understand what you're presenting. This is a powerful one-two punch that works every time. If you give people what they want, especially certainty and a clear direction, you will generally prevail. I felt pretty confident that I could get the membership on board with my plan.

Once our letter was out, Dave Fairman called Steve. He was livid. He reminded us that we couldn't buy the club—that only the membership could. He said his letter was very clear about the stipulations.

"I understand, Dave. I think you should read your letter to the membership and Bob's letter more carefully," Steve said. "I'll wait."

Steve could hear Dave rummaging through the pages of both letters. Nowhere did it state that the membership needed to own the club for any period of time before selling it. Usually there's a time restriction, but Crown hadn't put that in their letter. They hadn't even thought about it because they never expected the membership to step up. "Ugh," Steve heard Dave say as he realized what just happened.

There were still a few hurdles to get over, such as which plan the membership would vote on. We knew the membership had to buy the club or we would end up in the bidding war we were hoping to avoid, and there were all sorts of restrictions that we needed to adhere to in order to get my plan through. In the end, the members unanimously chose my plan to vote on. I believe there were around 146 members at the time of the vote. One hundred forty-five of them voted to approve the Bob Parsons plan. One member turned it down. Thankfully, we got the vote, and we did the deal.

Eventually, Crown understood where I was coming from, but they didn't like the outcome one bit. Once I had the vote, we had until mid- to late September to close. There was a lot of information we needed to get from Crown Golf to make a closing decision. They weren't happy with the deal because, in the end, I bought 296 entitled acres in North Scottsdale with water rights, an operating golf course, a driving range, a clubhouse, a maintenance facility, and all the equipment for $100,000. That was it. Sure, I had to guarantee the liabilities, but that was no problem. As I've said, it was the deal of a lifetime.

In early August, I asked Steve how things were going, and he expressed his annoyance with the lack of transparency and cooperation from Crown. I've never been great at hearing "can't" or "won't." "No" is fine, because it's definitive. It's an answer. "Can't" and "won't" are defiance, and that can usually be turned around. One thing I'm certain of is that for every problem, there's a solution. The other person may not like the outcome, but there's always a solution. If you don't find it, you're just not thinking hard enough, or you're looking at the problem the wrong way. But I'll tell you one thing: I love to solve complicated puzzles. I thought about our situation and then told Steve to have Dave come back to Scottsdale to meet with me. Steve, Dave, and I sat down together. It was just the three of us in the room.

"So, Dave, Steve tells me you're making it a little challenging to close this deal," I said matter-of-factly.

"Oh, no, Bob. There's this process we must go through," Dave said, but then I cut him off.

"Let me ask you something: How about I kick in an extra $500,000 if the deal gets done during the month of August. Would that help?" I smiled and didn't say another word. It was worth it to me to grease the skids and get this thing over with.

"Yes, it would," Dave said.

And it was smooth sailing from there.

Even at $600,000 it was a hell of a deal. I knew it, and so did they. But this allowed Dave to walk away with a win, which made a big difference in getting things done. And, ultimately, closing was what I was after.

We signed our deal in September 2013, and the Golf Club Scottsdale officially became Scottsdale National Golf Club, under new ownership. I've made a few amazing deals in my life. Selling Parsons Technology and GoDaddy were two of them. And without a doubt, buying Scottsdale National is the third.

In the end, about thirty members left. I paid them half of their initiation deposits, making them happy. The rest of the members were, for the most part, beyond thrilled. But the day I took over the club, it became exclusive again. There would be no hotel guests coming over to play, and no reciprocation with other clubs. There would be no player on the course who we didn't know. All of that got shut off right away. This was once again *our* club, and the members and their guests were the only people who would be allowed in. Period.

Later, in early December, I began to notice that the members who used the club the most spent the least. They would never eat in the clubhouse, never buy dinner, never bring guests. They didn't like using a cart, or worse, they wouldn't take a cart for eight or nine holes and then would grab one for the back nine without being charged. It was frustrating, and it wasn't the type of member behavior I wanted. To be fair, there were many existing members who met the criteria I envisioned for Scottsdale National, and they wanted the same type of place I did. I was looking to make our club über-exclusive. It would be top of the line—whether rated for the course or the hospitality, food, or beverages, it was going to become the best place to play golf in Arizona, if not the country and, potentially, the world. This was what we set out to accomplish. But to do that, we first had to fix the membership.

It was time to send out another letter to the members. This time, it would have a slightly different tone. The letter started off like any other message: it laid out our plans to redesign and build a new clubhouse and to add other amenities. It was in the final third of the letter where things took an unexpected turn, and it caused quite a stir. Immediately after I hit send, the letter went viral on the internet. Why? The members who used the club the most but supported it the least were my targets. It was a classic carrot and stick. The stick was they weren't going to be allowed to do that anymore. The carrot was if they wanted to leave, I'd give them back all their money. I certainly didn't have to do that; I only had to give them back half, as I did the thirty members who left when I took over the club. Additionally, I was instituting a one-hundred-dollar service fee for every day a player used the course. This included the cost of the cart rental. For those utilizing the course seven days a week, that would become quite an expense. Further, members would be able to play only thirty times a year without bringing a guest, and the rate per guest was now $200.

> Immediately after I hit send, the letter went viral on the internet.

I emailed the letter knowing it would create a ruckus. It was an intentional change to the value proposition. I knew that there were members who wouldn't take to the new rules, even if those rules would create a far better club. I made one thing very clear: if you terminated your membership, regardless of the reason, you could never come back. The rule was blind as to circumstance, so we always encouraged members to think long and hard about their decision before resigning their membership, because there would be no exceptions. A number of years after that rule went into effect and the members who'd stayed had gotten a taste of what the new club now offered, a friend of mine recounted a conversation he'd had with a couple who left when I took ownership. He was telling the couple how great the new Scottsdale National was and asked if they were still members.

"No," the husband quickly responded.

"Why not?" my buddy asked.

"Because my husband is an idiot!" his wife proclaimed.

In the end, we lost around seventy-six members from the time I bought the club until shortly after this letter went out. I was delighted to write them their checks. I even went back to those who'd left three months earlier and paid them the rest of their initiation fees. Again, that wasn't something that was required, but I chose to do it because it was fair. I didn't want anyone to think we'd given them a bait and switch. We hadn't. What I was making crystal clear, though, was that we were going to create a high-end club, and the way the club used to operate would not be the same way it operated in the future.

People were blown away. At the end of the day, I don't have to be liked, but I always want to treat people fairly. If you ask any of the people who left the club whether they were treated unfairly, they'd have to say no. They were all treated with respect and got more than their fair share.

> At the end of the day, I don't have to be liked, but I always want to treat people fairly.

In the beginning, membership stayed steady because while some people left, others joined right after I bought the club. A number of people caught on to my vision and wanted to get in. Of course, after the old members left, I changed the rules again, retracting the refunds for leaving. All I'd wanted was to get rid of those who didn't support my vision for the club going forward. Once I did that, it was all systems go.

Now that I'd bought the club, it was time to set the foundation for what I wanted it to become. I had a lot of work ahead of me to make my dream become a reality. We began to create construction plans for some things I wanted to do and changes I wanted to make. I hadn't spoken to Lyle Anderson since buying the club, but I knew that we needed to have a conversation about his land, which was directly adjacent to the club, and his proposed development, known as Sierra Reserve. The development was supposed to have 235 units, including a hotel. Lyle was ready to go. In fact, he had already started grading the property. He'd put a sales center on the premises too. Lyle's deal was with Crown Golf, and that deal carried over in our purchase agreement.

Lyle had gotten some really good zoning pushed through, which is hard to achieve in the area. He'd been in Scottsdale for many years, and as I've said, he's a great developer. His biggest concern was securing his membership allocation for homeowners. I was up-front with him, saying that I had no intention of honoring the allocation. Lyle reminded me that it was in his contract and I was obligated to make good on it.

The reality was, I wanted Lyle's land a lot more than I wanted those members. I certainly didn't want a bunch of homes there, and I didn't want to go through years of listening to construction noise while Lyle was building them. I wanted to avoid all that by just buying the land. It was the perfect place to build a second golf course and an outstanding clubhouse, and that was my priority.

Lyle and his business partner asked to have a meeting with me. They'd been speaking with Steve, who was keeping me well informed. I'm very attentive to the details of any deal I get involved in, even if I'm not managing the day-to-day conversations. To think otherwise would be a mistake—and a lot of people have made that mistake, including Lyle and his partner. They figured they would set up a meeting with me and get everything worked out. I could see what they were trying to do and knew exactly how to handle the situation.

When they came into my office, Steve and I moved into our usual good cop, bad cop mode. I like being the bad cop. This time, however, Steve was the moderately bad cop and I came in as the *really* bad cop.

"You guys think I'm stupid?" I asked Lyle and his partner matter-of-factly.

"We don't think you're stupid," Lyle said.

I slammed my hands down on the table, leaned in, and said, "I judge you by your actions!"

The meeting went downhill pretty fast from there. Steve walked the two men out of my office and sent them on their way. Within minutes, he received a call from Lyle saying that he never wanted to meet with me again.

"I told you," Steve said. "You thought I wasn't keeping him informed, but you were wrong."

From that point on, it was like a wrestling match. We played with what their memberships would look like, and Lyle's employees continued grading the property. Oftentimes, one of his employees would get on his bulldozer and grade while I was on the golf course. I'd hear the loud beeps every time he put the damn thing in reverse. Somehow Lyle had a sixth sense about when I was playing the hole next to his land, and of course, that's exactly when the bulldozer was always in reverse, "BEEP . . . BEEP . . . BEEP." For the next year, we slowly tried to find a solution and make an agreement to buy Lyle's 235 acres.

Once again, Steve and I pored over the contracts, where we discovered that Lyle's memberships were defined as "reserve memberships." We could set the rules for those memberships, so we did. We decided that reserve memberships would essentially be nighttime memberships. As such, those memberships could only play golf from thirty minutes after sundown to thirty minutes before sun-up. That sort of membership might be okay when there's a full moon—as long as it's a really bright one—but otherwise . . . well, you get it.

From our perspective, nighttime memberships were the thing that got the deal done.

By the summer of 2014, we had an agreement, one in which no one thought they'd gotten the better of the others. We all felt great about getting it done, even though Lyle got less than he wanted and I paid more than I'd hoped to. Lyle and I actually became friends after that. We closed in the fall of that same year. At the time, Lyle wasn't a member of Scottsdale National, so I asked him and his wife, Missy, to become members. And they did.

Launching Parsons Xtreme Golf

While we were deep in negotiations with Lyle, I began to develop an idea for another company, one that was just as important to me as buying the golf course. I wanted to start my own golf club company. I had never thought about a golf club company until after I purchased Scottsdale National. Whenever I would mention this idea, people would ask if I had lost my mind. There have been many times in my life when people have grossly underestimated me. You know what? It's an enviable position to be in, because I never try to persuade them otherwise. I just plan and scheme about how I'm going to make whatever I'm doing work, and when it does, I completely surprise them. I did it with Parsons Technology, GoDaddy, and Scottsdale National, and I was hoping I could do it with golf clubs too. Many people I greatly respected warned me not to do it. They pointed out it was a small mature industry with a number of well entrenched competitors.

**"You'll never succeed,"
they all said.**

"You'll never succeed," they all said.

Even the team at KKR, who'd played a key role in the GoDaddy deal, warned me. They'd gotten involved in golf and lost a stack of cash. Of course, they'd tried to do business the way everyone else was doing it, which made no sense. In the Marine Corps, they teach you not to run right into a machine gun. Instead, you go around it and attack from a position where you stand a much better chance of not getting shot. You have to be different in a good way—a way that resonates. I don't think this. I *know* it.

I have friends who are big gamblers. They can go to Vegas and drop hundreds of thousands of dollars in a night and not think twice about it. I also have friends who buy exotic cars or art, curating a collection worth millions. Me? I bought golf clubs. It wasn't until I first moved to Scottsdale and joined Whisper Rock Golf Club that I really began working on my game. There were guys there who would play high-stakes rounds. When I started playing with them, and there were thousands of dollars on the line, I started to care about my game a little more—okay, a lot more. I was like a check waiting to be cashed, an easy target for sure.

I was an aspiring golfer who was a middle-of-the-road player at best. I knew more about the golf swing than most people, but executing it was my issue. I was always looking for an edge, anything to help me improve, so I would always look at equipment. I'd noticed that sometimes the right equipment would make an evident difference in how I played. I often had custom fittings where experts would re-shaft and do this and that to my clubs. The bill would be thousands of dollars. They definitely loved me. Curious, I asked my executive assistant Francisca to look at my receipts for all the golf clubs I'd bought in the year before I started my golf club company. She stopped tallying at $300,000. Whenever there would be a new club that piqued my interest, I'd buy it and then have different shafts put in and so on. I spent a lot of time and money pursuing the best equipment in golf.

I noticed that most of the products I was buying didn't live up to the hype around them. They overpromised and underdelivered. Through mutual friends, I met Mike Nicolette, a former PGA Tour winner (at Bay Hill) and one of the chief designers at Ping, when we were at Whisper Rock one day. I asked him why clubs weren't getting any better. He told me that the designers did the best they could, but their creativity was limited by having to hit specific price points and meet strict deadlines for each design.

I couldn't stop thinking about what he'd said.

Unlike most golfers, I'd studied aerodynamics. I also knew something about ballistics and different metals. Let's just say I knew enough to be dangerous but not enough to accomplish anything on my own. There was a sector of the market that just wasn't being served, and that was people who had the income to stroke a check for something that would truly make a difference in their game. They're the people who will never ask what something costs. Now, granted, that's the smallest segment of the market, but for a start-up like us it was huge, because it was a segment that wasn't being served at all. That's when it occurred to me that there was an opportunity to change the game altogether.

What if we could make golf clubs that were different?

What if we could create clubs that *actually* improved your game?

I called Mike and asked him to meet me in my office. At that meeting, I posed the following question: "If you had as much time as you wanted to design clubs, and you also had as much money as you needed to spend on them—I'm talking about an unlimited budget—could you create clubs that were significantly better?"

"I'd like to think I could," he said.

I explained that I was thinking about starting a company that would do just that.

At first Mike tried to dissuade me from getting into the equipment business, but then his curiosity and creativity must have gotten ahold of him. "How much time would we have to do this?" he asked.

"At the moment, I can carry the company for at least twenty years. You can spend whatever the hell you want to spend and take all the time you need. Would you like to do that?"

"I'd love it," he said.

"Well, then, I'm going to start the company, and I want you to design the clubs for us," I said. I thought it was a done deal.

Not so fast.

He didn't want to leave Ping. They had been very good to him, and he felt a sense of loyalty to the company. I had to respect his position, so I told him that if he changed his mind, he should call me. With that, I shook his hand and said goodbye. After he left, I turned to Steve Gabbay and said, "I'll hear from him in three months."

It didn't take that long.

One month later, he called and said, "I want to do it. And I have three others who want to join me."

Whoa. I wasn't looking to hire a whole company. Even so, in September 2013, I hired Mike and his fellow Ping designer Brad Schweigert to join me in starting Parsons Xtreme Golf, aka PXG. Mike, Brad, and I shared a passion for the greatest game ever played and an equal obsession with club technology. Their task was to develop the finest golf equipment on the planet. At their suggestion, I also hired their patent attorney and a young engineer.

Ping was pissed.

Three of them had noncompete agreements, which meant they couldn't work in the business for a year. Arizona is one of the few states that enforces noncompete clauses, unless you're an attorney (of course!). We honored that agreement for a full year, doing only organizational stuff in that time, and I gave each of them a salary. I had them study 3D printing, how to make golf balls, and other non-club-related tasks. That time worked out well for us. By the end of the one-year term, they knew this stuff inside and out, and they were ready to get down to business.

The success of any business depends upon the leader. That person must be obsessed with the quality of their product. You'd better believe that's me to the core. PXG was born out of my desire to

The success of any business depends upon the leader. That person must be obsessed with the quality of their product.

make the world's best golf equipment. I wanted what most golfers dream about: a sexy set of irons that look like blades but perform like cavity backs. They had to launch higher, go farther, feel softer, and have a sweet spot the size of Texas. I told Mike and Brad that PXG clubs had to feel like butter, and the difference had to be noticeable. I wanted it all and was willing to pay for it. I also believed there were plenty of others who would be willing to pay for it too.

With no cost or time constraints, the team began the long process of researching various alloys, exploring new technologies, and identifying the unique properties that would make PXG clubs unlike any others.

I tried every incarnation they came up with.

I hit one club that went like hell and felt like shit. They made a 3 wood that would go forever, but the second time I hit it, the club collapsed. Apparently, we'd made the only disposable 3 wood in the game. There's not a big market for that.

Then one day we decided to try a hollow head. I said, "What if you had a filler in it, something that would soften everything and bring it all together?"

So, they experimented. They found a polymer and put it inside. "Bob, we've had a breakthrough," they said with great excitement.

And what a breakthrough it was. Nobody had ever done anything quite like that before. By using the polymer filler and the right pressure, we were able to make the face of the club much thinner, which gave it more of a trampoline effect. The filler also made the club feel soft. Ultimately, we had our initial set of clubs designed within six months. And what I realized was that we hadn't made clubs for a specific gender; we'd made them for golfers. No one had ever done that before. When they debuted, nobody could believe how good they were.

Our clubs were, however, also a little pricey. I did that for a reason: if you want to go into an established market where everybody is doing business the same way, don't do business the way they're doing it, because you'll get clobbered. They know how to do business that way, and they already have all the right resources, contacts, and customers. As I mentioned earlier, if you want to stand out, you've got to do something different. I priced my clubs very high. My quest for perfection was expensive, but I had put enough money into the development of the clubs to justify the cost. Unlike most irons, which are typically priced at $1,000 or less for an eight-piece set with steel shafts, our clubs started at $325 per iron. We were also offering $700 drivers and $500 fairway woods.

If you want to stand out, you've got to do something different.

Those prices got everybody's attention. People, especially other manufacturers, thought I was nuts. They didn't think anyone would pay what we were asking for our clubs. They were certain we'd be out of business in no time. Not so fast, fellas—I had people standing in line to buy them from me. And the best part? They had to buy the clubs directly from us. They weren't available in the big box stores. You couldn't find them in Dick's Sporting Goods, the PGA Tour Superstore, or any of the other big retailers. We sold direct to the consumer. The perception was that they must be good if we were charging so much money. And when our customers hit those clubs for the first time, *Ka-boom, baby!* They felt and saw a huge difference. It blew them away. Whenever someone asked how anyone would know that our clubs were better, I'd always say, "The moment they hit them, they'll know." And I was right.

We didn't attend any of the big golf shows either. Whenever the media asked if we were going to be at the PGA merchandise show in Orlando, I would tell them no, because we were in a different business. We were a luxury business. Every time I said that, they reported it. *Ka-boom!* First, they couldn't believe how good the clubs were, and then they had to admit that our clubs were more forgiving, more accurate, better looking, and superior in every sense of the word. I also had the flexibility to move my pricing whenever and however I chose.

My son, Sean, once taught me something about pricing. He said, "Dad, remember, you can shear a sheep many times, but you can only skin it once." That was stellar advice, which I loved. That's always on my mind, and I got it from him. Eventually, I started pricing the clubs below our top competitors—not by much, but by enough to get everyone's attention. And because we sold direct to the consumer, our margins were significantly higher than the competition's. Their sales are reported by all the resellers, which means I can track them, but they have no way of knowing our sales. About 5 percent of the business we do gets reported. They have no idea how much volume we move. PXG is a Trojan horse. It's a beautiful thing. Most significant golf companies, with the exception of Ping, are either public companies or on their way to becoming public, so they're stressed for sales, results, and revenue. They have to put numbers on the board, and to do that they've got to sell to the widest part of the market. They can't do the stuff we do when it comes to marketing and sales. They're solely focused on turning a profit, which precludes a long-term strategy. I don't focus on that. I just focus on getting better, improving execution, and finding new and innovative ways to get where I want us to be. Like I said, as you think, so shall you be. I just keep looking forward—never backward.

In the beginning, before we launched our first generation of clubs, nobody paid much attention to us. True Temper Sports, one of the larger shaft companies, wouldn't do business with us because their biggest customer was Ping. It's not that they had a better product than other companies as much as they had a better selection. However, after we released our first clubs and started to have some success, True Temper came around, and today we're one of their best customers.

As I write this, PXG has branched out into golf apparel and accessories to rival the best of our competitors' products. Our golf balls perform right with the market leader but for less money. Today, a significant number of pros play with our clubs.

I'm personally involved in the creation of all our ads. Yes, that's my voice you hear in most of our commercials. They're direct and to the point. Why? Because nobody makes golf clubs the way we do, period. *Ka-boom, baby!*

> Whatever we do, we consistently do the best.

We've opened a network of retail stores around the country, where of course we sell only our own products. Renee has done a wonderful job creating our apparel line and overseeing our retail operation. Even our clothing is different from everyone else's. We're all about using the highest-quality materials. We don't use buttons; instead our shirts all use snaps. Snaps are much easier, and they work much better than buttons.

We pay top dollar for those, but it's worth it. We use only the finest fabrics from top-shelf merchants. Finally, our design team is second to none. All our designs are original and unique to our brand. Renee has exquisite taste, taking a new angle on golf wear, making it as fashionable as any designer streetwear. She has even created après golf attire—clothes so stylish that you can wear them from the course to dinner. Renee has also designed an outstanding line of apparel for females. None of our competitors offer this. Whatever we do, we consistently do the best.

One other thing I'm extremely proud of is that all our products have a military bent. Our top-of-the-line clubs today are called 0311s—that's a Marine Corps number for an infantry rifleman. And we also extend a special welcome to consumers we call PXG Heroes. These are current or former military, police, law enforcement, firefighters, and EMTs. We give discounts to all these customers—always have, and always will. I don't do it for business. I do it for the men and women who serve our country, who are the first responders in a crisis. They deserve to be honored and appreciated, and this is our way of showing respect and saying thanks for their service.

30

Build It and They Will Come

By the time we launched our first generation of golf clubs, we'd closed on Lyle's land adjacent to Scottsdale National and some other nearby acreage we bought in small parcels from different landowners. We also acquired Lyle's sales trailers and turned them into PXG's first offices. Altogether, I was sitting on a little more than seven hundred acres of prime real estate in North Scottsdale. There was only one piece of real estate I overpaid for, a five-acre plot that now sits in the middle of hole 15 on the new course. I needed that land, and the owners knew it. Steve had the husband and wife who held the title to the property in his office and was doing everything he could to close the deal. They didn't want to sell—or they did, but they understood that we needed what they had. They were playing hardball, and when I walked into Steve's office to meet them, I could see they weren't going to budge. Five minutes later, I'd made them a once-in-a-lifetime offer, and we came to an understanding. Everyone got what they wanted and walked away happy that day.

Now that I had all that land, there were about three hundred acres I needed to secure entitlements and water rights for. There was also a power line that was supposed to go through the property that had to be moved. We acquired the land in 2014, and by the summer of 2015 we had our conditional-use permit to build out the remainder of Scottsdale National, which included the existing 18-hole golf course, a new 18-hole course, a new 9-hole par 3 course, several villas for members and their guests, a new clubhouse, and a host of other parts and pieces. In early July, at the last city council meeting prior to their late summer break, our development plans were approved. We started construction on the new golf course in August of 2015.

We used Jackson Kahn Design, a relatively new firm, to build the course. Tim Jackson and David Kahn were young and hungry. David's father, Stan, was a member of Whisper Rock, where I was also still a member. Stan approached me at the club to tell me about his son's firm.

"Have him send me an email," I politely said.

David reached out right away. I hired his team to do some remodeling work on the existing course, which I renamed the Mine Shaft Course. Jackson Kahn had worked for Tom Fazio as lead designers on several courses, so they knew what they were doing, but I still had some hesitation about handing the reins to them. Everything they'd done up until now was under someone else's name. They hadn't flown their own flag, so it was a risk, albeit a small one.

They started working through design ideas for the new eighteen-hole course and the par 3. They went through several iterations, which always led us to the million-dollar question: Should we hire them or not?

One of the challenges Tim and David had to contend with was my need to see things up close. I don't do well with renderings or one-dimensional presentations. I have to see whatever I'm working on in full. I tend to make everyone nervous when something is being built for me because I'm very particular.

At one point, Steve and I met with Bill Coore of Coore and Crenshaw. They're probably one of the top three golf course architects in the world, if not the best. Bill happened to live in Scottsdale, so when it was time to do that remodeling work, and again when we acquired the new land, I spoke with him, but he didn't want to design the new course. He doesn't like to move a lot of earth. He gets a piece of land and builds his courses right into it. Lyle had already graded a lot of the property we acquired from him, so there were no elevation changes or vegetation, just lot pad after lot pad. When Bill asked who else we were talking to about building the course, I mentioned Jackson Kahn and Tom Weiskopf, and that we were also planning on calling The Player Group too. I told Bill I liked the guys from Jackson Kahn a lot but I was concerned that they were young and green and had never designed their own course before.

Bill paused for a moment, took a breath, and said, "Mr. Parsons, I hadn't done it before until someone gave me a chance."

It was like a switch got turned on for me. I remembered saying the same thing many years ago when I couldn't get hired for an accounting job. Bill was totally right. I told Steve to cancel all our meetings with the other design firms and to call Jackson Kahn to tell them they'd gotten the job.

No one else could have done what they ended up doing. Their design was completely unique, which was exactly the mandate I gave. The new 18-hole golf course is not the typical desert course because it's continuous grass. It's more like a links course. You can play it in your bare feet. In contrast, the Mine Shaft Course is exactly what a desert course should look and play like.

Unlike any other course in the world, our new course has six par 3s, par 4s, and par 5s, and no two holes with the same par back-to-back. I wanted eighteen exclusive, signature holes, not a few signature holes scattered across the eighteen.

When Tim and Dave came to me with their designs, I had them line up all the par 3s, 4s, and 5s next to each other so I could make sure they didn't look alike. Every one of them had to have something unique or different compared to the others. I had them walk me through each hole until we had the perfect 18-hole course. Once I approved the plan, it was a go. I rarely went to see how things were progressing. Steve tried to get me out there, but I wasn't interested. I had PXG and other businesses to run, and that's where I put my attention. What I knew for sure was that if they just built the course I signed off on, everything would be swell. They wound up having to change a few things along the way, but it only made for a better course. In the end, we moved over a million cubic yards of earth to create one of the most beautiful and dramatic golf courses anywhere in the world. And it was all done in a short period of time so we could meet our schedule and timeline.

When I finally saw the finished course, I was blown away. We started to build it on August 1, 2015, and I played my first round of golf on the new course in September of 2016. I gave the new course a very understated name. I named it "The Other Course." This name belies the true nature of the course, which is absolutely magnificent. I named our 9-hole par 3 course "The Bad Little Nine." This course is a collection of the most difficult, unfair, par 3 9 holes Jackson Kahn could conjure up. You would think because of the difficult and unfair nature of this little course that golfers wouldn't play it. Exactly the opposite is true.

It was an exciting time for sure. We were so busy that I never had a moment to look back or just savor what we were doing. Like always, I was looking forward. I've been that way forever. Instead of asking what we could have done yesterday, I ask what we're doing tomorrow. How are we getting better? There's always room for improvement.

Scottsdale National has indeed become a legacy property. We have a great group of members, and we keep adding ten to fourteen highly selective new ones a year. Nowadays, it's expensive to join the club. That up-front money is no longer a deposit or equity. It's access. And this is what our members want: exclusivity, privacy, and to play one of the best damn golf courses available. I'm happy to provide that opportunity.

What a Long, Strange Trip

When a man and a woman get married, the man is usually hoping his new wife won't change, while the woman is almost always hoping her new husband will. Typically, they're both disappointed in this regard. In my marriage to Renee, I did change—eventually. Renee would tell you that I was a guy who had a lot of ups and downs in my mood. She was never really sure what the mood of the day was going to be. I know that must have been very challenging for her. Renee is such a positive person, with an inherently good outlook on life. She's even-keeled and has a very sunny disposition. Those are just a few of the reasons I married her. Despite our challenges—or, I should say, *my* challenges—Renee has stuck by me. I wasn't the easiest man to live with. My temper was often irrational and usually caught Renee off guard. For a long time, it was difficult for her to navigate.

While there were signs of my PTSD when we were dating, I don't think either of us really understood what it was, or the depth of it, the way we do now. I'm sure Renee didn't understand that she'd married a man with PTSD. How could she? She probably just thought I was an idiot sometimes. An idiot who loves her to pieces. And she loves me. I don't know why, but she does. We were married for nine years before I realized that my PTSD was impacting our relationship and figured out how to correct it. What my wife sees in me I'll never know, but like my buddies say, "I really outkicked my coverage here." She hung in with me during my worst days. God bless her for that.

> **What my wife sees in me I'll never know, but like my buddies say, "I really outkicked my coverage here." She hung in with me during my worst days. God bless her for that.**

There were countless moments throughout my life after the war when I had outbursts that no one saw coming, including me. As I've told you, I sometimes found myself uncontrollably sobbing. I retreated from those I loved the most. I relived the horrors of war. Carrying that hurt and pain had a profound impact on me and everyone and everything around me. Talking about this with my wife was off the table. And for her, approaching me about it was too. She was never sure what would set me off. That led to a period of no communication, which isn't healthy for any relationship. Sometimes we joke that she now has PTSD as a result of my PTSD. But it isn't really funny, because sadly, I think it's true. I think a lot of spouses endure that fallout, and that's a casualty I never expected to encounter. I had to find a way to do better and be better in our marriage. She deserved better—much better. I didn't want to let her down. Of course, I wanted all of that for myself too.

It wasn't until 2018 that I approached Renee with an idea. You see, I'd read a book that got me thinking—*How to Change Your Mind* by Michael Pollan—and it was a game changer for me. I read that the use of plant-based therapies is a natural complement to the more typical psychotherapeutic approaches to mental health in our culture. Plants were used historically in indigenous and tribal settings, predating ancient Greece. They've always played a role in the psyche, although their use was often in a religious context. Nevertheless, that's how those things were handled for numerous cultures over great spans of time. In many ways, we've gone through a very damaging interruption in the evolution of the treatment of mental health and the optimization of the psyche in the West due to the restriction of these plants and compounds over the last fifty-plus years.

I was immensely interested and intrigued by the possible impact that plant-based psychedelic therapies could have on me. Even so, I hadn't yet shared any of this with Renee. I was still doing the Cereset treatments, but I was looking for something that might have a greater and more lasting impact. As luck would have it, in January 2018, we were at our home on the Big Island in Hawaii. Some friends of ours were also there, so we invited them over for dinner. During the cocktail hour, Renee and the others were chatting, and one of the women in the group began sharing an incredible experience she had just gone through using psyche-delic plant medicines. Her experience sounded very positive, and she said it really helped her. Renee immediately noticed that she seemed more relaxed, present, and open. She had gone through some difficult challenges in her life, which had created a pretty tough exterior shell, but that all seemed to have gone away. Renee didn't share her conversation with me until months later. At the time, people weren't talking as openly about psychedelics as treat-ments for mental health as they do today. Even the terminology she used to describe her experience was foreign. So Renee didn't ask a lot of questions, and she chose to respect the woman's confi-dentiality and privacy by keeping it to herself.

Two or three months later, I told Renee I had recently read *How to Change Your Mind* and wanted to try plant-based psychedelic therapy. I asked her to help me find someone I could work with.

She was immediately on board. Her primary concern was that I was safe if I chose to experiment with psychedelics. Unbeknownst to me, she knew exactly who to call. Within two weeks, she had names and numbers—yet another reason I love that woman.

Renee found someone she felt comfortable with through another mutual friend. I also spoke to this person in advance. I knew I would need to feel completely relaxed with my decision if I were to reap the greatest benefits. Since psychedelic therapy wasn't exactly legal, this particular person flew under the radar. The only way to connect was through word of mouth. Even with my due diligence, I had some hesitation going in, but I had to weigh my symptoms against my fear. If I could feel better and be better, it would be worth it.

By July, we were set to meet in a private location where my psychedelic treatment would take place over the course of four days. It was comforting to get to know the guides a little before embarking on this journey. The more we talked, the better I felt about what was to come. I could feel myself connecting to them in a very surprising way. I suppose that's part of the process and the intention they set coming into these situations.

The first day, I took ayahuasca. It's not the tastiest stuff I've ever ingested. One thing is for sure—I'd never think about ordering it with dinner. Ayahuasca is used by numerous indigenous tribes throughout the Amazon for medicinal and ritualistic purposes, and scientists, physicians, and people like me are interested in its spiritual, psychological, and medicinal benefits. Ayahuasca is a mixture of chacruna leaves, caapi vine, and a bunch of supplemental plants. About half an hour after it's ingested, its psychedelic effects begin, and they can last for roughly six hours. I was warned that I might feel stressed at first and that I could have an increased heart rate, bouts of nausea, and possible hallucinations. I was also warned that vomiting and occasional diarrhea, known as the "purge," is quite common. In fact, some shamans believe that's an essential part of the experience. My guides said I might see vibrant light, which can sometimes turn into images. The impact can vary and can be both intense and healing. As for me? Well, I didn't hallucinate, except for the expected colors and lights that seemed to be jumping around on the ceiling, and I also didn't purge. I did a lot of talking with my guides and revisited a number of unpleasant memories from my childhood and the war.

On the second day, one of the guides made a pot of magic mushroom tea. While the pot held three cups' worth, I was told I would need only one cup, as it was very strong. Ha! I drank all three cups, and then (I'm not joking here) ate the tea bags too. When I finished the last tea bag, I asked, "Is that all you have?"

"That is all I've got," one of my guides said, smiling.

Magic mushrooms contain psilocybin, a psychedelic drug that has shown tremendous potential as a treatment for depression and PTSD. While the use of psilocybin is still illegal in most American states, Oregon and Colorado passed laws in January of 2023 that legalized its use as a treatment for mental health disorders, including PTSD, anxiety, and depression.

> Magic mushrooms contain psilocybin, a psychedelic drug that has shown tremendous potential as a treatment for depression and PTSD.

When consumed, psilocybin quickly metabolizes into a compound called psilocin, which binds to and activates a subset of neuronal receptors belonging to the 5-HT family. These receptors are normally activated by serotonin, which affects mood and emotional state and is the primary target of selective serotonin reuptake inhibitors, or SSRIs. It has a similar effect as taking an antidepressant. However, the use of psilocybin may actually facilitate a remodeling of neuronal circuits after a single dose—meaning that it just might fix what is broken.

Again, I didn't hallucinate, but for sure I was righteously buzzed. I talked for hours about my various experiences. There were a lot of tears. By the end, there was also a sense of relief and exhaustion.

We took the third day off. Renee and I played nine holes of golf. The feeling I had that day is hard to describe. It was incredible, like a waking dream. I could feel the trees and bushes being alive and breathing. I was glad to be with them, and they were welcoming me to the golf course as if it were my first time there. It felt like the golf course greens were talking to me, saying, "Hit it here, Bobby." I would hit the putt exactly where I was told, and the ball dropped right into the cup. I never putted better! Maybe the mushrooms lasted a little longer than I thought . . .

On the fourth day, I was treated with lysergic acid diethylamide (LSD), repeated doses of which are reported to be effective over time in reducing symptoms of stress-related anxiety and depression. LSD was discovered in 1938 by Swiss chemist Albert Hofmann, who synthesized it while in search of a method to reduce postpartum hemorrhaging. After accidentally ingesting a small dose, he became the first person in history to experience its effects. By the end of the 1940s, there was a lot of interest in LSD and its potential use as a therapeutic agent in psychiatry. In the 1950s, LSD was marketed in the United States and Europe as Delysid. The US Army and the CIA experimented with LSD as a truth serum and a potential incapacitating agent, although it turned out to be neither. LSD was banned in 1967, mostly due to its recreational use.

LSD is classified as a "classical hallucinogen," which is a fancy name for psychedelics. Along with psilocybin and dimethyltryptamine (DMT), LSD has a similar chemical structure to those found in indolamines, a group of neurotransmitters that includes serotonin. LSD causes an alteration in perception that has led some cultures to use it as an entheogen, a substance used to create an altered state of consciousness for spiritual or religious purposes. LSD is one of the most potent classical hallucinogens available. Its usual effects include distortions in one's sense of identity, alterations in depth and time perception, visual hallucinations, a sense of euphoria or utter certainty, delusions, and distorted spatial perceptions of objects, movements, colors, sounds, textures, and body image. My guides shared all the potential risks with me and told me what I could expect. As a recreational drug, LSD doesn't provoke the physical dependence or withdrawal symptoms commonly associated with hard drugs and opioids. In fact, it exhibits very low physiological toxicity, even at high doses. It's considered to be one of the safest psychoactive substances, although it remains one of the most stigmatized and legally restricted.

One's response to LSD depends on several variables, including dose, thoughts, mood, and expectations. Since it was being administered in a controlled environment by people I had come to trust and had now bonded with, I felt completely safe and secure about going all in.

Taking LSD was different from taking ayahuasca and mushrooms. It seemed to draw more out of me. Like the other psychedelics, I didn't hallucinate per se; I did see colored lights and felt buzzed, and again, we talked for hours about experiences that I thought might have been causing my PTSD. Once more, memories from growing up and from Vietnam dominated my thoughts. I was incredibly open and vulnerable—and, in the end, I was relieved to get it all off my

> I had gone into this experience believing my PTSD was all about the war; I came out of it understanding that that was merely a large piece of a very complex puzzle.

chest. I had gone into this experience believing my PTSD was all about the war; I came out of it understanding that that was merely a large piece of a very complex puzzle. I wasn't just a wounded warrior. I was also a wounded child. To be certain, it was a hell of a lot harder for me to talk about my childhood than about my time in Vietnam. I loved my parents. I never wanted to disparage their memories. But by going back and revisiting some of those experiences, I was finally able to let go of some anger and resentment I hadn't known I was still holding on to—and, of course, to write about it in this book.

Before undergoing this treatment, I had done a lot of work to forgive my parents and to understand them better so I could deal with my experiences. As I said back in the preface, I attended weekend workshops that explored my inner child and went through years of therapy. In a way, I think it was the challenges of my childhood that made it a little easier for me to enlist in the United States Marine Corps, and to succeed there. I was already hardened because of my upbringing and the lack of a loving, nurturing environment. No matter how much work I've done, those memories will always linger. How I process them has changed, though.

After those four days of psychedelic therapy, as crazy as it may sound, I was a different man. I was like I'd been before the war and how I would have been if I'd had a better childhood. It was like meeting up with an old friend I hadn't seen for many years. We picked up right where we'd left off. And man, that felt good. I was happier, more content, and calmer about things.

> No matter how much work I've done, those memories will always linger. How I process them has changed, though.

To be clear, happy isn't the same as joyful. Joy can only be felt in the moment. It's more euphoric. Happy is on the better side of content. What does that mean? It means accepting things and people as they are and not expecting them to be the way we want them to be. You don't have to like each and every moment, but it's important to remember that they're just windows of time. Change continues to move you toward where you want or need to be, even if you don't realize it in the moment. What I learned is that when you're happy, you're content and you enjoy your surroundings and your relationships, or at least most of them.

I'm a happier guy now. I'm blessed to have such good people in my life. Family, friends, and friends who feel like family. My wife. My children and grandchildren. Longtime employees who are with me day in and day out, including Francisca, who's been my personal assistant for more than twenty–one years; Juan, my driver; and countless others who have all noticed a huge change in me. If I'm not happy, it's because I'm somehow fucking something up. So I choose to be happy always. I'll admit to an occasional flare-up that hearkens back to the old me, but those are much less frequent, and they usually end with my putting my arms around the other person and apologizing. Believe me, if I were an asshole all the time, everyone would have left me by now. People stay, for whatever reason, so I guess I'm somehow doing all right.

After my psychedelic therapy session, people who knew me simply couldn't believe the change. They were saying things like "You seem so happy," "He stopped losing his temper," and "He's so complimentary." My son Sean told his wife, "I'm afraid Dad found out that he's going to die soon, because he keeps calling and he's never treated me that nicely." I had to laugh, but he was right. To set his mind at ease, I explained the psychedelic treatment I had gone through, and he was happy for me. Sean and I grew closer than ever. He finally got the father he always should have had, and I was the father I always should have been. This is also true for my two daughters, Marianne and Jessica. What a joy it is to have all of them in my life.

A few weeks later, I reached out to Sean and said, "You know what, son? I want to just be in your life. No more telling you what to do. No more judging what you do. You do what you do. If you want to talk to me for advice or you need help or anything, I'll be here. I just want to be in your life."

"Dad, I want to be in your life too," he said.

"Son, it's nice that we got to this point." I felt a sense of relief and comfort all at the same time.

Then Sean said something to me I'll never forget: "Dad, you may not realize it, but I've always been here."

So, in many ways, it was on me. I was the catalyst that kept us apart. These days, we're like two best buddies. We get together most Tuesdays, something his wife tells me he looks forward to almost as much as I do. Occasionally, Sean will play golf with me, but one of the best days of golf I ever had was when he caddied for me in the Cedar Rapids amateur golf tournament back in 1990. I shot a 71, the best round I'd ever played. And having Sean as my caddie was the reason. I will never forget that.

And I'll never forget a road trip I took with my daughter Marianne when she was in her late teens. She was going to work at a summer camp in Pennsylvania, which was about a thousand miles from where we were living in Cedar Rapids. She asked if I would drive with her. Of course I said I would. Marianne warned

If you're contemplating psychedelic therapy, it's *very important* that you not do it on your own. Should you pursue this therapy to help heal PTSD, anxiety, or depression, you must do it under the care of a responsible and experienced guide or therapist in case you have a bad trip—which is rare, but it can happen.

me that it was a straight shot on I-70, and I-70 is one long road. It wasn't scenic at all. However, it gave us quality time together, and we spent the bulk of the drive talking and getting to know a little more about each other. I loved every minute of that trip with Marianne, and I cherish it to this day.

Since this wonderful healing experience, I've been advocating for the legalization of psychedelics. I've been doing this by talking openly about my experience and donating to organizations that are actively involved in legalizing their therapeutic use.

If you're contemplating psychedelic therapy, it's *very important* that you not do it on your own. Should you pursue this therapy to help heal PTSD, anxiety, or depression, you must do it under the care of a responsible and experienced guide or therapist in case you have a bad trip—which is rare, but it can happen. Also, doing this treatment on your own won't result in the outcome you're seeking. Remember this golden rule: The therapy does the healing. The psychedelics make it possible.

32

To Whom Much Is Given,
Much Is Expected

In 2019, I received one of the greatest honors I could possibly imagine: I was given the Marine for Life Award. When fellow Marine Jake Wood called me and asked if I would accept the award, it took me a moment to realize what he was talking about. And then I couldn't believe it. I said, "Absolutely I would." After we hung up, I got to thinking about it and thought, *You know, I've got so many knucklehead friends. My staff better call back and make sure this is real.*

Well, it was. I was incredibly humbled by the honor and especially grateful to the committee who chose me, which included Zach Iscol, Gerry Byrne, and Jake Wood. I was thrilled to accept the award—not for myself but rather on behalf of my brothers and sisters who served in the Vietnam War.

As I became more successful over the years, I realized that money could be a very powerful tool. Having nothing as a kid and never wanting to ask anyone for help gave me an intimate understanding of that. My childhood experiences also made me aware of how important it is to look outside myself and help others in need. Renee and I both believe there is huge responsibility that comes with great success.

In 2008, Renee took a hiatus from work because her stepdad was dying of cancer. At the time, she was working for Starwood Hotels and Resorts. When she decided to go back to work, I suggested she come work at GoDaddy. I wanted Renee to quit her current job. Working for Starwood Hotels was great, but it was more regimented and didn't allow her the same freedom that working at GoDaddy would provide. Besides, we needed an events department, and I thought she would be perfect for the position. Thankfully, she agreed and joined us at GoDaddy. Not long after she started, she took on our community giving program, called GoDaddy Cares. She learned a lot about philanthropy and giving back to communities, and it became a passion, if not a mission, for both of us. Why? Because we can make a difference, big or small, in people's lives, especially through organizations that are actively doing the work. More important, we both feel a sense of responsibility and want to give back. Renee had those feelings long before she met me or started to work at GoDaddy. As for me? Well, I spent so many years giving back to my employees, the people in my life, and those in need, it was just second nature to me. I wasn't doing it for any reason other than to make somebody happy. I love the feeling I get when I know I might have changed someone's life by supporting organizations such as Free Arts. The Make-A-Wish Foundation is another group that pulls me right in.

> I love the feeling I get when I know I might have changed someone's life.

We started our personal foundation in 2012 after Renee watched an episode of *60 Minutes* featuring Bill and Melinda Gates talking about the Giving Pledge. The Giving Pledge's stated goal is to inspire the signatories to give at least half of their net worth to philanthropy, either during their lifetime or upon their death. As of June 2022, there are 236 signatories to the pledge, representing twenty-eight countries around the world.

Renee shared the Gateses' story and strategy with me. I was intrigued. We both really liked the way they'd leveraged their dollars toward their core causes. We'd done that to a point when we were giving at GoDaddy, but there was no strategic plan. When Renee suggested we start our own foundation post-GoDaddy, she kept telling me it would be my legacy. That wasn't exactly true. It was really *our* legacy.

Renee said, "You're very generous. You're very giving. You always have been through your companies. And now it's time to do the same thing through this new foundation."

I was all in—so much so that Renee and I agreed to take the Giving Pledge. We called our new charitable entity the Bob and Renee Parsons Foundation.

Renee came up with the name, worked on our logo, and did all the things necessary to get the foundation set up. We had a lot of conversations about directing the dollars in an intentional way. We wanted to focus on certain things that we cared about, which we already were doing in a loose way. We needed to define our intentions and set clear criteria for the things we would agree to support.

When we first started, it was less about the military and veterans. There were some veterans' groups that we supported here and there, but that wasn't our initial focus. We formed the foundation to reach low-income and underserved communities and causes that were often overlooked or underfunded by mainstream philanthropy. We supported groups that served children, education, undocumented citizens, and the homeless—all organizations that weren't glamorous but needed help and had a hard time raising funds. We were looking for the underdogs, if you will—those who needed us the most.

Our first significant donation was to Hope for Haiti. We had initially donated to this organization while I was still at GoDaddy. After the earthquake in 2010, Sean Penn's advocacy brought so much attention to the needs of the people of that country that I was compelled to donate half a million dollars. After that first burst of attention, however, the resources and money flowing into Haiti all but dried up, even though the people and country remained in shambles. Even today, many years later, the people of Haiti are suffering terribly.

Renee and I traveled to Haiti and fell in love with the people. We were especially taken with an orphaned child we met, who we wanted to adopt but weren't allowed to. This broke our hearts, because we knew we could provide a much better life for this beautiful little girl. Instead, we committed millions of dollars to help the incredibly resilient people of Haiti get back on their feet. Today, we fund two medical clinics and two schools.

Our giving eventually evolved to include military and first responders and groups dedicated to the pursuit of the American dream, but we still weren't making the major contributions I wanted to make. And then the Semper Fi and America's Fund approached us. We had already done all the research and due diligence on them when we made contributions from GoDaddy Cares and found them to be very fiscally responsible. But more than that, they barely took any money for themselves; in fact, 96 percent of the money donated to their organization goes to those they serve. Immediately, Renee and I both agreed that this group was special; we found that to be true when we first met them and certainly again when they came back around. They were a game changer for the veterans they helped, especially those who returned from Desert Storm, Desert Shield, and other missions with horrific injuries. That struck a chord, big-time.

When we first started the Bob and Renee Parsons Foundation, we found that a number of organizations had certain people they would help and certain people they wouldn't. We didn't agree with that. So we made it our policy that any organization we gave money to had to help everybody, or we would take our money elsewhere. Now, everybody helps everybody because many other foundations followed suit. We are really proud to have had a hand in setting that standard.

Today, through our foundation, Renee and I give away a little more than $1 million every fourteen days, or more than $26 million a year. It's a number I can do, and so we do it. In 2023, we gave $26.6 million, awarding thirty-two grants to twenty-three partners. We support many organizations, including Semper Fi and America's Fund; Hope for Haiti; the Boys and Girls Clubs of the Valley; Girl Scouts Arizona Cactus-Pine, a local chapter of the Girl Scouts in an underserved community; LGBTQ+ groups; research in psychedelics; and much more.

> Today, through our foundation, Renee and I give away a little more than $1 million every fourteen days, or more than $26 million a year. It's a number I can do, and so we do it.

I get a lot of satisfaction and gratification from knowing that we're helping to impact so many people's lives. It's heartwarming, and it's especially inspiring when we meet the recipients and see the difference our support is making. The people who run the organizations we donate to are so dedicated to their causes that it also inspires us. For the most part, theirs are really grassroots efforts, and what they do time and time again is make good things happen. It's truly rewarding.

33

Family Is Everything

Occasionally I think about what it means to be a man. In my opinion, it takes a certain degree of roughness, crassness, strength, and bravery. But it also takes gentleness, kindness, and empathy.

To be a man takes forgiveness of others and yourself.

You should be generous with your time and/or resources.

And a good sense of humor goes a long way.

To be a man, you've got to be somebody who's willing to go to war—to fight for what you believe in. I was and will always be a United States Marine. My responsibility is now for the safety of my loved ones. You hurt them, you'll have to deal with me. I am *their* United States Marine now.

I always tell Renee that if somebody breaks into our home, she should head straight to our safe room. "That's for you," I say. "I'll be out here taking care of business."

And I will.

All those things make a man a man.

My younger brother, Allan, had a saying he lived by "We're not here for a long time, we're here for a good time." It was something he read, but it surely defined how he lived. Allan had an infectious sense of humor. : He was kind, had a nice smile, and was a ladies' man all the way. He took after Pop in that regard. We grew up together like the Lone Ranger and Tonto. We couldn't have been more different from each other. I was an introvert; Allan was outgoing. Despite our differences, we were best friends, inseparable until I fought in the war. I joined the Marine Corps. He joined the Air Force. I went to Vietnam. He went to South Carolina.

> "We're not here for a long time, we're here for a good time."

When I was single, we would sometimes go to nightclubs. Women always came up and asked him to dance. Not me. It was the darndest thing.

"I'll dance," I would say, but none of Allan's rejects were interested in me.

One time we were in Spain for the running of the bulls. I did it. He didn't do it. And I got smacked by a bull. I was running in the street with the bulls coming up from behind me. I was hungover and thirsty, and I just got distracted. A bull or steer nailed me. *Woo!* His big horns went around me, lifting me right up and flipping me over his back. I came out of one of my shoes. I was bruised but not seriously hurt. I was incredibly lucky, because later, on television, I saw a dude in the crowd get gored in the crotch and dragged a hundred yards. That's gotta hurt!

If you play with *el toro*, you will surely get the horns.

But as fun-loving as Allan was, he was also a worrier. He had a lawn-care business, which he ran until he had his third heart attack and couldn't operate the equipment anymore. After he sold his business, I told him I would take care of him. He didn't have to worry about a thing.

> If you play with *el toro*, you will surely get the horns.

Yet Allan still worried about everything. He worried about the country, about the city, about his local golf course. You name it, Allan carried it around like a coat of heavy weights. He once told me he went to see his therapist and said he wanted to not worry, just like me. I am, as Allan said, the complete opposite of him: I never worry. It's wasted time and energy.

The therapist told him he had a different personality than I did, but he could learn to manage his worrying so that it didn't manage him.

That was some rock-solid advice, although Allan never did master that skill.

As his health began to fail, Allan became more dependent on the advice of his doctors. He did whatever they told him to do, even if it was doing more harm than good. No matter what the consequences were or the toll it took on his body, he blindly obliged. He took so many pills for his heart condition that he developed kidney cancer, which eventually metastasized and spread throughout his body to his brain.

That's how I lost my little brother.

Sometimes I think he worried himself to death.

The last time I went to see him, he gave me a hug and whispered in my ear, "I love it when you're here."

I said, "I love being around you too, brother."

Those were our last words to each other.

I miss him so much, but I don't have any more tears left in me. I grieved his loss for quite some time, until I just decided to quit thinking about how much I missed him and to stop feeling sorry for myself. Instead, I think about all the good times I had with him and how lucky I was to spend time with him when he was alive. And when I do that, I smile.

With Allan, Mom, and Dad passing, that leaves only me and my little sister, Beverly. Beverly grew up tough—probably tougher than I did. Because of our seven-year age difference and my time in the military, we were never very close during our younger years. My favorite memory of Beverly is from just after I came home from the war. At the time, I had a pretty solid smoking habit. Beverly would dump all my cigarettes out and circle each one about an inch from the filter to try to protect me from smoking the most carcinogenic part. I always enjoyed her company. When I got married and moved out, our lives went in different directions. Today, though, I'm happy to say that Beverly and I are getting closer and closer, and I love her so much.

There's no question that guys do stupid shit. As a kid, I was always doing stupid stuff, but it didn't hurt me in my development, and it taught me to always have a sense of humor. If I hadn't maintained that, I don't know how I would have gotten through some of those challenging times.

I suppose that throughout my life, I've felt a guardian angel watching over me. He, she, or it is probably exhausted by now and ready to retire. And I wouldn't blame whoever or whatever it is.

As we move through our lives, it's important to understand that we can't control everything. We can try, but I promise you, even the best of us have to deal with setbacks. That doesn't mean we aren't making progress. Since I founded Parsons Technology, I haven't started a company that failed. That's because I love what I'm doing. You've got to love what you're doing, too, because when you love something, it not only tells you all its secrets but it also makes you willing to work harder at it, spend more time with it, just for the sake of doing it right. And when you love what you're doing and compete against somebody who's doing it just to make a dollar, eventually you'll have them by the tail.

And another thing: in all my businesses, just like in my philanthropy, I want to make a difference. I want to do a job that nobody has done before. When you want to make a difference, you must commit to doing whatever it takes to get a business off the ground, and that especially includes working hard to create enthusiasm. If you look at something only from a profit and loss standpoint, it will make no sense. But if you look at it as creating enthusiasm and doing something to bring the customer closer to your business, it makes all the sense in the world. When you're doing that, you're thinking the right way—and when you think the right way, you have a greater chance of succeeding.

Conversely, when you're thinking the wrong way, you're dead in the water. I've got a lot of people who depend on me, from our employees to the recipients of our philanthropic efforts and all the other people we deal with in those endeavors. That keeps me motivated to continue.

> If you look at something only from a profit and loss standpoint, it will make no sense. But if you look at it as creating enthusiasm and doing something to bring the customer closer to your business, it makes all the sense in the world.

I'm often asked what retirement looks like for me. I just laugh and say, "I think I'm going to set a time when I'll make that decision, as opposed to actually doing it. And so far, that time is after I'm cremated. I don't see me returning after that." That's life. I don't think we wear out; I think we rust.

One of the things I believe is that everything in life moves on. I don't worry too much about anything, and certainly not about a legacy. I simply want to do the best I can, and I want to do right by the people I come into contact with. I always remind myself I'm still that guy who shot a snake during the Vietnam War and was not allowed to throw hand grenades. Like most guys, I'm just a knucklehead. I never lose sight of the fact that my people are the blue collar guys, the taxi cab driver, the policeman, the fire fighter, the veteran, the plumber, and on and on. These are my people, and I look up to them.

When the day comes that I move on to whatever the next life holds, I hope a few of my people, and maybe you, will think about me, once or twice. That'll be more than enough for me.

ACKNOWLEDGMENTS

I want to thank my coauthor, Laura Morton. Laura is the epitome of professionalism. Her strength, perseverance, creativity, wit, and humor brought out the very best in me.

Adam Mitchell, thank you for your tireless hours of transcribing and research. You've been a pleasure to work with.

Hope Innelli, your gentle nature, guidance, perspective, and skilled editing are greatly appreciated.

Benjamin Holmes, your attention to detail, fact checking, and suggestions helped make this a better book.

To my publisher, Jonathan Merkh, and your team at Forefront Books, thank you for your belief in *Fire in the Hole!*

To my support team at YAM Worldwide, especially my assistant, Marine Corps veteran Francisca Sanchez, who has been with me for over two decades. She keeps my train on the tracks. Thank you for your many years of service and dedication.

To my spectacular wife, partner, and sounding board, Renee. It was you who took the initiative to rescue me from PTSD. Life without you would be unimaginable.

To my beloved son, Sean, daughters, Marianne and Jessica, and grand and great-grandchildren, thank you for the joy you bring to my life. I love you. I appreciate you. I am so grateful for you.

To my little sister, Beverly, an outstanding writer and genealogist. Like me, you had a tough upbringing. I think this is why we relate to each other so well. I love you and treasure our long conversations.

To my little brother and sidekick, Allan. I have missed you so much since the Lord took you, I can hardly bring myself to write this. You're never far from my thoughts. You always told me "We're not here for a long time. We're here for a good time." How right you were.

Outside of my book, team, and family, I would be remiss not to acknowledge and thank Barbara Rechterman, who has worked with me in an executive capacity for over thirty-eight years and in four different companies. Barbara, in each business, you were the perfect counterpoint to me and played a key role in making the business success I had possible.

Beyond Barbara, individual acknowledgements would have taken up half this book and introduced the extreme and unthinkable possibility that I might have unintentionally left one or more individuals out. If you've been a part of my journey (you know who you are), I thank you for your friendship and wisdom. I am grateful and appreciative and love every one of you.

I want to thank you, the reader. I'm especially grateful you bought this book and hope my story resonates with and inspires you in your own life.

Finally, I want to thank the United States Marines I served with during the Vietnam War. You taught me the true meaning of responsibility, discipline, leadership, and brotherhood. I think of you most every day. Semper Fi and Welcome Home.

BIBLIOGRAPHY

"6 Ways Ayahuasca Works like a Good Trauma Therapist," Charcruna.net online, May 8, 2018, https://chacruna.net/6-ways-ayahuasca-works-like-good-trauma-therapist/

"8 PTSD Facts You May Not Know," Sepsis Alliance, June 2, 2022, https://www.sepsis.org/news/8-ptsd-facts-you-may-not-know/

"Emerging research on MDMA, LSD, and psilocybin for PTSD treatment," Campus Well, updated Jan 5, 2022, https://www.campuswell.com/psychedelic-treatment-ptsd/

"Everything You Need to Know About Psychedelic Therapy and PTSD," Harmony, updated July 20, 2021, https://www.grwhealth.com/post/everything-you-need-to-know-about-psychedelic-therapy-and-ptsd

"How Common Is PTSD in Adults?," U.S. Department of Veterans Affairs, accessed January 2, 2023, https://www.ptsd.va.gov/understand/common/common_adults.asp

"Post-Traumatic Stress Disorder Overview," National Institute of Mental Health, accessed January 2, 2023, https://www.nimh.nih.gov/health/topics/post-traumatic-stress-disorder-ptsd

"Post-Traumatic Stress Disorder Treatment with Psychedelic Drugs," NYU Langone Health, accessed on January 2, 2023,

https://med.nyu.edu/departments-institutes/population-health
/divisions-sections-centers/medical-ethics/education/high
-school-bioethics-project/learning-scenarios/ptsd-treatment
-psychedelics

"Psychedelic drug LSD may be effective as anxiety treatment,"
Medical News Today, accessed January 2, 2023, https://www
.medicalnewstoday.com/articles/psychedelic-drug-lsd-may-be
-effective-as-anxiety-treatment

"PTSD and Veterans: Breaking Down the Statistics," Hill and
Ponton Disability Attorneys online, accessed January 2, 2023,
https://www.hillandponton.com/veterans-statistics/ptsd/

"PTSD: National Center for PTSD," U.S. Department of Veterans Affairs, accessed January 2, 2023, https://www.ptsd.va.gov
/understand/common/common_veterans.asp,

"Repeated ketamine infusions reduce PTSD symptom severity,"
The Mount Sinai Hospital / Mount Sinai School of Medicine,
January 5, 2021, https://www.sciencedaily.com/releases/2021/01
/210105130121.htm

"What Is Ayahuasca? Experience, Benefits, and Side Effects,"
Healthline.com online, accessed January 2, 2023, https://www
.healthline.com/nutrition/ayahuasca#what-it-is

Caitlin Tilley, "Why Americans are turning to psychedelics over
traditional meds to cure trauma and mental health," Daily Mail
online, December 24, 2022, https://www.dailymail.co.uk/health
/article-11440675/Americas-bad-trip.html

Cassidy Morrison, "Researchers create an ayahuasca pill: powerful psychedelic could be coming to a pharmacy near you in
next 10 years," Daily Mail online, https://www.dailymail.co.uk
/health/article-11504263/Prescription-ayahuasca-come-decade
-Canadian-company-sets-sights-FDA-approval.html

Danica Jeffries, "Psychedelic therapies are on the horizon, but
who will administer the drugs? Schools are ramping up training

programs to teach therapists and other practitioners how to safely give psychedelics to patients," NBC News, Dec. 26, 2022, https://www.nbcnews.com/health/mental-health/psychedelic -therapies-are-horizon-will-administer-rcna61030

Dr. Brett Forrest Shenkman, "How is Ketamine Therapy Used for PTSD?," Sanctuary.net online, accessed January 2, 2023, https://www.sanctuary.net/blog/how-is-ketamine-therapy-used -for-ptsd/

Emma Yasinski, "Why Psychedelic Drugs May Become a Key Treatment for PTSD and Depression,", May 3, 2022, https:// www.smithsonianmag.com/science-nature/why-psychedelic -drugs-may-become-a-key-treatment-for-ptsd-and-depression -180979983/

Erika Edwards, "Could 'magic mushrooms' treat severe depression? A major study aims to find out.," NBC News online, Nov. 2, 2022, https://www.nbcnews.com/health/health-news/magic -mushrooms-treat-severe-depression-major-study-aims-find -rcna54856

Ernesto Londono, "After Six-Decade Hiatus, Experimental Psychedelic Therapy Returns to the V.A.," New York Times online, June 24, 2022, https://www.nytimes.com/2022/06/24/us/politics /psychedelic-therapy-veterans.html

Hannah Wiley, "California could decriminalize psychedelics under new bill," Los Angeles Times online, Dec. 19, 2022, https://www .latimes.com/california/story/2022-12-19/magic-mushrooms-and -ayahuasca-would-be-decriminalized-in-california-under-new -bill

Jamie Reno, "How Psychedelic Drugs Are Helping Veterans and Others with PTSD, Depression," Healthline.com online, November 20, 2021, https://www.healthline.com/health-news /how-psychedelic-drugs-are-helping-veterans-and-others-with -ptsd-depression

Jon Hamilton, "Psychedelic drugs may launch a new era in psychiatric treatment, brain scientists say," https://www.npr.org/sections/health-shots/2022/12/27/1145306096/psychedelic-drugs-psychiatric-disorders-brain-research

Juan Jose Fuentes, Fancina Fonseca, Matilde Elices, Magi Farre, Marta Torrens, "Therapeutic Use of LSD in Psychiatry: A Systematic Review of Randomized-Controlled Clinical Trials," Frontiers online, January 21, 2020, https://www.frontiersin.org/articles/10.3389/fpsyt.2019.00943/full

Katherine Cullent MFA, LCSW, "Should You Try Ketamine-Assisted Psychotherapy? A look into whom it's best for, how it works, and what it costs," Psychology Today online, December 29, 2022, https://www.psychologytoday.com/gb/blog/the-truth-about-exercise-addiction/202212/should-you-try-ketamine-assisted-psychotherapy

Katherine Dillinger, Deidre McPhillips, "Ketamine infusions improve symptoms of depression, anxiety and suicidal ideation, study says," CNN online, accessed January 2, 2023, https://www.cnn.com/2022/09/12/health/ketamine-infusions-help-depression-study-wellness/index.html

Kelly Servick, "A psychedelic drug may help treat PTSD. But questions remain on how best to use—and regulate—it," Science.org, May 19, 2021, https://www.science.org/content/article/psychedelic-drug-may-help-treat-ptsd-questions-remain-how-best-use-and-regulate-it

Lauren Gravitz, "Hope that psychedelic drugs can erase trauma," Nature.com online, September 28, 2022, https://www.nature.com/articles/d41586-022-02870-x

Lauren P. Carboni, David L. Rosen, "Psychedelic Drugs – Easing the Regulatory Hurdles for Development," Foley and Lardner LLP online, December 15, 2022, https://www.foley.com/en/insights/publications/2022/12/psychedelic-drugs-regulatory-hurdles-development

Mattha Busby, "Biden Administration Plans for Legal Psychedelic Therapies Within Two Years," The Intercept online, July 26, 2022, https://theintercept.com/2022/07/26/mdma-psilocybin-fda-ptsd/

Michael Eisenstein, "The psychedelic escape from depression," Nature.com online, Sept. 28, 2022, https://www.nature.com/articles/d41586-022-02872-9

Morgan Mandriota, Christie Craft, "Experts Suggest MDMA Could Heal PTSD: Here's How," Psych Central online, March 31, 2022, https://psychcentral.com/ptsd/mdma-for-ptsd

Robert t. Muller PhD., "Ayahuasca and Its Potential to Treat PTSDA new use for the Native American ritualistic psychedelic," Psychology Today online, August 20, 2020, https://www.psychologytoday.com/us/blog/talking-about-trauma/202008/ayahuasca-and-its-potential-treat-ptsd

Sonya Collins, "Ketamine for Depression: What to Know," Web MD online, updated December 29, 2023, https://www.webmd.com/depression/features/what-does-ketamine-do-your-brain

Wesley Thoricatha, "Soldiers of the Vine: Healing PTSD with Ayahuasca," Psychedelic Times online, Aug. 11, 2017, https://psychedelictimes.com/soldiers-vine-healing-ptsd-ayahuasca/